TOPOGRAPHIES
OF HELLENISM

A volume in the series

MYTH AND POETICS

edited by GREGORY NAGY

A full list of titles in the series appears at the end of the book.

TOPOGRAPHIES OF HELLENISM

Mapping the Homeland

ARTEMIS LEONTIS

CORNELL UNIVERSITY PRESS

ITHACA AND LONDON

Library of Congress Cataloging-in-Publication Data

Leontis, Artemis.
    Topographies of Hellenism : mapping the homeland / Artemis Leontis.
       p.   cm. — (Myth and poetics)
    Includes bibliographical references and index.
    ISBN 0-8014-3057-7
    1. Literature, Modern—Greek influences.   2. Greek literature—History and
criticism—Theory, etc.   3. Civilization, Modern—Greek influences.   4. Geography,
Ancient, in literature.   5. Mythology, Greek, in literature.   6. Greece—In literature.
7. Greece—Historiography.   8. Hellenism.   I. Title.   II. Series.
PA3071.L46   1995
809—dc20   94-41498

Contents

Foreword

GREGORY NAGY

This book is about the mythology and poetics of a space, the culturally defined topography of Neohellenism. Like other Hellenisms of the past, most notably the Panhellenism of Homeric poetry, Neohellenism finds its most powerful self-expression in a poetics of its own, unifying a vast array of different groups into a single people, the Greeks of today. This poetics, as Artemis Leontis demonstrates, is all-pervasive in modern Greek literature.

The space created by the poetics of Neohellenism becomes the ever re-created homeland of the Greeks. In its concreteness, it is a real space. At the same time, its reality is infused with myth, always resituated by the groundedness of Neohellenism in all the Hellenisms of the past. Any *topos* of modern Greek literature may reactivate a corresponding *topos* from the archaic, the classical, the Hellenistic, the Roman, and the Byzantine periods. The poetics of the space that is Hellas is the myth of a Hellas eternally recovered in the literary imagination.

Acknowledgments

This book was written between 1987 and 1993 while I was studying and teaching in Classics, Comparative Studies, and Modern Greek at the Ohio State University. Earlier versions of portions of the text have appeared elsewhere: parts of Chapter 3 in the *Journal of Modern Greek Studies* 8; Chapter 5 in the *Journal of Modern Greek Studies* 5 and in *Homer*, edited by Katherine King (New York and London: Garland Press, 1994); and Chapter 6 in the *Journal of Modern Greek Studies* 9. I thank Johns Hopkins University Press for permission to reprint material that appeared in the *Journal of Modern Greek Studies*.

The book has as long a prehistory as any. It saw me through graduate training, during which time I benefited from studies with Eugene W. Holland, Stephen V. Tracy, and Marilyn Robinson Waldman, as well as the administrative support of Charles Babcock, Frederic Cadora, and Micheal Riley. To Gregory Jusdanis I owe special thanks, for he cultivated an interpretive community of young scholars, invested it with his integrity and enthusiasm, and encouraged its members to share work. In part as a result of his efforts, I found myself caught in a powerful new wave of Neohellenists. Panayotis Bosnakis, Vangelis Calotychos, Van Gegas, Stathis Gourgouris, Martha Klironomos, Eva Konstantellou, Tracy Lord, Neni Panourgia, and Maria Papacostaki all responded to ideas found in this book.

As the book took shape, many colleagues helped me develop my thoughts, improve the manuscript, and find a home for it. Margaret Alexiou gave me *topos*. Eleni Vakalo and Nanos Valaoritis surveyed it. Khachig Tölölyan recalled its diasporas. Charles Williams reversed compass points. And Andreas Mylonas found that one obscure article that helped me connect the dots. I also thank Elizabeth J. Bellamy, John Chioles, Ernestine Friedl, Katherine King, and Charles Stewart for their encouragement and advice. I am very grateful to Bernhard Kendler for his confidence. Marian Shotwell's impressive learning in Greek, modern and ancient, and her scrupulous editing were especially helpful. I appreciated her fine work. Above all, I am indebted to Gregory Nagy, whose optimism never waned. He remains for me a model of courage and open-mindedness.

For as long as the book has been in the making, Vassilis Lambropoulos has stood by my side, gently and persuasively pointing out what routes of inquiry there are for thinking and being. This work owes its life to him and to Daphne Polymnia, a parallel achievement.

Finally, I acknowledge today what I could not always appreciate in the past: my parents' vigilance in retaining a bilingual household. They zealously bridged two distant worlds and enabled me to frequent both sides. With Neocles Leontis, I have enjoyed exploring the circuitous paths of border crossing. I dedicate this book to my parents, Thomas E. Leontis and Anna P. Leontis, for their love of letters and their firm belief that women should be equal sharers of learning.

A. L.

Columbus, Ohio

Note on Translations
and Transliteration

Most translations in this book are my own and reflect my understanding of the original Greek. Where I have used English translations of others, I indicate the translator's name or the title of the translated publication.

In transliterating modern Greek terms, I have followed the phonetic system of the *Journal of Modern Greek Studies,* which reproduces the sound as opposed to the spelling of Greek words. Transliterated words of more than one syllable normally bear a stress accent. I retain well-known Latinizations or Anglicizations of proper names, place-names, and Greek words that circulate in English. The names Elytis and Seferis and the river Ilissus, as well as the names of ancient authors and heroes and words like *topos* and *cosmos*, are prominent examples of this practice. For ancient and Byzantine Greek names, I have followed the more traditional, nonphonetic system of transliteration, in which each Greek letter is rendered into English, and accents are omitted. I follow these two different systems for modern and ancient transliteration because their phonetics differ; furthermore, there is a lack of consensus on ancient Greek pronunciation.

TOPOGRAPHIES
OF HELLENISM

Mapping the Territory

In the present-day collectors' market, the value of old topographical materials—maps, travel books, drawings, paintings, engravings—depends on the economic vitality of the country they depict: the stronger the economy, the higher the value of these items. The logic of the market follows familiar rules. Collectors exist in larger numbers in countries where economies are expanding enough to produce surplus capital. Collectors of maps, travel books, and engravings tend to invest in items representing their homeland. Hence the demand is greatest for topographical materials that register older layers of today's strongest national economies. The higher price of these items reflects the higher demand.

Greece presents a modest exception to the rule that a perennially ailing economy should hinder people from investing in nonessential items like old travel books, or from finding the leisure to discuss and enjoy them. Greeks are avid collectors of topographical items, particularly those that depict historical remnants of the Hellenic world. These representations also continue to interest collectors from other national groups. Topographies of Hellenism carry a relatively high price.

Perhaps the present-day demand for Greek topographies follows another rule, as inviolable as the rule of markets. Neohellenes, the unapparent heirs of the Hellenic past, continually seek to ascertain their origins. To this end, they are compelled to reinvest in a past shaped by the interests of several modern European states. European interests in Hellas accrued in the form of diplomacy, the disciplines of archeology and philology, the collection of antiquities, and travel, as well as in their by-products: buildings, museums, poetry, etchings, paintings, drawings, travel writing, and maps. Another by-product was the Greek state, established in large part through Western diplomatic efforts, military intervention, and financial support. Greek collectors of topographical materials seem to be posthumously repaying their brokers: the artist who engraved their ruins, the antiquary who carried them away, and the scribbler whose journals abused them.[1]

The Greek case suggests that maps, images, and descriptions of a place may be not surplus but ineluctable elements of a homeland. These items confirm that others have valued one's territory enough to cite it. Furthermore, they allow a nation to "verify with its senses, as Locke and Condillac proposed, that the body of the homeland exists."[2] In its topographies, a nation accrues symbols, pictures, narratives, and reports of its physical presence. Topographies are substantive markers of a homeland. They seem to affix culture to place. Indeed, there have been few cases in modern history where a group of people has achieved sovereignty within a territory without creating topographies. Thus we can anticipate that the Greeks themselves not only value the topographies that visitors to Greece produce, but also engage in their own map-making activities.[3] The task of resurrecting Hellenism in the Balkan peninsula has been a cartographic as well as a political, cultural, and linguistic enterprise.

The mapping of a homeland is the subject of this book. What is a homeland? It may be a place where one builds a home, or a place where one can feel at home; but it must be a place one calls one's home. The citation of "home" is the provision of a homeland. One may have a place of residence without claiming a homeland. Conversely, one may call a territory that is not one's place of residence a homeland. Whether it exists on an imaginary plane or settles into the domain of the real, a homeland requires that one narrate a past, claim a present, and proph-

---

[1] In his notes to *Childe Harold's Pilgrimage*, canto 2, Byron protested with irony his compatriots' accounts of present-day Greeks' obligations: "They are to be grateful to the Turks for their fetters, and to the Franks for their broken promises and lying counsels! They are to be grateful to the artist who engraves their ruins, and to the antiquary who carries them away! To the Traveler whose janissary flogs them, and to the scribbler whose journal abuses them" (*Byron's Works* [1899], 2:191).

[2] Kóstas Vergópulos, Η δυναμική του 1821 (The dynamic of 1821) (1990), 85.

[3] From the early modern period, beginning a few decades prior to the Greek assertion of independence (1821), we have the example of Rígas Feréos (1760–98), poet and revolutionary, who was before all else the cartographer of Hellenism.

esy a future. A homeland must have a history one recalls, a topography one describes, a culture one envisions spreading its roots in the depths of time. In this sense, a homeland emerges not when it has been inhabited but when it has been mapped.

It is my thesis that topographies are embedded in the homeland they map. To become a homeland, a place requires topography. To understand how a place becomes a homeland, one must know its topography. By topography I refer to any conceptual map that cites a place.[4] Topography is the *graphē* of a *topos*, the writing of a (common)place.[5] Topographies assign to a place a sequence of symbols readable through the codes of verisimilitude, mapping, description, or narration. Emergent nations engage in topography when they name a geographical expanse and represent it as their own bounded territory, fundamental to their existence and brimming with their history. Mapping a homeland is both a process and a product. Topography is a process: it requires the persistent return to history, the systematic unearthing of ruins, the conscientious recovery of traditions, and, generally, the reactivation of an inherited past. But topography is also the product of these reactivations: it consists in the archive of shared images, evolving traditions, literary works, and visual maps, as well as in the geopolitical entity itself. Literary topographies take different forms. The political oration, the travel journal, the linguistic treatise, the novel of ideas, the philosophical treatise, the essay on art, even the lyric or epic poem, may shape a place and, conversely, make geography and climate matters of a national destiny, which culture is bound to express. Literary topographies give *logos* to a place and so deliver that place, in the modern era at least, to the logic of national culture.

The critical work of analyzing topography might be labeled topology, a term I borrow but dissociate from its mathematical usage. Topology is the study of a *topos*. In a sense, topology is yet another topography, yet another representation of place. It is a distinct activity, however, in that it makes topography its object of study. It examines how others have envisioned a place. The work of the topologist

---

[4] Postmodern geographers use the related term "cognitive mapping." In "The Politics of Space" (1991), Louise Jezierski traces the term to Kevin Lynch, a geographer who in the 1960s proposed mapping how people's perceptions of significant barriers, landmarks, modes, and pathways structure space (180). With Edward Soja a leading theorist, postmodern geography analyzes how culture and politics organize space, and how space then "becomes an instrument of power and resistance" (179).

[5] For a definition of *topos*, see Chapter 1.

involves not describing a site or digging on location but rethinking the constellation of factors that have shaped our sense of place. Topology may analyze how people give to a spatial plane symbolic value, how they construct centers, boundaries, passages, monuments, how their everyday life and artistic self-presentations organize their domain of activity. Topology thus investigates its two constituent elements: the *logos* that refers to a place and the *topos* (both the literary commonplace and the geographical site) to which this *logos* may give shape through a tradition of citations.[6]

The terrain I study is Hellas. Hellas is the name by which modern Greeks refer to their geopolitical entity, established as an independent kingdom in the early 1830s and renamed a state in the 1970s.[7] But Hellas is also a major ideal of modernity. It represents the political, cultural, and philosophical value of the Hellenic heritage for Western Europe. During the late eighteenth century, the idea that Hellas is the harmonious origin of civilization became popular in the West; it became a kind of *topos* of the Western imagination that continues to feed upon itself, at times more avariciously than at other times. Hellenism, the study of Hellas, has been a quixotic though grossly self-consuming enterprise. To this day, it seeks to apprehend artifacts of the past while also producing out of these a "symbolic universe" that imposes "meaning on the present."[8]

The symbolic universe of Hellas is the domain of Hellenism's topographies. In this domain, Greeks themselves also traverse. In general, Greeks have favored the medium of language for assigning symbols to a place and imposing meaning on their present. In oral communication, Greeks may cite literary commonplaces to aid physical orientation. Their relationship to visual maps is unusual, for although they collect them, Greeks do not use them. They do not commonly recognize the points of a compass or orient themselves by north, south, east, and

[6] On this dual signification of *topos*, see Chapter 1.

[7] In a national referendum held in 1974, 69 percent of the population voted against restoration of the monarchy and for the establishment of a republic. Seven years earlier, King Constantine II had flown his family to Rome after the failure of his countercoup against the military junta of the Colonels. On the history of the period 1967–74, see Richard Clogg, *A Short History of Modern Greece* (1979), 186–210. Clogg informs us that "the December 1974 referendum was the sixth such referendum on the constitutional issue to have been held in the twentieth century (the others took place in 1920, 1924, 1935, 1946, and 1973)" (207).

[8] Tamara M. Green, "*Black Athena* and Classical Historiography: Other Approaches, Other Views" (1989), 57.

west. Yet they have a strong sense of place, which they define in other ways. Within cities they sense the slightest inclination of the land and speak of a trajectory up or down, left or right. They also orient themselves toward or away from geographical landmarks like the sea or a mountain range. They recognize neighborhoods, public squares, the local *stéki* 'hangout', the smallest *periohí* 'district', the odd building or sign, window displays, churches, kiosks, railway lines, bus routes, alleys, cemeteries, and ruins from the many layers of their past. They mark the distance traveled by the number of cigarettes it takes to arrive. They know a place by its landmarks, venders, taverns, edible vegetation that they can cut with a pocketknife and carry home to boil. They also recognize historical references, literary citations, and myths related to these places. They measure territory by its most prestigious cultural layers. One must know historical landmarks, even texts, to get around. In Thessaloniki today the answer to any query for directions usually begins with another question, ποὐ εἶναι ο Λευκὸς Πύργος; 'where is the White Tower?' which assumes its own ambiguous history.

More important for my study, Greeks have created a category of writing that deserves special attention, the literary map of their homeland. Their literary topographies are fictional and nonfictional, poetic and prosaic. What these genres have in common is that they affix a *logos* to a place and so shape that place through their *logos*. Like visual maps, their literary topographies serve many purposes, including urban development, on the one hand, and tourist information, on the other. Like visual maps, too, they may feature the historical monuments of a given site, though their mode of presentation gives another dimension to these monuments. Here place comes alive through literary language and historical citations: the more learned the language, the more the reference to the place resounds. Visual maps, too, may develop their own *logos*; but conceptual maps resonate with literary citations, since these maps come to life through citations and may themselves circulate as another citation.

In this critical study of Hellenism's topography, I thematize the idea that literature and geography are interdependent. This idea is expanded on in the first chapter. In general terms, my contention is that geography is always cited, identified, and organized. Conversely, literature requires a site. Literature takes place, in the sense that it assigns cultural identity to a territory, even when that territory is extraterritorial or utopic. In Hellas we find texts interacting with place with the explicit goal of constructing a homeland; and the physical site of a reconstructed Hellenic world frequently dictates the form modern texts may take. Even the narrow rubric of imaginary writing that aspires to artistic achievement is inextricably connected to geography. There is a geographical plane where national narratives takes shape, to which they assign identity, on which they impose order, within which they teach an audience to get around. On the level of theory, then, I argue that places produce meanings and meanings give roots to place.

One way to understand the interdependence of geography and literature is to learn how Neohellenism forged a Panhellenic union out of distinctly regional homes.[9] Before the foundation of their nation-state, speakers of Greek were organized under different systems of governance, subject to different rulers, connected to different centers of administration, and emotionally tied to different regions. During the period of Ottoman rule, Greeks fit into the administrative category of Rum, the Orthodox millet that surrendered final authority to the Sublime Porte. This religious category offered a conceptual framework within which Greek-speaking, Orthodox subjects were able to identify their extraregional ties and to distinguish themselves from their Muslim rulers. But their territorial identification was regional, as folk culture of the Ottoman period attests. Neohellenism, the ideology of a Hellenic national culture, emerged when Greeks articulated in their literature an abstract principle of territorial identification. One of its first tasks was to link heterogeneous peoples, onetime Ottoman subjects, to the evolving centers of the Greek Kingdom. These centers included physical sites such as the capital of Athens or the citadel of the Acropolis; institutions such as the state, religion, education; concepts like origin, history, beauty; and the expressive media of the neoclassical, romantic, and modern styles and the standardized Neohellenic language. Neohellenism derived the content of this new homeland from the fragments of other milieus such as towns, villages, monasteries, ethnic communities, the isolated countryside, and, most notable of all, the ruins of older communities. The home retained elements of these milieus; but state institutions decoded them, removing them

---

[9] Panhellenism is a historically relative term for a recurring trend that first appears during the eighth century B.C., as "evidenced in particular by the following institutions: Olympic Games, Delphic Oracle, and Homeric poetry" (Gregory Nagy, *Pindar's Homer: The Lyric Possession of an Epic Past* [1990], 52–53). I would like to adapt Nagy's "hermeneutic model of Panhellenism" to a specifically modern pattern of administrative centralization and intellectual activity coordinated within the ideological framework of a national territory.

from their prior contexts and cutting off their relations to each other. It then recoded elements that followed a different logic, giving them another value, making certain features common to all, and subjecting them to taxation, verification by title, conscription and national defense, exploitation of natural resources, and the disposition of public power. Although to this day one's region continues to be one's home and one's fellow villagers one's *simpatriótes* 'compatriots',[10] gradually Hellas became one's bigger homeland: the symbol of national destiny, principle of unification, plane of cultural activity, and rule of reconstruction.

A recurring question in Neohellenism's debate about its national fate concerns the physical depth and expanse of its cultural terrain. In this discussion, Greeks link the fate of their territory to the literary and artistic heritage of classical Greece. Furthermore, they attempt to specify the physical features of this inheritance. Then they set their administrative sights on embracing the larger geographical terri tory that reveals traces of these features. The tautology of this national project should come as no surprise.[11] Contemporary studies in the fields of political and cultural geography suggest that the attachment of a unified, though richly layered, historical identity to a continuous territory is a core doctrine of nationalist ideologies. Cultural geographers refer to territorial identification as "geoethnicity" or "group politico-territorial identity." Geoethnicity "involves the historical identification of an ethnic group with a given territory, an

---

[10] The Greek vernacular word for homeland, *patrída* (ancient Greek *patrís*), derives from an ancient poetic form of *pátrios* 'of one's father' that assumes the referent "land"; it denotes a place of origin, from one's native village to one's country. On metaphors and metaphorical practices that territorialize space by linking places of origin to kinship, on the one hand, and to earth or soil, on the other hand, see Liisa Malkki, "National Geographic: The Rooting of Peoples and the Territorialization of National Identity among Scholars and Refugees" (1992), 25–28.

[11] Relevant contemporary discussions of nationalism are too numerous to cite. Some works I have found useful are Benedict Anderson, *Imagined Communities: Reflections on the Origin and Spread of Nationalism* (1983); John Breuilly, *Nationalism and the State* (1985); Elie Kedourie, ed., *Nationalism in Asia and Africa* (1970); Gavin Kitching, *Development and Underdevelopment in Historical Perspective* (1982); George L. Mosse, *Nationalism and Sexuality: Middle-Class Morality and Sexual Norms in Modern Europe* (1985); Boyd C. Shafer, *Faces of Nationalism: New Realities and Old Myths* (1972); and Hugh Seton-Watson, *Nations and States* (1977). For a good bibliographical guide, see Anthony D. Smith, *The Ethnic Origin of Nations* (1988). *The Encyclopedia of Nationalism* (1990), edited by Louis L. Snyder, offers a comprehensive bibliography and broad historical overview of more than two hundred nationalist movements.

attachment to a particular place, a sense of place as a symbol of being and identity."[12]

The particular pattern of nation building in Greece allows me to visualize the connection between geography and culture. Crucial to the evolution of Neohellenism is the fact that the inheritance of classical Hellas haunts the Greek present. From the time of the Greek drive for self-determination to the present, speakers of Greek, like their philhellenic supporters,[13] have traced their lines of descent to the classical heritage. The remnants of this heritage exist in physical space. More important, Neohellenes have repeatedly found in these remnants a principle of unity. They have created a pattern of intensified intercommunication among local regions, following an archaic and classical precedent. They have sought to reconcile local dialects, generalize history, consolidate traditions, and feature the Hellenicity of their self-governance within the reconstructed city of Athens. Evidence of Panhellenism can be found in the formation of a nation-state and in the recomposition of oral traditions and of a long written heritage that reflect the continuous and unique history of the Greek nation. In the twentieth century, modernist literary recompositions of classical texts energetically seek to recover common Hellenic elements. Often mapping an imaginary or desired space, these literary topographies nonetheless refer their readers to existing sites like the Aegean, the Attic peninsula, Greek islands, the Greek village.

Certainly the theme of literature and geography's entwinement assumes current developments in academic discussions about culture, the arts, and everyday life. It is now commonplace for literary scholars to assert the interdependence of high culture and ideology, politics, or the economy, as well as the dynamic part culture plays in the con-

[12] Josiah A. M. Cobbah, "Toward a Geography of Peace in Africa: Redefining Sub-State Self-Determination Rights" (1988), 73.

[13] Philhellenism is non-Greek sympathy for modern Greeks, particularly the Greek cause of emancipation and self-determination. This sympathy derived from a love for the cultural heritage of ancient Hellas, but it should be distinguished from Hellenism, the antiquarian interest in Hellas. On this distinction, see Richard Jenkyns, *The Victorians and Ancient Greece* (1980), 3; and Robert Byron, *The Byzantine Achievement, an Historical Perspective,* A.D. 330–1453 [1929] 1964), 17–23. In a little-known address, Cedric H. Whitman defined the difference between the classicist and the philhellene as "chiefly this: . . . a philhellene likes the living Greeks, and a classicist likes the dead ones. By that definition," he observed, "I qualify as both, assuredly, for I spend my professional life with the dead ones and my spare time with the living" (*The Vitality of the Greek Language and Its Importance Today* [1954], 5).

struction of gender, race, class, and, most recently, nation and empire. Despite efforts to achieve autonomy, it is argued, culture has not been able to escape the tumult of world history so as to find a room of its own. Even when it seeks transcendence, culture may share in power, support revolutions or counterrevolutions, and become a willing or unwilling accomplice in colonial and postcolonial orders.

To the growing list of fields to which we can relate literature, I would add geography, the *graphē* of the *gē*, the writing of the earth. Geography refers to human activity, not natural space. Although usually defined as the science of measuring the world, geography also involves social practices that inscribe identities in places. These practices range from the drawing up of boundaries to the writing of foundational narratives. Whether aspiring to accuracy, expediency, or aesthetic value, geography has a common effect. The charting of physical terrain, the counting of human populations, the positioning of identities, the mapping of places, the definition of dwelling, is continuously—sometimes subtly, sometimes conspicuously—refashioning the physical terrain we occupy. Thus the writing of the earth demarcates spheres of influence, grids of power, and lines of division as well as lines of flight.

Until recently, geography was the domain of geographers, who tended to favor visual over verbal forms of representation. As boundaries between the disciplines of the humanities and social sciences shift, however, some geographers are relocating their center of interest from visual to oral and written descriptions of place. The work of some cultural anthropologists is converging with that of cultural geographers as the former begin to pay attention to their own placement vis-à-vis their subjects and to their subjects' narratives of place. Literary study, too, now at its own crossroads, has begun to explore the connection between narration and nation, ethos and ethnos, literary *topos* and geopolitical territory. The poststructuralist interest in power, identity, and position seems to have given a spatial twist to metaphors for change even as declarations of the end of history have revived interest in the place of history.

There are several things I wish to accomplish here. One important goal is to describe Neohellenism's contrapuntal relationship with Western Hellenism. Classical revivalism in the West preceded Neohellenism, though we should not perceive Western precedence as necessarily delimiting Neohellenic self-presentation. The ideal of Western Hellenism was subject to the realpolitik of changing policies vis-à-vis the

Ottoman Porte and the Greeks. Travel accounts bear witness to these changing attitudes. To grasp changes and continuities in Western views of Hellas, I search the major cities of Europe for descriptions of Hellas's archeological sites. In the second chapter, I study the accounts of European travelers, in order to document typical attitudes toward Hellenism's most sacred site, the Acropolis. I view these texts both as statements of knowledge and as symbols of Europeans' willingness to appropriate and sometimes ravage cultural remains that may support their own claims of civilization. Thus I move from the theoretical exposition of a topological approach to the study of travelers' topographies. Travelers typically described Hellas as an extension of home. Their perspective allows me to explore an important dimension of the Hellenic *topos*. I examine how the real space of Hellas—the geographically circumscribed area brimming with its overvalued ancient history—has served as a countersite to European cities.

A second goal of this book is to view Hellenism through the lens of Neohellenism. To this end, in the remaining chapters of this book, I study Neohellenic topographies. Neohellenism offers an unusual intellectual adventure for the Western scholar interested in Hellas. Although modern Greece is the usual point of departure for a pilgrimage to ancient sites, contemporary Greece remains obscure next to the preeminent culture of ruins. Interest in the past rather than the present prompts westerners to travel to Greece. Yet I would propose that Neohellenism has the power to unfold in an intricate labyrinth where the venerated texts, language, museums, and excavation sites of Hellas stand at crucial, if sometimes ambivalent, junctures. Its meandering passages through the classical heritage inevitably return to their contemporary points of origin: the forces of change during the nineteenth and twentieth centuries that transformed Hellenism into a national institution and site. Greek reactivations of the Hellenic past inevitably face the dilemmas of national culture. Following an important nationalist ideal, Neohellenism has fashioned itself with the hope that it might somehow embody, that is to say, physically incorporate, an inherited standard. Against this standard, however, Neohellenism has had to measure most of its accomplishments and has often found itself short. Rhetorical appeals to the "miracle" of Hellas, which today seem to lose their once deferential audience, continue to serve as the emollient that covers, without eliminating, the wrinkles of Hellenism's mixed project.

In the third chapter, I trace the genealogy of the word *topos* in

Neohellenic literary topographies. In the Greek literature I have read, *topos* appears as the preferred term for the imaginary space in which the nation finds its self-fulfillment. In its intersection with a national tradition, *topos* gives historical roots to an imagined community. Neohellenism's topographies align the physical expanse of the homeland with the discursive field of a shared heritage or, better, common ground. On this ground, Greek authors are encouraged to tread in order to excavate their cultural resources and reconstruct their homeland.

Because the precise historical and geographical boundaries of Neohellenism are subject to endless debate, the tracing of an imaginary map of the "Hellenic" (as distinguished from the "Helladic")[14] homeland has become a major enterprise in Neohellenic politics and culture, especially during our own century. We shall see how the mapping of a homeland confers a spatial and temporal site on an aggregate of individuals who once held stronger regional ties. The *topos* of Hellenism becomes a symbolic center that governs political decisions, from choosing the nation's capital to articulating foreign policy. It coordinates cultural output and regulates the coexistence of an imagined community of Neohellenes.

My genealogy of *topos* extends temporally to the postwar era. Chapter 4 provides the theoretical framework for a discussion of the modernist turn in Greece from the late 1930s to the early 1960s. The framework is again contrapuntal: I read Neohellenic reterritorializations of Hellenism against Western modernism's skeptical reassessment of the Hellenic heritage. Greek modernism achieved consolidation during the first two decades of the cold war. Sundered by the global division between East and West, torn apart by a civil war between Left and Right, Greek society sought to purify itself of non-Hellenic elements even as it opened its doors to foreign investment. Mainstream Neohellenic poets, at the service of the nation while also in search of international recognition, reconstructed a "Hellenic . . . racial, historical, and human" *topos* in the literary text.[15] Some of the same poets and critics who in the early 1930s had combatted the rigidities of national culture now proffered their work as a bulwark

---

[14] "Hellenic" refers to the entire nation, including territories historically occupied by speakers of *elliniká* 'Greek' and at present "unredeemed," while "Helladic" refers to mainland Greece, the original Greek state.

[15] Andréas Karandónis, Η ελληνική αίσθηση στην ποίηση του Σεφέρη και του Ελύτη (Hellenic feeling in the poetry of Seferis and Elytis) ([1962] 1980), 151.

against indiscriminate internationalism. They attempted to resolve questions of national identity not by debating outright issues of continuity, language, religion, geopolitical orientation, or race but by incorporating uncontextualized fragments from Hellenism's past in a portable, disengaged, but nonetheless emphatically *Hellenic* literary corpus. Their goal was to Hellenize international flight, thus demonstrating Hellenism's special contribution to the foundations of a free world.

A wide range of authors, liberal and conservative, from the critic Andréas Karandónis to the philosopher I. N. Theodorakópulos, reimagined their homeland as a *topos* with its own *ontología* 'logos of being', which demanded its own proportional *deontología* 'logos of moral necessity'.[16] The homeland had its own cultural logic, dependent on its natural features. The Greek language was the crystalline reflection of the physical environment. The traditions of the Greek people become products of the same unchanging climate and geography that gave the world classical Hellenism. It was the responsibility of the Greek artist to tap into Hellenism's natural resources, including its popular traditions, and to make these universally available. To this end, George Seferis, Greece's first Nobel laureate, whose work I discuss in Chapter 5, attempted to resurrect Everyman from his modern slumber. Seferis's poetry makes its literary journey into the depths of the *Odyssey* and so reenacts the drama of homecoming. Odysseus Elytis, Greece's second Nobel laureate, discussed in Chapter 6, tried to discover the natural language of Greece's landscape, which was beginning to be exploited for mass tourism at the time when Elytis was completing his literary masterpiece, the *Axion Esti*. In my afterthoughts at the book's conclusion, I try to map another Hellenism beyond the boundaries of the postwar Greek homeland—after Greece, so to speak.

In writing this book, I have faced several challenges. The most difficult one has been how to describe the interaction between Western Hellenism and Neohellenism without reducing this to a simple pattern of dominance and resistance, on the one hand, or genesis and imitation, on the other. I have tried to avoid ascribing blame for unequal power relations. It is my belief that even where an excess of power has led to intervention, the marshals of a new order are not necessarily

---

[16] See Ioánnis Theodorakópulos, Το πνεύμα του νεοελληνισμού (The spirit of Neohellenism) ([1945] 1967), 137.

aggressors, and the recipients of what may be an inspiring blow are not necessarily victims. The most powerful empires and states have their civilizing ideals; they may also have a few good women and men who seek to understand the civility of seemingly "uncivil subjects." Conversely, the smallest minority or ethnic group may adopt with a vengeance another civilization's ideals, which it then adapts to serve its own interests. In the modern period, Hellenism has been an ideal for Europeans and Greeks alike. Greeks have used Hellenism sometimes to their advantage, though they have also faltered under its weight. It does not seem tenable to suggest that without Western Hellenism there would be no Greek state, yet one could argue that without Hellenism there would be no Neohellenism. Greeks might have fashioned a different entity and mapped a different kind of homeland.

Another challenge is to address an audience representing different disciplines, knowledgeable about different societies and historical periods. Modern Greek is a minor, interdisciplinary field with a small number of scholars working in diverse areas of study, including history, sociology, economics, political science, anthropology, literature, and linguistics. Greek study includes those who would reconstruct Hellenism's older layers and those who would explore the contemporary Greek world. Unfortunately, students of ancient and modern Greek are usually cons apart, and few have successfully bridged the wide chasm between the dead and the living, a task I humbly undertake.[17] Since I claim a theoretical topic, I am also compelled to tread where theorists meet, though theorists dwell in diverse fields and reap different particulars. So I have faced the problem of gathering the

---

[17] There have been several distinguished scholarly attempts to approach both living and dead Greeks. George Thomson worked diligently to develop a program for studying Hellenism that worked through recent layers of Greek before excavating older ones. See Thomson, *The Greek Language* (1972), and "The Continuity of Hellenism" (1971). For a discussion of Thomson's interest in the continuity of Greek culture, see Dimitrios Tzióvas, "George Thomson and the Dialectics of Hellenism" (1989). Noteworthy, too, is the contribution of Margaret Alexiou, whose *Ritual Lament in Greek Tradition* (1974) stands in my eyes as one of the most successful scholarly efforts to treat all layers of Hellenism. See also Paschalis M. Kitromilides, "The Last Battle of the Ancients and Moderns: Ancient Greece and Modern Europe in the Neohellenic Revival" (1985); David Ricks, *The Shade of Homer: A Study in Modern Greek Poetry* (1989); and Speros Vryonis, "Recent Scholarship on Continuity and Discontinuity of Culture: Classical Greeks, Byzantines, Modern Greeks" (1978). For a more recent, though less comprehensive, attempt to discuss the difficult topic of the continuity of Greek culture, see Bernard Knox, *The Oldest Dead White European Males and Other Reflections on the Classics* (1993), 107–30.

necessary particulars of the Greek case while also cultivating a theory useful to nonspecialists. The result is a compromise that may sometimes leave readers unsatisfied, since it will occasionally forgo specifics that the specialist recalls as relevant, while it also makes a narrow path through unfamiliar ground where the nonspecialist may not wish to follow. In the interest of putting Neohellenism in the spotlight of today's most stimulating academic discussions, however, I am willing to make this compromise.

Finally, I face the dilemma of my own position. Any claim about the interaction of culture and place carries the burden of situating itself. The narrowest context of the present study is personal, in this case also professional, since I have chosen to make academic fodder of a sustaining provision of diaspora: that one search endlessly for roots discovered only through displacement. I am fortunate to have entered the academy at a time when dislocated identities have become a popular *topos*. The dilemmas of diaspora, an ancient phenomenon though a new area of research interest, seem to express several predicaments of our era. Yet just how does a diaspora intellectual interact with the familiar but foreign culture of the West, or with the alien but familiar national culture on which her special identity may depend? What role does her work play in the global context of expanding international markets, which continue to extract resources from less-developed nations, on the one hand, and renewed nationalisms that build walls of hostility between once-friendly neighbors, on the other? In my own case, I perceive the dichotomous relationship between westerner and Neohellene breaking down not only when I ascend the acropolis and assume the lofty height of the theorist who claims critical distance but also each time I descend to be with my own. It seems impossible for me to locate a single audience.

In the chapters that follow, I study Hellenism's topographies as drafted by European travelers, diplomats, archeologists, architects, and historians and by Greek intellectuals, critics, poets, artists, politicians, and urban planners. I explore how European "outsiders" and Greek "insiders" map a Hellenic homeland: how competing groups lay claim to the culture of ruins, give shape to Hellenism, fortify territorial claims, and combat the claims of others. I approach my subject as a topologist: that is to say, my aim is not simply to retrace Hellenism's topographies but to reshape the *topos* of Hellas.

PART I

RELOCATING THE ANCIENT SITE

CHAPTER I

The Topological Approach

One only knows a spot once one has experienced it in as many dimensions as possible. You have to have approached a place from all four cardinal points if you want to take it in, and what's more, you also have to have left it from all these points. Otherwise it will quite unexpectedly cross your path three or four times before you are prepared to discover it.

—Walter Benjamin, "Moscow Diary"

Hellas is a disputed province of Western thought. A recurring *topos* of the modern literary imagination, it represents neither a monolithic essence nor an unchanging truth. The centers and limits of Hellas, both actual and imaginary, are constantly shifting, as different groups approach their ideal from distinct paths, with differing objectives. Some sojourners in Hellas have followed the course of travel, an acquisitive mode of displacement; others have excavated antiquities, a displacing method of acquisition. Some hold nationalist aspirations, engaging in linguistic, political, and cartographic battles in order to reclaim the territories of Hellas; others work the field of indigenous practices, in which they may wish to discover ancient survivals. Still others have followed the literary paths of classicism, with its idealization of ancient Hellas, or high modernism, with its skeptical reassessment of Hellenism. All have played their part in relocating the temples and backwaters of this revered and reviled place. They have also produced interesting topographies: travel narratives, essays on the identity of Neohellenes, and modernist verse, to name only a few items discussed in this book.

Knowledge of a place is more than any academic study should promise, especially when that place exists on the level of both ideas and geography. Yet intellectual journeys are not randomly made.

Knowledge about a place is intertwined with the place of knowledge. Knowledge follows common vectors, well-beaten paths, cherished sites to which others have returned. These define one's course of study. They are landmarks in an open field, cardinal points of reference one cannot avoid. If one approaches a place through as many of these as possible, one may reach the modest goal of passing through some point of understanding from several different directions.

Hellas

Two intersecting axes define the coordinate plane we call Hellas, which is crossed by vectors of travel to and from, lines of exploration through, and points of return within Greece. They are conceptual maps and physical sites. Where maps of Hellenism and physical sites of Hellas intersect, we can locate the imaginary point from which knowledge about Greece emanates. This point is the *topos* of Hellas.[1]

In ancient Greek rhetoric, *topos* represented a site of learning to which speakers returned again and again for reliable phrases, expressions, and motifs that regularly impressed an audience. In its more general Greek usage, *topos* designated a physical location considered worthy of description: a burial place, a public building, a monument, a district, or a territory. Although *topos* has lost its physical referent in modern rhetorical terminology, it retains its spatial resonance in important English derivatives such as *topography*, *utopia* 'no place', and *dystopia* 'bad place'. Perhaps it is useful to dwell on this dual resonance: *topos* as citation and *topos* as physical place. To think of *topos* simultaneously as a site of learning and of geography is to raise the question of the reciprocal interdependence of literature and place. By historical coincidence, *topos* retains both rhetorical and spatial referents in modern

---

[1] I have assimilated into my theorizing of *topos* Gilles Deleuze and Félix Guattari's uses of "territory" in *A Thousand Plateaus: Capitalism and Schizophrenia* (1986), as well as the following discussions: Paul Alliès, *L'invention du territoire* (1980); James Anderson, "Nationalist Ideology and Territory" (1988); Cobbah, "Toward a Geography of Peace in Africa"; Jean Gottman, *The Significance of Territory* (1973); D. B. Knight, "Identity and Territory: Geographical Perspectives on Nationalism and Regionalism" (1982); Juval Portugali, "Nationalism, Social Theory, and the Israeli/Palestinian Case" (1988); R. Sack, "Human Territoriality: A Theory" (1983); id., *Human Territoriality: Its Theory and History* (1986); Rokkan Stein and Derek W. Urwin, *The Politics of Territorial Identity* (1982); Philip Wagner, "Rank and Territory" (1969).

Greek.[2] While it refers in certain cases to territory, piece of ground, place, position, or opportunity, *topos* also indicates a passage in a text or, more generally, a common citation, a commonplace.[3] Even in this last sense, however, *topos* in Greek marks a physical place of return, a site where the past makes its presence felt.

One fact is not coincidental to the unfolding of a Greek history: the classical Greek heritage is the particular past that haunts the Greek present. The entwinement of literature and place dictated destiny for the famed philhellene and romantic poet, George Gordon, Lord Byron (1788–1824). Hellas under Ottoman rule represented an odd piece of real estate.[4] Though a "sad relic of departed worth," yet it was "consecrated land": "Where'er we tread 'tis haunted, holy ground." Moreover, each site had its literary citation, and each citation consecrated that site and defined its cultural significance and geopolitical potential. The territory of Hellas could exist for rebelling Greek-speaking Ottoman subjects as the sacred land of historical restitution, if only Greeks would inform themselves of their glorious ancestry. They might turn, for example, to literary descriptions of the battle scene at Marathon, "when Marathon became a magic word." Recollection of such a *topos* of remarkable heroism promised to rescue their souls from enslavement and to transform each man to fit the place, so that the Greek could once again become "the true-born son of Greece." The result would be the wholesale recovery of Hellas.

But Byron's reference to Marathon in *Childe Harold's Pilgrimage* may be too familiar a citation to convey the message that Marathon, like Thermopylae, Dodona, Delphi, Macedonia, Athens, or Hellas itself, refers not only to an ideal but also to a place. Conversely, these places became common topics of learning in education, particularly in the revived classicism of the European Enlightenment that extended into the twentieth century. The point is that they exist both as sites of learning—citations in texts to which one might refer in order to make

[2] *Topos* is the name of a "journal of urban and peripheral studies" circulating in Greece. Two issues of another Greek journal, *Topos epikoinos*, from the ancient Greek 'topos common to many', had been published by the Department of Communications and Mass Media of Pandio University in Athens by December 1992.

[3] As in the ancient Greek *koinos topos* and the Latin *locus communis*.

[4] Byron even entertained "some idea of purchasing the Island of Ithaca" in his letter to Hobhouse from Patras dated 4 October 1810 (*Byron's Works* [1902], 1:305). The quotations that follow are from Byron's *Childe Harold's Pilgrimage*, canto 2, secs. 73, 93, 88, 89, 83; see *Poetical Works* (1979), 205, 208, 207.

a particular point or to call upon a particular model from the past—and as locations that one can visit, excavate, ravage, fence off, or mark on a map. The effect I wish to achieve here is to halt the mythic immediacy of the place-names, an immediacy that sends us directly to ancient sources. We must stop to consider the constellation of factors in recent history that have shaped Hellas.

This tactic of interruption may also bring to rest any tendency to conceive of the *topos* of Hellas as utopian, that is to say, existing in nonreferential space. As evidence of a utopian tendency, one has only to recall how Georg Lukács found it "fruitful to inquire into the transcendental topography of the Greek mind" found in Homeric poetry.[5] Through his analysis of the Greek epic form, Lukács claimed to have discovered the structure of the Greek world: integrated, homogeneous, rounded, an "archetypal home."[6] I might add that such a formalist approach assumes, paradoxically by its negation of physical space, that the referent Hellas has an exteriority to which language has the option of *not* referring because its significance transcends space. Surely the transcendence of space is the product of a certain view that holds space to be nature's last refuge where meaning can take root and grow.[7] Conversely, to deny the exteriority of the spatial referent is not to suggest that space does not exist. Rather it is to say that the *relationship* between knowledge and place is fundamental and constitutive, even in the making of utopias.

The physical consequences of certain literary commonplaces for Greeks themselves, on the one hand, and the rhetorical determinants of the Greek homeland, on the other, may become clearer when we consider a literally concrete site where the *topos* of the *logos*, the site of knowledge, and the *logos* of the *topos*, the story of the site, stand juxtaposed. Such a (common)place can be found in the river Ilissus, now paved in asphalt.[8] Plato's *Phaedrus* cited the Ilissus as the mythical

---

[5] Georg Lukács, *The Theory of the Novel* ([1920] 1971), 32.

[6] Ibid., 33.

[7] Uri Eisenzweig analyzes this view of nature as it relates to Zionism in "An Imaginary Territory: The Problematic of Space in Zionist Discourse" (1981). The common utopian elements in Zionism and Hellenism and the frequent utopian conceptions of Israel and Hellas are not unrelated to the important roles that Jerusalem and Athens have played in the modern European cultural and political imagination. See Vassilis Lambropoulos, *The Rise of Eurocentrism: Anatomy of Interpretation* (1992).

[8] See Panayótis Turnikiótis, Ο Ιλισσός του Πλάτωνα· Για την ιδεολογική παρουσία του παρελθόντος στη σύγχρονη Αθήνα (Plato's Ilissus: On the ideological pres-

site where "Boreas seized Oreithyia" (229b), while it was also the *topos* that inspired the Socratic *logos* on love, which Plato's dialogue, in turn, transformed into a commonplace for philosophical inspiration.

This literary recollection is not incidental to the river's destiny in modern times. The Ilissus remains an exemplar of the quiet location removed from the hurried activities of everyday life that engendered philosophical dialogue.[9] It epitomizes the place that inspires by its verdure, beauty, and peacefulness. On another level, it signifies the achievement of ancient philosophy: it attests to the harmony of ancient Hellenism, Lukács's "integrated" homeland. For modern Greeks, however, the Ilissus also represents the physical site described in detail by Pausanias, the topographer of late antiquity whose guidebook on the ruins of ancient Athens attached to the riverbed the *logos* of Oreithyia's rape and made the site *theās axion* 'worthy of contemplation'.[10] The dry banks of the Ilissus cut through the modern capital city and for decades divided wealthy from working-class neighborhoods. The struggle to identify the river's precise ancient location, to clean up its perennially polluted bed, to remove from its banks unscenic elements, and, above all, to recreate the semblance of cultural activity along its edges began in the mid-1800s and continued into the 1950s,

---

ence of the past in modern Athens) (1991), for an inspired discussion of the river Ilissus as a site where modern Athenians have struggled to recover past glories. He develops the thesis that the Ilissus was never a remarkable place, even in ancient times. It was Plato who transformed an insignificant river into an exemplar of the idyllic landscape that inspires philosophical thought. Plato's *logos* became "the starting point for the journey of the idea in Western thought" (81) that the Ilissus was physically imposing. Furthermore, it produced a *topos* that referred "not to a concrete place or object but to a situation without a material dimension" (81). Greek efforts to locate in physical space what is really a literary *topos* are a vain pursuit, Turnikiótis concludes.

[9] It is also identified as the site of the Panathenaic Stadium and the Lyceum where Aristotle taught.

[10] Pausanias's method was to relate what was best known to citizens of a polis through their *logoi* and *theorēmata* 'sights'. See Pausanias 1.39.3 on his methodology for describing Athens. Yánnis Tsifopoulos describes Pausanias's project thus: "Pausanias . . . may be better understood as an exegete, i.e., an author who, within the broad framework of a description of Hellas, is purveying various stories that survived to his time about the history, archaeology, religion and mythology, geography and topography, *inter alia*, of a particular place. For these stories the most trustworthy evidence available were the inscriptions, the monuments, and the local periegetes/exegetes" ("Pausanias as a Steloskopas: An Epigraphical Commentary on Pausanias' ELIAKON A and B" [1991], 14).

when city officials finally agreed to fill it in, thus creating the Leofóros Vasiléos Konstandínu 'Avenue of King Constantine'.[11]

Throughout this period of more than one hundred years, literary recollection surely shaped not only the Greek cultural unconscious but also town planning, which always proceeded on the assumption that the modern city of Athens had to retain distinct paths beneath antiquity's burdensome shadow. "Ilissus," the ancient literary prototype, existed both as an opportunity and as a quagmire. The story of Socrates' contemplative stroll with Phaedrus alongside a river lined with trees offering a bucolic refuge from the daily grind of city life somehow doomed efforts to recover the physical site of that "happy summer day." It made the dry bed of the Ilissus the symbol of a lost resource perennially crying for recovery, symbolizing severance and present disharmony. For Greeks, then, the Ilissus not only became the *topos* of a rich philosophical inheritance that they felt somehow obligated to transmit;[12] it also remained a "watery mirage . . . made to wet the far ends of the earth with the glory of a city now washed by a waterless river."[13]

Topology

The present era of intellectual activity, though sober in its antiromantic will to dispel watery mirages like the Ilissus from preceding eras, has been bountiful in its production of theories. Today's theories generally promise to deliver readers from one imaginary order to another. To produce a critical work is to create another plan for clearing the dry riverbed of past knowledge while standing quite self-consciously on a new mirage. Although the promise is a weak one, the work is hard, the debate lively, and the interchange between once-entrenched disciplines of the humanities and social sciences has be-

[11] Gustave Fougères mentions the existence of outdoor cafés, in particular the café-theater "Paradise," along the dry banks of the Ilissus in 1912 (*Athènes* [1912], 250; quoted in Turnikiótis, Ο Ιλισσός του Πλάτωνα [Plato's Ilissus], 85). A photograph of the "Paradise" from 1890 is extant. See Turnikiótis, 82.

[12] *Ilissós* was the title of a Greek philosophical periodical published in the 1950s.

[13] From Nicholas Calas's poem Αθήνα 1933 (Athens 1933). Cf. John Cam Hobhouse, who refers several times to the "small gravelly channel of the Ilissus. . . . If full to the margin, [it] could never have been more than an insignificant brook" (*A Journey through Albania, and Other Provinces of Turkey in Europe and Asia, to Constantinople, during the Years 1809 and 1810* [1813], 1:318).

come quite rich. I offer topology as another approach—not a new orthodoxy but a way to reflect on what we know. It is a lens through which to examine with a critical eye from below sacred constellations that have guided modern women and men, then to reconnect what appear to be fading points of light. Or one might identify the topologist with the critical spectator, the *theōros*, if you will, who surveys from above collective fantasies about the mythic origins of a civilization, then engages in redirecting these fantasies and reshaping the cultural terrain.[14]

Topology follows two directions of thought. It studies how a place makes power and knowledge immanent. And it seeks to determine how knowledge and power seize that place. In general, topology scrutinizes the complex interaction between the conceptual map, the *logos*, and place, the *topos*. It considers both how the *logos* constructs its plane of activity and how the *topos* makes meaning possible by providing landmarks, monuments, lines of connection, lines of flight, and barriers that facilitate or hinder representation.

Topology further aims to situate the knowledge *it* generates within the *topos* it occupies. While it develops a *logos* about place, its comprehension of that place is not linear but chiasmic. The chiasmus is that folding rhetorical trope that inseparably intertwines two phrases of thought through deft reversal. Examples can be dizzying. Knowledge of a site becomes a site of knowledge. The citation of a site shapes the site of citation. The *topos* of a *logos* nourishes a *logos* about the *topos*. Topology is not a *logos* about a *topos* acquired through successive incursions. Instead, topology enters the perpetual exchange between intersecting terms: the *topos* and the *logos*; the place of citation and the

[14] In ancient Greece the *theōros* is an emissary, one "who sees [root *hor-*] a vision [*theā*]" (Nagy, *Pindar's Homer*, 164). J. Peter Euben explains: "A theoros was either an ambassador sent by a polis to the sacred festivals of another state, or, more likely, an envoy sent to consult the Delphic oracle, the arbiter of sacred law, religious ritual, and rites of purification. . . . Gradually the meaning of theoros became more general and included going to witness religious and athletic festivals (spectacles) abroad. . . . As the role of theoros broadened, such spectating became less passive. . . . It demanded the capacity to explain and understand what one sees, distinguish what is essential to a performance or ritual from what is incidental, and transmit such knowledge to the polis in honest, useful form. Because theory entailed undertaking a journey abroad to see, a theorist and theory came to be associated with traveling, particularly over vast distances to non-Greek cultures. . . . Thus theory came to mean seeing with an eye toward learning about different lands and institutions, alien practices and experiences, distilling and comparing the pattern of things seen while engaged in travel ("Creatures of a Day: Thought and Action in Thucydides" [1978], 33–34).

citation of place. In this exchange, the *logos* of topology never fully occupies the *topos*, even as the *topos* of topology does not exercise complete control over the *logos*.

Let us consider again the example of Hellas. Hellas represents a historical, philological, and literary *logos* as well as a *topos* of social, economic, and cultural activity. In Western Hellenism, Hellas occupies the realm of the imagination and intellect. It is a country of the mind, even when put on tour. The *logos* of Hellenism may seize the *topos* of Hellas through literary citation or archeological excavation; but it can never entirely claim Hellas. At the same time, the *topos* of Hellas, the place cited as historically belonging to Hellenes, sets limits on the ways the *logos* of Hellenism can develop. Hellas gives Hellenism position and weight. It also gives it a geography, climate, and people to speak of. Yet the *topos* of Hellas never determines fully the *logos* of Hellenism. Topology must not privilege either the *topos* or the *logos*. Instead it should sustain the tensions between its two constituent elements—the *topos* of the *logos* and the *logos* of the *topos*.

It may be helpful to name some things that topology is not. Topology is not archeology. It does not participate in the patient reconstruction of monuments, the unburying of stones long underground, the recovery of culture's fragments from a nature that would subsume them. Yet topology may consider how the obsessions and techniques of this important discipline organize a site, and how the organization of the site in turn affects the discipline. Topology, furthermore, is not an analytical version of travel writing. It does not speak of the ambivalence of escape. It does not describe the nostalgia of return. It does not promise the vicarious pleasure of visiting a foreign place. Yet topology may reflect on how travel literature has afforded an audience the place it desires or expects. It might also aspire to the fluency and popularity of travel writing—something I do not do in this book.

Finally, although topology is a kind of topography, a kind of *graphē* of the *topos*, it is not just any topography. Perhaps I should reckon here with a tension in my own thinking about *topos*, which arises from my tendency to pass back and forth between the terms *topography* and *topology*. There is some system to my usage. Topography refers to cultural production, while topology is the critical enterprise that traces a culture's mappings of place. I assume that it is one thing to draw borders, to assign names to places, to describe one's encounter with a sacred space such as the Acropolis, and so to map one's identity as politician, nationalist, poet, citizen, critic, or traveler. It is quite a different activity to group together the makers of culture or nations based on the commonality of the site they reclaim; to study the emergence of national groups within that site; to map people's perceptions of place as they travel across its boundaries; to evaluate how social relations structure space and how space, conversely, structures social relations; or to study how ideas, movements, and genres change as they pass through a place. This is the work of topology.

It is important to realize, however, that there is no epistemological distinction between topography and topology—between mapping a homeland, on the one hand, and marking places that resonate on maps. The distinction lies not in how one knows but in the tools of knowledge one puts to use. The nationalist, for example, may use narrative or descriptive tools, while the topologist relies on analysis and exposition. There is also a difference in the level of representation. The nationalist may refer to an actual territory, whereas the topologist fixes her attention on representations of territory and brackets discussion of the "actual." Furthermore, the two classes of topographers may play different political roles, the one actively intervening, the other professing neutrality or preaching restraint. Yet it should be clearly stated that both orders of topography are drafting maps of place and creating territories of knowledge. Both are imagining a world, inserting vectors and signposts in space, and locating sites where the past makes itself present, where pleasure may be discovered, where knowledge is expounded, money expended, resources expropriated, and leisure consumed.

Tradition Extraterritorial?

Because topology studies the place of citation, it is by definition concerned with the topic of tradition.[15] Though frequently conceived

[15] Tradition is an unsettling territory of the modern imagination: both a burdensome repository of outmoded values and an inevitable, if lost, center of return. A focal point of study in a variety of disciplines throughout this century, tradition has received attention during the past several decades under various rubrics, including canon and evolution (Tynjanov, Wellek), literary history (White, Weimann), influence (Bloom), poetic authority (Guillory), and even paradigm (Kuhn). In contemporary criticism, one can point to studies of the development of Panhellenism in Greek antiquity that emphasize poetic repossessions of the past (Nagy), accounts of the relationship of modern poets to their literary precursors (Bate, Briggs, Gilbert and Gubar, Highet, Jenkyns, Mileur, Perl, Ricks, and Turner), descriptions of the continuous play between

as an imaginary vessel containing the resources of a shared past, tradition's "well-wrought urn" in fact holds an important place in the territory of the nation. The instrument of a narrative that asserts the value of the past for the present, traditions are invented wherever individuals or groups "refer to old situations, or . . . establish their own past by quasi-obligatory repetition" as they respond to "novel situations."[16] "Novel situations" in modern times have included modernization and the institution of nation-states. These are some of the same situations to which groups have responded by producing topographies. Tradition, frequently serving the goals of topography, also comes to the aid of topography. The relationship is as interdependent as the interchange between citation and place. Certainly topographies have invented traditions through their repeated collocation of

---

tradition and innovation in the history of religions (Eikelman, Eisenstadt, Gusfield, Mani, Rudolph and Rudolph, Shils, Waldman, and Werblowsky), or, more generally, a pervasive interest in the contradictory condition of modernity (de Man), with its impulse to embrace the new and its secret wish to resuscitate the old. These critical projects all explore the meaning and nature of tradition. On the classical tradition, see Highet, and Reinhold and Hanawalt. (The relevant references are, in order of mention above, Jurij Tynjanov, "On Literary Evolution" [(1927) 1987]; René Wellek, "The Concept of Evolution in Literary History" [(1956) 1963]; Hayden White, "The Problem of Change in Literary History" [1975]; Robert Weimann, *Structure and Society in Literary History: Studies in the History and Theory of Historical Criticism* [1984]; Harold Bloom, *The Anxiety of Influence* [1975]; John Guillory, *Poetic Authority: Spenser, Milton, and Literary History* [1983]; Thomas S. Kuhn, "Postscript—1969" [1970]; Nagy, *Pindar's Homer*; Walter Jackson Bate, *The Burden of the Past and the English Poet* [1972]; Asa Briggs, "The Image of Greece in Modern English Literature" [1987]; Sandra Gilbert and Susan Gubar, *No Man's Land: The Place of the Woman Writer in the Twentieth Century* [1988]; Gilbert Highet, *The Classical Tradition: Greek and Roman Influences on Western Literature* [(1949) 1976]; Jenkyns, *Victorians and Ancient Greece*; Jean-Pierre Mileur, *Literary Revisionism and the Burden of Modernity* [1985]; Jeffrey M. Perl, *The Tradition of Return: The Implicit History of Modern Literature* [1984]; Ricks, *Shade of Homer*; Frank M. Turner, *The Greek Heritage in Victorian Britain* [1981]; Dale F. Eikelman, "Ideological Change and Regional Cults: Maraboutism and Ties of 'Closeness' in Western Morocco" [1977]; S. N. Eisenstadt, "Continuity and Reconstruction of Tradition" [1973]; Joseph R. Gusfield, "Tradition and Modernity: Misplaced Polarities in the Study of Social Change" [1967]; Lata Mani, "Contentious Traditions: The Debate on SATI in Colonial India" [1987]; Lloyd I. Rudolph and Susanne Hoeber Rudolph, *The Modernity of Tradition: Political Development in India* [1967]; Edward Shils, *The Torment of Secrecy* [1969]; id., *Tradition* [1981]; Marilyn Waldman, "Tradition as a Modality of Change: Islamic Examples" [1986]; R. J. Zwi Werblowsky, *Beyond Tradition and Modernity: Changing Religions in a Changing World* [1976]; Paul de Man, "Literary History and Literary Modernity" [1983]; Highet, *Classical Tradition*; Meyer Reinhold and Emily Albu Hanawalt, *The Classical Tradition: Teaching and Research* [1987].)

[16] Eric Hobsbawm and Terence Ranger, eds., *The Invention of Tradition* (1983), 1–2.

sites. And traditions have served topographers of all kinds, particularly nation builders.

Current research on national institutions shows that culture is a standard vehicle for defining the nation's plane of activity, the homeland. Culture's citation of a shared past may circumscribe the expanse of the homeland, unify that expanse, and deepen a people's "roots" in a place.[17] Indeed culture renders the connections between people and place natural and symbolic by citing the distinctiveness of a people's history in place. "Nations, like states, are not simply located in geographic space—which is the case with social organisms—rather they explicitly claim particular territories and derive distinctiveness from them. . . . Nationalists typically over-emphasize the particular uniqueness of their own territory and history."[18] The specific geographical plane in which a national idea organizes itself does not in and of itself define the uniqueness of the nation. Instead it is culture's reactivated sense of a shared past that marks the territory, rendering territory foundational and essential, rather than functional and transitory. One is again reminded of the dual resonance of *topos*, the reciprocal interdependence of citation and place. National culture both cites the tradition of place and seizes the spatial expanse that traditions may claim.

Tradition occupies physical place. This means that there is a physical plane on which a shared inheritance takes shape, to which it assigns identity, on which it imposes order, within which it may teach an audience to get around. The examples of the Acropolis, Athens, and, by extension, all of Greece may help to illuminate this point. Athens is the capital of Hellas. It locates itself in Greece's present by relating itself to its past. Its temporal situation is both physical and philological. The Acropolis, the conspicuous landmark standing high above the center of Athens, is carved into Athens's urban plan, but it is also engraved in the topography of Hellenism, which Greeks collect, study, and cite.

---

[17] "Nationalist ideologies have sought to interpret the occupation and control of space, both in the past and as a plan for the future" (R. J. Johnston, David B. Knight, and Eleonore Kofman, eds., *Nationalism, Self-Determination, and Political Geography* [1988], 3). On territory and the nation, see also Gottman, *Significance of Territory*; Roy E. H. Mellor, *Nation, State, and Territory: A Political Geography* (1989); Stein and Urwin, *Politics of Territorial Identity*; and Wagner, "Rank and Territory." For an excellent bibliography on territory, nation, state, and self-determination, see D. B. Knight and Maureen Davies, eds., *Self-Determination: An Interdisciplinary Annotated Bibliography* (1987).

[18] Anderson, "Nationalist Ideology and Territory," 18.

Through several complementary determinants, Greece as a whole, Athens in particular, has been condemned to realize unsuccessfully two urban projects: to be Hellenic and to become modern. Not incidental to Greece's modern history, other national groups also fiercely fought for the right to claim the same characteristics. Although not entirely unique to Greece, this situation is undeniably peculiar.[19] Greeks found themselves defined by their historical dislocation, disinherited from a past whose genealogical tree was made to grow upward in the direction of the British, Germans, and French, Greece's supposed cultural descendants. In Western Europe, everybody aspired to be more Greek than everyone else and even more Greek than the Greeks themselves (ancient and modern). Not oblivious to foreign uses and abuses of its history, monuments, and terrain, Greeks legally staked out their homeland around the capital center of Athens.[20] To be Hellenic, then, Greeks have felt the relentless necessity to reconstruct the ancient city of Athens as no other Europeans could. To be modern, however, they have had to model their cities on European urban centers. In both cases their archetype, the arche-*topos*, if you will, lay elsewhere. More concretely, the story of what Hellas had been and the map of what it had become in the ideal European capital shaped the here and now of the modern city of Athens. Athens has therefore been built upon maps of other cities: on older layers of itself and on present models designed and realized elsewhere. It is physically saturated with its own history and with other people's maps, two sites of return that have both obstructed and enhanced its physical potential.

National literature, a more traditional subject of critical analysis than urban planning, makes special use of the resources of a shared past to posit a distinct origin for the present. One of literature's distinct roles is to excavate verbal remains from the nation's previous occupants, now "dead, absent, or conquered."[21] By rescuing traditions from oblivion, national literature has "defined a native ethos and justified the claims to autonomy and independence of that entity."[22] Even though literature tends to obfuscate the interests at stake in its citation

[19] Egypt and Israel present analogous examples. On Egyptians' relationship to their ancient history, see Mary N. Layoun, *Travels of a Genre: The Modern Novel and Ideology* (1990), chap. 2.

[20] In 1833, Ottoman authorities abandoned the defense of the Acropolis to the Bavarian Otto, king of Hellas. Within the next year, Otto moved the capital of his new Greek kingdom from the Peloponnesian port of Náfplion to Athens.

[21] Shelly Errington, "Fragile Traditions and Contested Meanings" (1989), 50.

[22] Vassilis Lambropoulos, *Literature as National Institution: Studies in the Politics of Modern Greek Criticism* (1988), 9.

of tradition, nevertheless these interests remain evident. Through deliberate citations that relate past to present, literature serves to relocate the present world practices inherited from the past. As literary citations become commonplace, they take their place in place. Literature's act of repossessing the past thus aids in possessing the site of the nation.

The territorial dimension of tradition, though fundamental, is certainly not obvious. Much criticism today imagines the territory of traditon through extraterritorial images. Tradition is not geographically located; rather it is a canonic corpus, a textual (written or oral) point of departure for building a new world order out of the wasteland of the old. Critical attention therefore converges on formal techniques by which writers and artists recode the traditional elements of narratives, myths, heroes, images, and expressions in their imaginative works: for example, how they fragment and spatialize time by the modernist techniques of montage, quotation, and collage, and so recreate the past as text.[23]

Where critics make reference to territory, it is to show how a (good) work crosses national boundaries. George Steiner was perhaps the first to feature "extraterritoriality" as a positive literary attribute. Steiner began one book of essays, aptly entitled *Extraterritorial* (1975), in search of authors whose work transcends the goal of incarnating the genius of native speech. Praising the example of Vladimir Nabokov, Steiner asserted that a pattern of "cross-writing," epitomized by Nabokov's work, appropriately expressed today's "civilization of quasi-barbarism which has made so many homeless, which has torn up tongues and peoples by the root."[24] Steiner's other examples are Proust, Joyce, and Beckett.

Gilles Deleuze and Félix Guattari, too, have taken up the theme of

[23] For a critical discussion of spatial form in modern literature, see Paul de Man, "Spacecritics: J. Hillis Miller and Joseph Frank" (1989); Joseph Frank, "Spatial Form in Modern Literature" ([1945] 1963, 1968); Elrud Ibsch, "Historical Changes of the Function of Spatial Description in Literary Texts" (1982); Richard Jackson, *The Dismantling of Time in Contemporary Poetry* (1988); Stephen Kern, *The Culture of Time and Space, 1880–1918* (1983); W. J. T. Mitchell, "Diagrammatology" (1981); id., "Spatial Form in Literature: Toward a General Theory" (1980); and William Spanos, "Modern Literary Criticism and the Spatialization of Time" (1970). For postmodernist discussions of space and modernity, see David Harvey, *The Condition of Postmodernity* (1989); Jezierski, "Politics of Space"; Kristin Ross, *The Emergence of Social Space: Rimbaud and the Paris Commune* (1988); Edward W. Soja, *Postmodern Geographies: The Reassertion of Space in Critical Social Theory* (1989).

[24] George Steiner, *Extraterritorial: Papers on Literature and the Language Revolution* (1975), 11.

writing across territories. In the interest of defining a "minor literature"—the characteristics of which are not easily distinguishable from
certain high modernist tendencies—they focused attention on literature "effected" by "deterritorialization."[25] In their now standard work
Kafka: Toward a Minor Literature (1986), they celebrated a "minor
literature" written within a major language with a major cultural
referent but against a system of investment that would extract constants from a national tradition. Not coincidentally, they, like Steiner,
drew their examples of "minor" authors—Kafka, Joyce, Proust—
from the canon of modernists whose reputation is already sizable.
They, too, featured the unstable linguistic situation of both authors
and works. Cross-writing epitomized the (dis)placement of nondominant cultures in the world.

Although it is a valiant project to define the revolutionary potential
of dislocated literary works, by promoting guerrilla acts of cross-
writing do we not merely demonstrate our dependence on the modern
library? The library, not the world, remains our point of reference.
The library-encyclopedia may be the most familiar image used to
describe the cultural reserve that can be sorted, rearranged, and transported across the borders of nations, languages, and divisions such as
gender, race, religion, and class—at least within the framework of
stacks.[26] What should not be lost in the metaphor of the library,
however, with its collections of works national and extraterritorial,
major and minor, is the condition of each borrowing: the specific
contexts of translation, migration, occupation, exile, uprising, forced
removal of minority populations, importation of goods, and international trade that make possible the reactivation of an older work in the
territory of the new. It seems to me that "extraterritorial" is too general

[25] "Deterritorialization" is the movement or "line of flight" out of a territory.
"Reterritorialization" compensates for or hinders a "line of flight." It is the "standing
for" (*valoir pour*) a territory that has been deterritorialized. For a condensed discussion
of these important terms, see the conclusion of Deleuze and Guattari's *Thousand
Plateaus* (501–14). On Deleuze and Guattari's cartographic enterprise, see Charles J.
Stivale, "The Literary Element in *Mille Plateaus*: The New Cartography of Deleuze and
Guattari" (1985).

[26] Witness Flaubert's "library-encyclopedia" in *Bouvard and Pécuchet*, Mallarmé's
search for The Book, and Borges's "The Library of Babel." For critical discussions, see
Debra A. Castillo, *The Translated World: A Postmodern Tour of Libraries in Literature*
(1980); Eugenio Donato, "The Museum's Furnace: Notes toward a Contextual Reading of *Bouvard and Pécuchet*" (1979); and Michel Foucault, "La bibliothèque fantastique"
(1967).

a term to grasp the geopolitical contexts of today's literary production, which range from political exile, statelessness, minority oppression, and unemployment to the internationalism and cosmopolitanism of the world's intellectual or economic elite. It is important to distinguish whether a work emphasizes dislocation, motivates relocation, celebrates the pleasures of dissociation, or creates roots that might make it harder for another group to contest one's particular claim on a territory. In the present world, the unity against which modern literature's "extraterritoriality" must be measured is the national territory from/ for which uprooted people are fleeing/writing.

As uprooted as people have been throughout this century, it seems strange that critics have overlooked the tools of mapping, border crossing, imaginary geography, or any other conceptual means of assigning tradition to a site and giving a place to *logos*. Surely this follows from the tendency of criticism to isolate the rhetorical sense of *topos* from its geographical resonance. Yet, upon reflection, we can see that tradition, the mental archive of learning, must relate to some physical place and that the delineation of the geographical terrain requires the precedent of myth, history, or some form of literature. Contrary to common assertions, then, tradition, particularly a "minor" tradition, is not extraterritorial. Rather its grain runs along some territories and against others. The place tradition occupies is not just the space of a book on a shelf, or the public arenas involved in a book's publication, distribution, or reception. Traditions *take place*, in the sense that they assign cultural identity to a geographical referent—even when this referent is extraterritorial or utopic. To be sure, geographical referents are themselves always imaginary, but only in the sense that their hypostasis is imaginary, just as any map is imaginary because it spans a different horizon from the territories we traverse with our feet. The interaction between the map and the territory is *not* fully described in Jean Baudrillard's postmodern statement that "territory no longer precedes the map," which follows the suggestion of the Borges tale where the cartographers "draw up a map so detailed that it ends up exactly covering the territory."[27] The obverse is equally true: the map does not precede territory. Instead, map and territory, tradition and place, though of different orders, remain in continuous interaction and tension.

[27]Jean Baudrillard, *Simulations* (1983), 1. In "Simulating History: A Cockfight for Our Times," (1990) Leonard Tennenhouse criticizes Baudrillard's "collapse of the map/territory distinction" (138).

Cardinal Points

In its journey through sites of knowledge, topology approaches a spot through several cardinal points. Let us consider briefly a few examples relevant to this study. Travel literature is the *logos* taken up in the next chapter. Increasingly a topic of interest to cultural studies, travel accounts lend themselves easily to the study of representations of place, since they give to a place literary usage. A previous generation of scholars tended to focus on the literary status of the genre: its relationship to the development of other fictional genres such as the novel; its use of literary themes such as the journey, the quest, self-discovery, and return. Today, as travel becomes a (somewhat inappropriate) metaphor for the postmodern situation of displacement, while people's geographical disorientation remains pervasive, theories of travel and travel literature are beginning to multiply. Critical analysis of travel literature would do well to begin rather pedantically by plotting the course of the world's travelers, both real and imaginary, on a received map and considering the motives for travel, the important matter of financing, the market for travel accounts. It could then draft conceptual maps of the world that name literary signposts: places frequented, places written about, places set apart from the ordinary, sites made to stand out against everything else that is rendered either too foreign or too ordinary to warrant careful description.[28]

A growing number of critical works are devoting attention to the accounts of travelers to Greece, sometimes erroneously referred to as *Greek* travelers, from the mid-eighteenth to the early twentieth century. Discussion focuses on what these accounts may tell us about the way that Western Europeans perceived Hellas and situated themselves as Hellenes in the world. These studies are useful to the extent that they make evident travelers' interests and prejudices: how Hellas played on their imaginations, how they felt, what they saw, what they ignored, what they liked, what they despised, how Hellas cast its spell on them, stimulated them, bored them, lured them, disturbed them. Hellas holds a literary place in the minds of many of these authors much more than it reflects a literal place. We may observe certain patterns of representation: many travelers saw themselves moving into the realm of their own past as they traveled south; they also may have viewed the

---

[28] Mary Louise Pratt's *Imperial Eyes: Travel Writing and Transculturalism* (1992) is exemplary in its analysis of travelers' views and local responses.

journey through present-day Hellas as a journey into the Orient. Their vision of Hellas as past and the Greek peninsula as East presented to them, as moderns and westerners, a venerated place of origin that present-day inhabitants of the peninsula, unlike themselves, could not truly occupy.

It has been suggested that Hellas, like the Orient, is not a mere geographical fact but a place actualized by and simultaneously acting upon the imagination of its visitors from the north. Few contemporary studies of travel to Greece, however, go on to discuss how the site of Hellas exerts its power on travelers' topographies. We have entered a critical mode where representation itself presents a problem worthy of analysis. Of geography, this would mean that we might consider how a displaced body traveling from north to south, west to east, reflects on the passing image. Yet we tend to stop here rather than to view things from the other side. Should we not also consider how the place of citation organizes itself locally, how the *topos* cited by travelers exerts is force on the *logos* of the local inhabitants? In the present division of disciplines, it seems that only anthropologists study a site *epi topou* 'on site', though they frequently ignore Western citations of the place.[29]

Certainly there is another reason for our silence about the local organization of space. As long as the study of travel literature duplicates the vectors of leisure travel, as long as critical interests remain invested in a culture of return, rooted in the West we seek to flee, the fact that the textualized traces of westerners' encounter with a foreign place cut through the local terrain at some expense to its inhabitants can present only secondary interest. Given that the Hellenic past was so systematically appropriated by the West, one can make room for the study of local inhabitants' repossessions of Hellenism only if one relates these, in turn, to prior Western appropriations. Otherwise the Hellenic terrain remains outside the *topos* of academic study as it has been organized for the past fifty years.

[29] Nenny Panourgia's *Fragments of Death, Fables of Identity: An Athenian Anthropography* (forthcoming) is a notable exception on many counts. In contrast to most anthropological studies of Greece, which take rural subjects, it focuses on the metropolitan center, Athens. And while its point of reference is the "native" anthropologist's self, family, and city—another exception—it does not underestimate the import of literary references from abroad. See, for example, the chapter entitled "Athens," which begins by reviewing what travelers said they expected to find in Athens, then presents what they did not find, that is to say, what they could not see in Athens: the pastiche of identities that constitute a modern Athenian woman's experience of the city.

To put topology on the map of humanistic disciplines is to reshape the field of cultural studies. As I have suggested, a topological approach compels the student of world cultures to move in two directions simultaneously: to pass back and forth between the *logos* of the *topos* and the *topos* of the *logos*. The study of travel literature must therefore concern itself not only with how texts make territory significant but also with how this territory "imbued with meaning" simultaneously becomes "an instrument of power and resistance" for local inhabitants.[30] Our critical blind spot duplicates the pattern of travel literature and travel itself. To overcome the effects of years of neglect, topology must also study the present situation of the local host. It is compelled to reckon with what is left over of *topos* after the literature of displacement assigns citations to sites. The central axis of study must shift, then, from the *logos* of travel to the *topos* of citation: the place that gives structure to a "native" *logos* and the maps of identity that the local occupants render of themselves.

In modern history, people around the world have embraced nationalism. Indeed there are few groups in the world today that have not at some time defined their particularity, often in the face of other transnational incursions, through this most influential ideology, the "global theology of the modern age."[31] Nationalist movements present a new map of the world. We are reminded of nationalism's cartographic enterprise by recent developments in Eastern Europe, where emergent nations, following in the footsteps of nations that evolved during the past century, redefine their borders through the claim that they embody a unique culture, language, and history. Through language, they affirm a majority occupation; through historical narratives of self-fulfillment, they legitimize that occupation; through culture, they prove the continuity of a rich inheritance.

Because the nation is conceived as a territorial entity, territory (or *topos*) is a standard rubric of the nation, as I shall show. Territory both shapes the nation and is shaped by the nation. On the one hand, the nation may choose its past, use the authority of cultural inheritance to stake out a territory, deploy tradition within that territory, assign textual citations to sites, and, generally, use evidence from historical, archeological, and linguistic studies to defend or expand existing boundaries, create a capital center, and set up its monuments. On the other

---

[30] Jezierski, "Politics of Space," 179–80.

[31] Gregory Jusdanis, *Belated Modernity and Aesthetic Culture: The Making of a National Literature* (1991), 165.

hand, the territory may precede the dream of emancipation, as it did in Hellas, where the *topos* cited by Western humanism shaped the unique particularity of the imagined national community.

In the event that dislocated populations such as diaspora intellectuals intervene in defining the nation or choosing a site, topology must also allow itself to be drawn into a much-needed though rather nascent discussion about the self-imagining of diaspora groups. Two scenarios of diasporic intervention present themselves. In one case, a diaspora may converge on the idea of settling a single, nonspecific territory to solve the specific ills of pogroms or unemployment it suffers. In this case, the territory of a utopian homeland—an otherwise "empty" space, unoccupied, at least in the imagination of the diaspora, by any other inhabitants—becomes a gathering place. The acquisition of territory means the end of diaspora, even if not all the diaspora pours into the territory. In another scenario, the diaspora may settle on the idea of self-determination within a specific territory, for example, the sacred site of Hellas. To establish a homeland does not require recollecting the diaspora if the diaspora does not pose itself as the problem to be solved. Instead the diaspora poses two questions about territory: what might it take to repossess control of an already-occupied territory, and what might it take to remake the present occupants of Hellas into Hellenes?

In either case, one must study how the diaspora, perhaps alongside or in counterpoint to an "indigenous" population, chooses the *topos* of its past, or, conversely, how this *topos* chooses the diaspora. How does an emergent nation use the past to create a homeland, to set up monuments, choose a capital, define itself as an entity? Where does it locate this past? Does the site of return correspond to the present definition of location? Do appeals to tradition emphasize dislocation, motivate relocation, compensate for migration, call for expansion? Do they seek to create roots that entrench the identification of a group in a homeland? Do they contest another group's competing claim?

Topology should not rest, however, after investigating the *logos* of the nation. Equally influential in mapping modern identity is the "counter-discourse" of modernism, which claims to transcend national territory in the interest of internationalism or cosmopolitanism.[32] Present-day cultural criticism seems to conflate modernism

---

[32] "Counter-discourse" refers to "a series of techniques and practices by which 19th-century intellectuals and artists contested the dominant habits of mind and expression of their contemporaries" (Richard Terdiman, *Discourse/Counter-Discourse: The Theory*

with the "minor," another counter-*logos* that develops outside national territory, in willful contradistinction to a hegemonic *logos* of power, investment, and occupation. As noted above, it has become commonplace to stress the multilingual, cross-cultural, extraterritorial situation shared by authors whose contribution to a language of resistance one seeks to affirm. There sometimes follows a serious, informed discussion about how the resource of labor seems to be continually extracted from postcolonials and other uprooted peoples.

As the "minor" evolves into a *logos* in its own right, however, and "minority" begins to occupy more visible sites, at least in the academic world, one should be careful to anticipate certain counterproductive trends. Paradoxically, though perhaps predictably, cherished references to the "minor" now tend to confirm the value of "major" works already central to the organized study of the culture in a few Western countries. The inevitability of this development rides on the economic fact that modernists were the first to experience the luxury of discovering their international situation in the modern world. Moreover, it reflects the institutional fact that the hierarchy of the disciplines of humanistic study has not changed; at the very most, it has adjusted itself in small ways to significant demographic shifts.

As a general rule, "extraterritorial" does not describe important features of the modernist *logos* developed by minority groups or by members of national cultures whose relative power in the world economy of cultural exchange has been secondary if not negligible. More frequently, this *logos* buttressed claims of particularity through the tautology of territorial, racial, and climatic determinism. I refer to the *logos* of the *topos* that prescribes its own necessary features. This *logos* finds no cracked window of opportunity, as it were, between culture and place. Instead it settles (national) culture firmly in place. Although it may employ techniques commonly associated with literary modernisms in France, England, Germany, and the United States—the unassimilated quotation, shifting narrative points of view, temporal simultaneity, the unreliable narrator, the device that lays bare the device—it presents these as local options. They seem to grow out of native roots. They achieve perfection in the place of home. These ideas anticipate the discussion of Odysseus Elytis in Chapter 6. Elytis denied that there is any "chasm" between modernist poetics and Hellenic tradition.

---

and Practice of Symbolic Resistance in Nineteenth-Century France [1985], 12). On "discourse," see Paul Bové, "Discourse" (1990).

Surely the effect of his creative energies was not, as one critic suggested of a Caribbean work, to "force . . . us as readers to abandon monolithic reading and to open our minds to multiple readings of reality."[33] Instead, Elytis's poetry grounds the *logos* of internationalism in an almost monolithic *topos* of valued communal inheritance, from which it encourages its readers to extract constants.

National cultures have evolved in many places around the globe that are easily ignored. In most cases, the relationship of the less-powerful *logos* to a more powerful standard represents no easy reproduction or inversion. If one focuses on the specific points of intersection between the *logos* and the *topos* it seeks to shape or, alternatively, that gives it structure, one is compelled to describe the continuous processes of self-institution that any *logos* may undergo. Minor, marginalized, minority, colonized, and decolonized cultures and their histories require comparison when they are studied in the institutional setting of the American university. One must consider how ideas, movements, genres, forms, and ideologies travel through space. How does a minority group transform the majority standard? How does the minor define itself vis-à-vis the major? How does the periphery institute *its* center in relation to another, more powerful center? What mode of transportation, what set of economic relations, has made possible the travel of culture in space? How do genres, ideas, techniques, movements, transform themselves when they reach a new site, and in relation to a set of pressures? Under what conditions might they duplicate a majority standard? What sorts of distinctions do local populations make between foreign and indigenous products? How do they describe their very own indigenous local space? How do they define and defend its borders? Is there any persistent fear of invasion? resistance to occupation? awareness that one's history, monuments, borders, sites, may be appropriated by the out-side?

I have developed my theory of *topos* through study of the *topos* of Hellas. This fact is not irrelevant to my theory or to my proposal for a topological approach to cultural studies. The centrality of *topos* in Neohellenic debates about identity cued me to the importance of topography in the creation of the Greek homeland in particular and emergent nations in general. Overlapping uses of two important Greek words suggested examination of the interaction between literature and place; I

---

[33] Josaphat B. Kubayanda, "Minority Discourse and the African Collective: Some Examples from Latin American and Caribbean Literature" (1987), 130.

found it significant that *topos*, the sign of the familiar place, can be easily conflated with *topos*, the sign of the commonplace citation, while "Hellas" refers to both a geopolitical entity and a cultural ideal. That "Hellas" itself is still a commonplace in the modern imagination also alerted me to the rich interaction of citations and sites. It suggested to me how frequently we rely on rhetorical commonplaces, figures of language, and habits of thought to visualize geography, and how covertly sites of knowledge may influence an argument—as Hellas has done in shaping this book.

The decision to carve an area of expertise out of a field of limited interest in the present organization of disciplines has made me sensitive to the fact that the methods and conclusions that other critics bring from their areas of study must be made to serve my own field, and that I must relate my work to theirs. I believe that the topological approach, developed through the interaction of my critical *logos* with a very minor field of study—though a very major territory of the modern imagination—can be useful to other fields. Indeed, the current interest in the spatial contexts of literary and artistic production encourages me to think so.

Frequently, however, the use of spatial metaphors in the titles of new books, articles, and conference presentations represents nothing more than a fashion in nomenclature rather than a substantive turn of thought. In the present climate of uncommitted flirtation with the topics of geography, cartography, borders, and maps, it is heartening to hear Edward Said's call for a critical "shift . . . to geographical analysis." "These are the two parameters of my work," Said recently announced, "on the one hand, the theme of history—the problem of how a work produces or gives birth to another while passing through the horizon of specific traditions . . . —and, on the other hand, the theme of geography and the problem of perpetual migration."[34] This is a welcome change from a previous era when literary artifacts such as the novel were seen to "have an almost negligible spatial aspect (the size of the book)."[35] The *topos* a *logos* occupies is certainly more than the space a book (not to mention its numerous extant copies) occupies on a library shelf. The more concretely we visualize this fact, the more capable we become of understanding how the products we peddle through importation, translation, analysis, commentary, or borrow-

[34] Stathis Gourgouris, Με τον Ed. Said (With Edward Said) (1992), 401.
[35] Frank Kermode, *The Sense of an Ending: Studies in the Theory of Fiction* (1967), 178.

ings of any kind interact with the places they represent and those to which they are transported.

Thus we can begin to understand how certain *logoi* have cut vectors into the *topos* of our shrunken globe. These line up with deeply ingrained routes of passage followed by migrant laborers, intellectuals, political exiles, and refugees in the one direction, and travelers, tourists, and the dropouts of the Western world in the other. The path of labor collides with the path of spirit, leisure, and emotion in a familiar pattern of exchange that always seems to deposit now-dwindling resources in the same regions of the world. The geographical inversions of exoticism and the everyday, leisure and labor, whiteness and color, compulsive consumption and the depletion the world's resources, are inscribed in Western texts, even in the "extraterritorial" ones that refuse to center their *logos*. To these texts, nonhegemonic cultures of the modern era frequently respond by drawing fortification lines around themselves. The literary utopias and dystopias they create may be *topoi* of the imagination: dream nations, imaginary homelands, countries of the mind. But they also attach identity to geography. In this sense, they are supremely territorial, firmly grounded in a geopolitical world order.

Above all, I would hope that my theorizing of *topos* might encourage others to use discretion when they employ words like "cartography," "geography," "topography," "topology," "borders," and "mapping." The case of Hellas remains instructive about the uses and abuses of topographies. It reminds us that any *logos* about *topos* bears responsibility for its effects. If we ignore the complex interaction between the place of knowledge and our knowledge of a place, we may quite unexpectedly cross the paths of the place we claim to know numerous times before we are prepared to understand how it has shaped our ways of knowing.

CHAPTER 2

Heterotopia:
Visitors to the Culture of Ruins

Let us begin with one observation: the Parthenon on the surface has
been worn down: it has disappeared into textual, visual, or photographic commentary; it has been stepped upon by tourists. . . . Yet it
can at every moment emerge again, as it does emerge, new and
different, each time historians like Vidal-Naquet, Vernant, Loraux,
or Finley—to mention only a few—speak about it.
　　　　　—Yánnis Tsiómis, Επιστρέφοντας από την έκθεση
　　　　　　(Returning from the exhibition)

The entablature of a cruel rigidity crushes and terrorizes. The feeling
of a superhuman fatality seizes you. The Parthenon, a terrible machine, grinds and dominates; seen from as far as a four-hour walk and
one hour by boat, alone it is a sovereign cube facing the sea.
　　　　　—Le Corbusier, *Journey to the East*

　　Hellas, "the most classical country in the world,"[1] is a *topos* of
architectural and sculptural ruins. This is true especially of Athens,
Greece's cosmopolitan capital, with its crowning Acropolis. In modernity's secular imagination, "this ground is holy."[2] Certainly the Acrop-

---

[1] William M. Thackeray, *Notes of a Journey from Cornhill to Grand Cairo* ([1844] 1991),
52.
[2] Georg Brandes, *Hellas: Travels in Greece* ([1926] 1969), 170. A self-declared atheist,
Brandes described his encounter with the Acropolis as the realization of a dream that
filled him with "a feeling of awe. . . . These curiously tarnished marble columns,
bathed in the warm, caressing March sunlight, are a festive sight to the eyes, both by
their color and their form. The longer one has thirsted for this sight, the profounder is
one's rapture" (170).

olis was holy for ancient Athenians, too, but in a very different sense.[3] In the modern period, artists, diplomats, and scholars traveling from France, Austria, Scandinavia, and especially Britain have conjured up a different spiritual landscape in their descriptions of this place. A necessary stopping point in their travels, the Acropolis becomes a starting point in travel journals.[4] It is the *topos* par excellence of a European *logos* about Hellenism.

Travel annotations, letters, journals, newspaper articles, and scholarly texts representing nearly two centuries of travel to Greece and acquisitions from Greece claim the Acropolis as a home away from home. These texts make the Acropolis European, the traveler Hellenic. This is one of many patterns of expression, thought, and practice commonly found in texts. In discussing an array of works from different national traditions, I am seeking to define recurring patterns. I will not be reconstructing the chronological development of a European presence on the Acropolis, or, more generally, the phenomenon of travel in Greece.[5] My focus is on the reciprocal relationship of the

[3] A genealogy of the Acropolis in ancient times would have to study its "transformation from the political and military center it was [during the Mycenean period] into an exclusionary cult site" (George Dontos, *The Acropolis and Its Museum* [1979], 6) at the beginning of the first millennium.

[4] The list of famous women and men of letters who visited the Acropolis in modern times and wrote about their experience is truly endless. A few works I do not discuss here are F. A. Chateaubriand, *Itinéraire de Paris à Jérusalem* (1811); W. M. Thackeray, *Notes of a Journey from Cornhill to Grand Cairo* (1844); G. de Nerval, *Voyage en Orient* (1851); Herman Melville, *Journal of a Visit to Europe and the Levant, October 11, 1856–May 6, 1857*; Julia Ward Howe, *From the Oak to the Olive: A Plain Record of a Pleasant Journey* (1868); Isadora Duncan, "The Parthenon" (1903 or 1904); Henry Miller, *The Colossus of Maroussi: A Celebration of the Uninhibited Pagan Spirit of Greece* (1941); Lawrence Durrell, *Prospero's Cell* (1945), *Bitter Lemons* (1957), and "Acropolis" (1966), James Merrill, "After Greece" (1962); Cyril Connolly, "On Revisiting Greece" (1963); Stephen Toulmin, *Night Sky at Rhodes* (1964); Patrick Leigh Fermor, *Roumeli: Travels in Northern Greece* (1966); Martin Heidegger, lecture on Athens (1967); and Derek Walcott, "Greece" (1981).

[5] Works on the phenomenon of travel to Greece include Olga Augustinos, *French Odysseys: Greece in French Literature from the Renaissance to the Romantic Era* (1993); Sophie Basch, *Le voyage imaginaire: Les écrivains français en Grèce au XXe siècle* (1991); David Constantine, *Early Greek Travellers and the Hellenic Ideal* (1984) and "Poets and Travellers and the Ideal of Greece" (1977); Robert Fisher, *Travelers to an Antique Land: The History and Literature of Travel in Greece* (1991); Emile Malakis, "French Travellers in Greece (1770–1820): An Early Phase of French Philhellenism" (1925); W. G. Rice, "Early English Travellers in Greece and the Levant" (1933); John Pemble, *The Mediterranean Passion: Victorians and Edwardians in the South* (1987); Kiriákos Simópulos, Ξένοι ταξιδιώτες στην Ελλάδα (Foreign travelers to Hellas) (1970); Richard Stoneman, *Land*

literary and physical *topos*, the *logos* of the *topos* and the *topos* of the *logos*. For example, nearly all British gentlemen travelers, schooled as they were in Greek and Latin from their public education, "would be equipped with a copy of the *Itinerary* of Greece by Pausanias."[6] It seems that classical learning directly affected the travelers' experience of the ruins; travelers' prior schooling, including perhaps a visit to the British Museum, which housed the Parthenon Marbles, heightened their sense of the Acropolis as a holy place. The travelers' notes on the ruins in turn verified classical learning and substantiated an individual traveler's claim to be Hellenic. Indeed, it seems, the one *topos* actualized the other.[7]

Certain questions follow from my broader problematic. What does occupying space on the Acropolis mean to the numerous Europeans who arrive in Greece fortified with a good classical education? How do travel narratives distinguish this tentatively occupied space from its physical surroundings? How do the authors use myth and the disciplines devoted to its study to relate the Acropolis to their distant homes? What modes of expression and procedures of knowledge about the Acropolis disassociate, metaphorically and literally, the idyllic site of ruins from its contemporary surroundings in Greece? How do they discipline the seemingly uncivil population currently inhabiting the *topos* of Hellas?

Consideration of the complex interrelationship between the *logos* of European Hellenism and the physical site of the Acropolis—between

---

of Lost Gods: The Search for Classical Greece (1987); Hugh Tregaskis, *Beyond the Grand Tour: The Levant Lunatics* (1979); and F. M. Tsigakou, *The Rediscovery of Greece: Travellers and Painters of the Romantic Era* (1981). Helen Angelomatis-Tsougarakis, *The Eve of the Greek Revival: British Travellers' Perceptions of Early Nineteenth-Century Greece* (1990), uses travel narratives as historical documents providing supplementary information on the Greek world prior to the Greek state. For a cogent discussion of present-day tourism, see Susan Buck-Morss, "Semiotic Boundaries and the Politics of Meaning: Modernity on Tour—A Village in Transition" (1987).

[6] Tregaskis, *Beyond the Grand Tour*, 9.

[7] Commenting on eighteenth-century Grand Tourists, Eisner remarks: "Of course one reason early travelers packed their accounts with learned references was because it was only as texts that many of the classical places existed as sites. So many of the antiquities remained below ground . . . and those above ground were rapidly losing their loveliest portions to the plunderers. And so, it was only by reading Pausanias or Aeschylus *in situ* that one might feel historically situated, or only by annotating the tour once back at home that one might feel thoroughly experienced in the famous places where civilization had arisen and fallen. Such places long remained, even for those who had been there, more literary *topoi* than geographical realities" (*Travelers to an Antique Land*, 67–68).

the system of statements about Hellas and the geographic location defined in the Western imagination as existing always already outside time and space—has led me to explore the analytical potential of a recently coined term. The term is *heterotopia*, a spatial metaphor deriving from the ancient Greek pronoun *heteros* 'other' and the noun *topos*. Coined by analogy to utopia and dystopia, *heterotopia* means, quite literally, "a place of different order" and refers to an actual place conceived as being otherwise and existing outside normative social and political space. In a lecture dated March 1987 entitled "Des espaces autres" (Of other spaces), Michel Foucault defined heterotopias as effectively enacted utopias that simultaneously represent, contest, and invert other sites; they are places "outside of all places, even though it may be possible to indicate their location in reality. . . . These places are absolutely different from all the sites that they reflect and speak about."[8]

Heterotopias are real countersites. They may be places instituted elsewhere, which purportedly reproduce the originary source (colonies); places set apart within a geopolitical entity, which are tangential to and potentially contaminating of its social and economic activity yet function to control crisis or deviation (prisons, nursing homes, inner cities); or places instituted elsewhere *or* within, which enclose in one location artifacts from all cultures and all times and thus purportedly save these from extinction (libraries, museums, archeological sites).

What defines a heterotopia as a place of another order is not its physical location. The relation of the *topos* of the "other" to the *topos* of the "same" is determined less by physical position than by the confluence of discourses, institutions, and procedures deployed in a place. A heterotopia's difference results from its discursively and institutionally defined form, function, meaning, and value. These simultaneously relate it to and cut it off from the normative space that surrounds it.

The term *heterotopia* should be distinguished from *periphery*, used by political economists to designate the impoverished outside of an

[8] Michel Foucault, "Of Other Spaces," trans. Jay Miskiewic, 24. Heterotopias that Foucault identifies are prisons, rest homes, psychiatric hospitals, boarding schools, military service facilities, honeymoon hotels, boats, and colonies including "the Puritan societies that the English had founded in America" and "those extraordinary Jesuit colonies that were founded in South America" (27). For discussions of heterotopia see Edward Soja, "Heterotopologies: A Remembrance of Other Spaces in the Citadel-LA" (1990), and *Postmodern Geographies*.

economic core or center. Though useful for indicating the position of greater and lesser economic forces in post–World War II global markets,[9] the terms *center* and *periphery* seem inadequate to the task of describing worldwide cultural exchange. The monocentric circular metaphor suggests a unidirectional flow from a single cataract of advantage to surrounding minireceptacles for outdated goods. It cannot adequately account for differences in the time and manner that various societies receive things, for example, modernizing trends. Furthermore, it tends to reduce societies on the outside, with their own variegated spaces, to discard bins: points on a radius along whose entire length the remainders of Western goods are sequentially deposited. Finally, this metaphor does not offer itself for analysis of the value that economically weaker societies may themselves present to the dominant West.

Heterotopias have various points of reference around the globe. Their value derives not from a single center but instead from their relationship to a set of "remaining spaces," which may include the immediate surroundings or territories lying at a great distance from the marked site. In addition, each heterotopia has its separate genealogy and its own time frame. It may be charged with social and cultural meaning by the "complex juxtaposition to cosmopolitan simultaneity of differences in space."[10] Furthermore, a heterotopia's layers of meaning that accrue through repeated efforts to reconstruct and interpret some originary model may make this heterotopia opaque to human understanding while they also give it the glow of transcendence.

Although Foucault mentions colonies as one class of heterotopias that lie outside a state's borders yet operate as a great reserve for that society's imagination, I have in mind another kind of place. What of the site that lies outside powerful Western states but that nonetheless appears as a place of origin within Western societies' collective imaginings? Here I refer to the numerous sites of ruins from classical antiquity forming a circuit known to the West as "Hellas." Certainly these occupy a special place in the collective imaginings both of the West as an entity that seeks to unify itself and of separate national traditions, including the Greek, that view themselves as exemplars of the West. Hellas itself is a heterotopia, a space set apart precisely because it contains classical ruins. Of individual sites of ruin in Greece, the

[9] See Wlad Godzich, "The Further Possibility of Knowledge" (1986), xi.
[10] Soja, "Heterotopologies," 9.

Acropolis is the most frequented and the most formidable—the one in which all meet their measure of sacredness, harmony, beauty, and grandeur.

The Romantic Traveler's Home Abroad

The documents that interest me derive from a period between 1800 and the early twentieth century.[11] Beginning in the late 1800s, Hellas provided Europeans with a powerful reserve of the imagination to which they could return again and again to define the value of their own national traditions. Predictably, travel to Greece became increasingly popular during this period. A peak era of British travel to Greece was the period between 1800 and 1821. For the British, the immediate cause for diverting the Grand Tour to the southwestern province of the Ottoman Empire may have been Napoleon's brief occupation of Italy (1796), another very popular destination, or his naval blockade and occupation of Egypt (1798–1801).[12] Travel to Greece was, to a degree, an extension of travel to Italy, Egypt, and the Holy Land, all places implicated in Europeans' search for origins. But a more substantial motive leading wealthy Englishmen to travel to Epirus, Delphi, and Athens came from the spirit of Greek Revivalism promoted at home in architecture, the decorative arts, painting, literature, and scholarship. The taste for the classical developed hand in hand with "a taste for travel and topography."[13] These were "dominant forces leading Englishmen towards Hellenism. . . . With this sentiment of pilgrimage" mingled with "a spirit of almost boyish adventurousness,"[14] they reached a place situated between home and the more exotic Orient. As elsewhere in the Mediterranean basin, here they seemed to travel back in time as they moved southeast around the globe. Here they could reflect on their present condition even as they developed a passion for their past: for "in the Mediterranean world antiquity seemed to be still

[11] Adventurous English noblemen began visiting Athens in the late seventeenth century. Among the first were Jacob Spon and Sir George Wheler (*Journey into Greece*, 1682). Travelers in the eighteenth century included the painters James Stuart and Nicholas Revett (*The Antiquities of Athens*, 1762); John Montague, Fourth Earl of Sandwich; Richard Chandler (*Travels in Greece*, 1775–76); and the critic Robert Wood (*An Essay on the Original Genius and Writings of Homer*, 1775).

[12] See Tregaskis, *Beyond the Grand Tour*, 7.

[13] Jenkyns, *Victorians and Ancient Greece*, 13.

[14] Ibid.

present."[15] Here, facing breathtaking ruins, architectural marvels such as the Parthenon, they sometimes overcame the fatigue of their modern world, although they also frequently pined away for northern convenience.[16]

As a general rule, European diplomats, intellectuals, and gentlemen were drawn to Hellas through their study of ancient Greek literature, their interest in the aesthetic value of classical art and architecture, their wish to see the values and styles of Hellenism resurrected (at least within their own society), their desire to amuse themselves, and, more than occasionally, some spiritual drive: "All of us on this strange boat . . . haunted by a dream, a yearning, a madness."[17] For some, travel to Hellas also promised financial gain. Gérard de Nerval (1808–55) supported himself from 1844 to 1847 by publishing his travel journal on Greece in the French magazine *L'artiste*, then in 1851 republished the material in a book entitled *Voyage en Orient*. The French poet and journalist Théophile Gauthier (1811–72) decided to make a stopover in Athens on his way home to Paris for purely economic reasons— "since a few articles about the Acropolis would be paid for dearly by the editors of newspapers."[18] Others, including Georg-Christian Gropius (1776–1850), Louis-François-Sébastien Fauvel (1753–1838), and Thomas Bruce, Lord Elgin (1766–1841), pilfered antiquities without worrying about Ottoman authorities. Indeed before the Kingdom of Greece existed to institute its own protective Archaeological Society (1837), Europeans found it easy to carry back to the "safety of home" major artifacts (the "Elgin" Marbles, Venus de Milo) from Hellas's most famous sites. Apparently without diminishing the value of the original site, these stolen objects seemed "to find their *proper* context"[19] in another heterotopia "proper to the culture of the 19th century":[20] the exhibition space of the national museum.[21] Here the

---

[15] Ibid., 44.

[16] See Byron's letter to his mother from Prevesa, dated 12 November 1809, which describes his valet's sufferings in Greece: "Fletcher like all Englishmen is very much dissatisfied. . . . He has suffered nothe but from cold, heat, & vermin which those who lie in cottages & cross mountains in a wild country must undergo, & of which I have equally partaken with himself, but he is not valiant, & is afraid of robbers & tempests" (*Byron's Works*, 1:33–34).

[17] Le Corbusier, *Journey to the East* (1989), 208.

[18] Váso Méntzu, Τρεις Γάλλοι ρομαντικοί στην Ελλάδα (Three French romantics in Greece) (1990), 26.

[19] B. F. Cook, *The Elgin Marbles* (1984), 4 (my emphasis).

[20] Foucault, "Of Other Spaces," 26.

[21] There is a growing bibliography on the museum as national institution. See, for example, Edward P. Alexander, *Museum Masters: Their Museums and Their Influence*

unearthed fragments functioned to enrich the state—with all the ambiguities this expression suggests—and to raise the level of aesthetic discourse, moral sensibilities, and historical understanding of its citizens.

Motivated by such desires, travelers made their way from home to Greece by sea or by land on the southern Balkans' rocky roads. To approach Hellas, they relied on existing descriptions of the place and its ruins—to such a degree, in fact, that literary expectations created by works like Thomas Love Peacock's *Gryll Grange* (1861) frequently colored their sentiments. Foreign policy might further complicate their emotional response. Even the Acropolis proved to be initially unattractive to Alphonse de Lamartine (1790–1869), the French poet and statesman, who arrived in Greece during the Crimean War—when France had allied itself with the Ottoman Empire.

At least two geopolitical entities seem to stand outside the Acropolis and simultaneously to serve as points of reference. These make up the spaces remaining outside the Acropolis. For most European travelers, there exist two main geographical axes: home and the local surroundings. Moreover, home exists on the horizon line dividing the ideal from the actual. The local surroundings, in contrast, represent the fallen present. To describe the complex relationship between the Acropolis and these remaining spaces, one is compelled to map out the international entwinement of spaces that occupy the imagination of the traveler occupying the site of the Acropolis.

One might reflect, first, on how the Acropolis becomes a place of homecoming set apart, quite literally, from home.[22] Here one finds unexpected reversals of colonial powers' self-representation as mother to pockets of civilization outside the West. Travelers held the Acropolis to be logically and historically prior to their society's institution, the

---

(1983); Joseph Alsop, *The Rare Art Traditions: The History of Art Collecting and Its Linked Phenomena Wherever These Have Appeared* (1982); Howard S. Becker, *Art Worlds* (1982); Pierre Bourdieu and Alain Darbel, with Dominique Schnapper, *L'amour de l'articles musées europeéns et leur public* (1969); and Douglas Crimp, "On the Museum's Ruins" (1980); id., "The End of Art and the Origin of the Museum" (1987); Kenneth Hudson, *A Social History of Museums: What the Visitors Thought* (1975); Oliver Impey and Arthur MacGregor, eds., *The Origins of Museums: The Cabinet of Curiosities in Sixteenth- and Seventeenth-Century Europe* (1985); H. Seling, "The Genesis of the Museum" (1967).

[22] The image of Greece as home still sells. In 1986, a year after the TWA hijacking at the Athens airport, the Greek Tourist Organization conducted a publicity campaign in the United States that featured American celebrities of various ethnic backgrounds. Each celebrity named her or his family's place of origin (England, Germany, Italy, Ireland), then joyfully announced: "This summer I'm going home—to Greece."

lost origin of a common heritage. Yet throughout this period of travel, they repeatedly affirmed, to a greater or lesser degree and often after intense scrutiny, a fundamental resemblance between the Acropolis and their European home. The mode of scrutiny was aesthetic. By the aesthetic, I refer to the modern discourse on beauty. This discourse assigns supreme value to the artifact as a kind of autonomous object. Indeed it distinguishes the artifact from other kinds of objects by relating it directly to human subjectivity. The aesthetic not only shapes the individual's experience of beauty but also defines a mode of encounter that liberates the individual from social, historical, and political contingencies. The cause of beauty, the ideal of unity and integrity, the desire to liberate the soul—all these things governed the encounter between the enlightened European and the Acropolis.[23] Quite literally in pursuit of what Friedrich Schiller (1759–1805) referred to metaphorically as the "path of aesthetics," which leads "through Beauty" to "arrive at Freedom,"[24] the European traveler made the annoying passage through the contemporary village and negotiated the difficult climb up the well-worn path that led to the gates of Nike. Face to face with the architectural and sculptural wonder, the Parthenon, one seemed to recover the intrinsic values of beauty, truth, reason, and freedom. One found one's spirit at home.

The view of the Acropolis might also induce a crisis of identity, however. Initially its effect was estranging. It produced "a sensation of unreality"; it made one the "victim of delusion"; it transformed the body's functions, "obtruded itself upon common sense,"[25] and generated reflection even on the reliability of one's perceptions.[26] One may recall Sigmund Freud's (1856–1939) incredulity, his feeling of *Entfremdung* 'derealization' at the sight of the Acropolis upon his visit in 1904:

> When, finally, on the afternoon of our arrival, I stood on the Acropolis and cast my eyes around upon the landscape, a surprising thought suddenly entered my mind: "So all this really *does* exist, just as we learnt

[23] One should be careful to distinguish between reactions conditioned by an Enlightenment versus a romantic sense of perfection. While the former finds emotional satisfaction in the Parthenon's classical perfection, the latter either remains untouched or finds pleasure in its present fragmentary condition. For a typical romantic reaction, see Nikos Kazantzakis, *Report to Greco* (1965), 136.

[24] Friedrich Schiller, *On the Aesthetic Education of Man, in a Series of Letters* (1965), 27.

[25] Robert Byron, *Europe in the Looking Glass*; quoted in Richard Stoneman, *A Literary Companion to Travel in Greece* (1984), 148.

[26] Le Corbusier (1887–1965) described this physical response to viewing the Acropolis: "The body, the mind, the heart gasp, suddenly overpowered" (*Journey to the East*, 212).

at school!" To describe the situation more accurately, the person who gave expression to the remark was divided, far more sharply than was usually noticeable, from another person who took cognizance of the remark; and both were astonished, though not by the same thing. The first behaved as though he were obliged, under the impact of an un-equivocal observation, to believe in something the reality of which had hitherto seemed doubtful. . . . The second person, on the other hand, was justifiably astonished, because he had been unaware that the real existence of Athens, the Acropolis, and the landscape around it had ever been objects of doubt. What he had been expecting was rather some expression of delight or admiration.[27]

To the "divided" observer, the Acropolis at first activated feelings of both discredited disbelief under the compulsion of hard physical evidence and "justifiable" astonishment that the encounter with a place so real in schoolbook illustrations might itself generate such doubt when it materialized before one's eyes.[28]

But the sum effect of this divided response was only apparently negative. For the modernist poet and essayist Hugo von Hofmannsthal (1874–1929), another Austrian lover of Greek antiquity, the "demonic irony" of his trip to the Acropolis sometime before 1910 was that the first view of "impossible antiquity" induced a sense both of the place's own unreality and of his "aimless searchings." He himself admitted: "The harshness of these words pleased me.—Nothing of all this exists. Here, where I had hoped to touch it with my hands, here it is gone, here more than anywhere else."[29] This feeling of grasping at the unattainable was oddly pleasing, not because it exorcised antiquity from the narrator's burdened soul, but because it finally deepened his understanding of his relationship to the "Unattainable."[30] There took place a fundamental communication between his innermost being and his irretrievable past as he reached behind the Acropolis statues' mournful gaze and sought to comprehend the inexhaustible depths of their expression.[31]

[27] Sigmund Freud, "A Disturbance of Memory on the Acropolis" ([1936] 1964), 241.

[28] For Thackeray, who resisted classical learning in school, the effect was the reverse: "Musing over this wonderful scene, perhaps I get some feeble glimpse or idea of that ancient Greek spirit which peopled it with sublime races and heroes and gods; and which I never could get out of a Greek book—no, not though Muzzle [the schoolmaster] flung it at my head" (Notes of a Journey from Cornhill to Grand Cairo, 53).

[29] Hugo von Hofmannsthal, "Moments in Greece" (1952), 184.

[30] Ibid., 187.

[31] The "mournful" gaze of the Acropolis statues is another common topos in travelers' accounts. Mark Twain's description in Innocents Abroad ([1869] 1984) is exemplary:

The experience was as nearly religious as the modern aesthetic encounter could be: "If the Unattainable feeds on my innermost being and the Eternal builds out of me its eternity, what then still stands between me and the Deity?"[32] The soul received its "direction" from these "messengers" of the past.[33] Here we see the initial crisis of being (the physical transformations, the obtrusion of the senses, the delusion of unreality) resolving itself in the European observer as a kind of aesthetic deification: a near union of being and beauty. Even the ruthlessly unsentimental Gustave Flaubert (1821–80) apologetically mentioned his temptation to pray on the Acropolis. In a letter from Patras, dated 10 February 1851, Flaubert described how "the pieces of sculpture found on the Acropolis" produced an "ecstatic" response within him:

> I noticed especially a bas-relief representing a woman. There remains only a fragment of the torso, just the two breasts, from the base of the neck to above the navel. One of the breasts is draped, the other un-covered. What breasts! Good God! What a breast! It is apple-round, full, abundant, widely spaced from the other: you can feel the weight of it in your hand. Its fecund maternity and its love-sweetness make you swoon. The rain and sun have turned the white marble to yellow, a tawny color, almost like flesh. It is so calm, so noble! It seems about to swell; one feels that the lungs beneath it are about to expand and breathe. How well it wore its sheer pleated drapery! How one would have rolled in it, weeping! How one would have fallen on one's knees before it, hands joined! Standing in front of it, I felt the beauty of the expression *Stupet aeris*. A little more and I'd have prayed.[34]

Ecstasy before "the ideal" beauty of lost pagan deities "incarnated in Pentelic marble" found its ultimate (and very influential) expression in the "Prière sur l'Acropole" by Ernest Renan (1823–92). During his

---

"As we wandered thoughtfully down the marble-paved length of this stately temple, the scene about us was strangely impressive. Here and there, in lavish profusion, were gleaming white statues of men and women, propped against blocks of marble, some of them armless, some without legs, others headless—but all looking mournful in the moonlight, and startlingly human! They rose up and confronted the midnight intruder on every side—they stared at him with stony eyes from unlooked-for nooks and recesses; they peered at him over fragmentary heaps far down the desolate corridors; they barred his way in the midst of the broad forum, and solemnly pointed with handless arms the way from the sacred fane" (274).

[32] Hofmannsthal, "Moments in Greece," 187.

[33] Ibid.

[34] Gustave Flaubert, *The Letters of Gustave Flaubert, 1830–1857* (1980), 136.

journey to Greece in 1865, Renan, a professor of oriental studies and cofounder (with Auguste Compte) of positivism, described his pious reaction to Athens and, more particularly, the Acropolis in the most unpositivistic terms:[35]

> There is only one place, not two, where perfection exists: it is this place here. I never imagined that there existed anything like it. What I encountered before me was the very ideal incarnated on Pentelic marble. Until this time I believed that perfection was not of this world. . . . But here before my eyes there appeared the Hellenic miracle next to the Judaic miracle: something that could only have occurred once, that had never appeared before, that would never be seen again, whose impression would be preserved eternally. I mean to say: it is a type of eternal beauty without local or nationalist color. . . . When I saw the Acropolis I accepted the revelation of the divine. . . . Then the entire world seemed barbarous to me.[36]

One should not overlook Renan's interesting juxtaposition of "the Hellenic miracle next to the Judaic miracle"—a parallel that sustains the religious tone of the description.[37] Hellenism, alongside Judaism, is said to fulfill the promised incarnation, eternity, and revelation, three important theological principles. With Hellenism, however, it is not grace but beauty that achieves "miraculous divinity." The incarnation of an eternal and universal beauty on the site of the Acropolis brings the viewer to "the revelation of the divine." The Acropolis becomes for the viewer a place where the highest aesthetic values of Western culture escape the ravages of time and limitations of "local or nationalist color" that obstruct modern incarnations. Next to the Acropolis, "the entire world seemed barbarous," perennially burdened by temporal considerations and national differences.[38]

[35] It may be relevant to note that Renan is known for his application of positivism to literary and cultural studies. With this intent, he wrote his "scientific" *Life of Jesus* (1863).

[36] Ernest Renan, "Prière sur l'Acropole" ([1865] 1925), 15–16. A Greek translation of Renan's prayer (Προσευχή επάνω στην Ακρόπολη [Prayer on the Acropolis], trans. Xenofóntas Steph. Dántis) is "dedicated to the worshippers of the Good and Beautiful" (title page).

[37] At least two other sources explicitly compare Greece to the Holy Land. Brandes arrives at the conclusion that "Greece, not Palestine, is the Holy Land" (*Hellas*, 192–93), as we saw above, and Lamartine calls Athens the "Jerusalem of nations" (*Voyage en Orient*, 57).

[38] Humanity's present-day limitations are conveyed in Lamartine's "deep and humble reverie" before the Acropolis: "We set before ourselves disquieting questions, we

The dialectic of self-contemplation inevitably leads to an affirmation of the ancient site's reality, often at the expense of the prestige and priority of one's actual homeland. Although it occupies no socially identifiable ground but only collects within a designated space the ruins of other eras, the Acropolis finally acquires an aura of virtual reality so powerful that it replaces Europe as one's real home.[39] According to the Danish critic Georg Brandes (1842–1927), "a first glance on this world of marble bathed in sunlight" even has the power to repair one's habit of associating the classical style with "the Dano-Greek neoclassicism of Thorvaldsen, the Germano-Greek architecture of the Glyptothek, to the French style of La Madeline, Greek statues as coarsened by Roman technique, Sicilian landscapes and coastlines as a substitute for those of Greece, the pitiable imitation known as Athens of the North, but now the true Athens, the only, true Athens!"[40]

Travel accounts frequently challenge their readers to rectify distorted images of the ideal home that circulate at home in neoclassical buildings, photographs, and, according to the English traveler and writer Robert Byron, in "water-colour sketches of the Russell Flint school that depicted the Parthenon as . . . grooved cinnamon ninepins against a sky the colour of a faded butcher's apron."[41]

Disciplining Local Populations

With its reality, perfection, eternity, and universality affirmed, the Acropolis not only replaces the traveler's home in travel accounts; it

---

ask whether human genius, which believes itself to be running with swift step along the road of progress, may have followed instead a backward path; and we think that, despite all its new religions and inventions of all kinds—the compass, printing, and steam—the idea of beauty has been lost from earth, or that children are unable to represent it" (*Voyage en Orient*, 162).

[39] In our postmodern era, the site of the Acropolis has acquired yet another dimension of the "real": computer-generated "virtual reality." The *Chronicle of Higher Education* reported on experiments with virtual-reality systems at Rensselaer Polytechnic Institute that produced a universe of the Parthenon. Students could stroll through the reconstructed building simply by "wearing a helmet that envelop[s them] in computer-generated images that citizens of ancient Athens would have recognized" (David L. Wilson, "Researchers Hope to Lead Students into 'Virtual Reality'" [1992], 23).

[40] Brandes, *Hellas*, 72–73. In this passage, Brandes refers to the Danish sculptor Albert Bertel Thorvaldsen (1770–1844), a leader of neoclassicism known for his adherence to Greek art and respect for ancient prototypes, and to the Glyptothek, a museum in Munich.

[41] Byron, *Europe in the Looking Glass*; quoted in Stoneman, *Literary Companion*, 148.

also overshadows the local populations—contemporary Greeks or, at
an earlier stage, "Greeks and Turks"—who never ceased to dwell in
the surrounding areas.[42] For most travelers, the current state of Hellas
was of little matter even after the independent Greek Kingdom took
the place of the Ottoman Empire as custodian of the Acropolis. Contemporary Greek reality was either unworthy of comment or deeply
troublesome because it apparently lacked civility. What mattered instead was to see Hellas as if through Plato's eyes. Thus, when Lamartine reported in an entry to *Voyage en Orient* dated 18 August 1832 that
the contemporary city of Athens was "desolate and entirely barren,"
he was not documenting a demonstrable fact but creating the scenery
for revelation.[43] His literary account discursively prepared Athens's
supposedly desolate modern surface to reveal only its most eternal
layers. The deepest of these, the Acropolis, arose apocalyptically out
of present cursed barrenness to reach great physical heights.[44]

At the peak of the Acropolis, his narrative shifts temporal registers.
From here Lamartine views Athens from the eternal viewpoint of the
founding philosopher. He reconstructs in his "mind's eye the Parthenon in its original form"—together with "the reverent population
of Athenians ascending to worship Athena," the temples of "Hephaes-
tian divinities," and all the surrounding ancient but not antiquated sites
of Athens in their original splendor.[45] That is to say, he imagines them
as "Plato would have seen them when Athens, alive and decorated
with its countless other temples, buzzed at his feet like an overflowing
swarm of bees."[46] Nothing of Athens's contemporary presence appears in this picture. So, too, Gauthier relates the eternity of the
Parthenon's beauty to the nonreproducibility of Athenian genius. The
Parthenon is born of itself. "Parthenogenesis," its essential characteristic, is also a mythical feature of the patron goddess Athena: "Parthenon, temple of the Parthenos [Virgin]! For Athena, Pallas Athena of
the Hellenes, was the purist creation of pagan mythology; she came
out of the head of Zeus fully armed and fully grown. . . . For this

---

[42] Edward Gibbon mentioned that of the "eight to ten thousand inhabitants" of
eighteenth-century Athens, "three-fourths are Greeks in religion and language; and the
Turks   compose the remainder" (*The Decline and Fall of the Roman Empire* [1932],
1177).

[43] Lamartine, *Voyage en Orient*, 60.

[44] Lamartine refers to Athens as a "land of the apocalypse which appears stricken by
a divine curse, a prophetic utterance" (*Voyage en Orient*, 57).

[45] Lamartine, *Voyage en Orient*, 71.

[46] Ibid., 70.

reason her temple was the brightest of all pagan temples; on this temple Attic genius spent its highest effort."[47]

The nineteenth-century reports tend to repress national affiliation. Only in the twentieth century has the question of the Acropolis's national ownership been forced upon Europeans, in part through Greece's efforts to recover stolen items. It is only a few foreign visitors who have argued, against the better judgment of powerful people like Lamartine, that to confirm the atemporal nature of the Parthenon's beauty is to whitewash the Acropolis of all native (if not also actual) color—whether this color is seen to derive from the surrounding Greek landscape or from distant European societies. These criticisms of the discourse of Hellenism, faintly heard during the first half of the century, grew louder after World War II.[48]

One may nevertheless find in certain descriptions an unexpected emphasis on the national affiliation of *others*, particularly after writers begin to identify tourism as a phenomenon incongruous with the sacredness of the Acropolis.[49] When Virginia Woolf (1882–1941) ironically refers to "grey and purple mackintoshes" as the garb of contemporary suppliants on the Acropolis, she identifies them as belonging not to the English but to "10 million *German* tourists": "Have I described our afternoon on The Acropolis—when a storm rushed up from the Aegean, black as arrows, and the blue was as blue as hard china, and the storm and the blue fell upon each other and 10 million German tourists rushed across the temple precisely like suppliants in their grey and purple mackintoshes—no I haven't described the

---

[47] Théophile Gauthier, *L'Orient* ([1877] 1990), 161.

[48] Among twentieth-century authors, André Malraux took strong exception to the physical violation done to the Acropolis when "the whole past" is seen to have "reached us . . . colorless" (*The Voices of Silence* [(1953) 1974], 47). Here Malraux refers to the surface of all the buildings and statues, systematically conceived as colorless even after an excavation in the 1880s had unearthed vividly painted archaic sculpture and architecture from beneath the embankment of the Acropolis.

[49] For postwar authors, it is not nationality so much as technology that intrudes on the sacredness of the Acropolis. Contemporary Canadian author Gwendolyn MacEwen describes the "unreality" of "the Acropolis lit by night; . . . the same unreality that surrounds two other 'high places' I have seen which have become the victims of the hellish *son et lumière* shows—the fortress of Saladin in Cairo and the great pyramids in Giza. . . . For me, however, those huge waves of unreal light create a nightmarish quality I can do without. When the Parthenon was built, nobody anticipated that one day hundreds of viewers would sit entranced before its holy pillars, half blinded not by the light of God but by that of Edison. Some things can only be understood in pure sunlight or in the discreet illumination of torches" (*Mermaids and Ikons: A Greek Summer* [1978], 16–17).

Acropolis."[50] Like so many others, Woolf's description of the Acropolis, or, better, her claim never to have described the Acropolis, delivers the Acropolis to a universality of taste: it must stand above personal, national, and economic interests. But what it also reveals in its ironic margins is the national and quite exclusive competition for the Acropolis's rightful inheritance. Perhaps the ideal state of the modern soul defied national boundaries; perhaps, under the best of conditions, everyone might freely pray to the immaculate Athena. But a visit to the Acropolis proved to individual European visitors that for *another* national group to conflate *its* identity with *one's own* purest origin was to do violence to the integrity of Western civilization. In the eyes of the British, French, German, or Austrian traveler (or, after World War II, the American tourist), only *one's own* national group reached the soul's eternal "home" when entering the gates of the Propylaia.[51] Defining the proper circumstance of one's soul when one strolled among the ruins of the Parthenon finally proved to be a matter of *national* honor.

But whatever distortion the view of the Acropolis revealed in *other* European groups, this could not be compared—in the traveler's imagination, at least—to the flagrant violation found in the local surroundings. By surroundings I refer to the town of Athens with its modern inhabitants, rather than to the physical landscape with its clear atmosphere and uncompromising light, which Europeans have consistently appreciated as a natural extension of the ancient *topos*. Yet the local population constitutes a major axis of remaining space; it cuts through the Acropolis in important ways. For Europeans, the Acropolis reflected below first on the ruling Ottoman Empire, which used several of its buildings for the storage of gunpowder, then on the Greek Kingdom, with its "uncivil" society, as a parody of the original brilliant performance. To follow another line of thought, " 'Modern Greek' is flavoured with a suspicion of contempt as inevitable as that aroma of human perfection which attaches to Ancient," according to Robert Byron, a philhellene who rejected this narrow attitude.[52]

[50] Virginia Woolf, *The Letters of Virginia Woolf* (1978), 52–53.

[51] Germans did not regularly visit the Acropolis or even Greece before the twentieth century. Hellenists like Wincklemann, Lessing, Goethe, Schiller, Nietzsche, and Heidegger (until very late in his life) instead imagined the Hellenic ideal through texts and decontextualized statues, without ever witnessing the architectural monuments in their physical surroundings. As Jenkyns observes, "to the German mind Hellas became a sort of heavenly city, a shimmering fantasy on the far horizon" (*Victorians and Ancient Greece*, 13). American tourism to Greece is a postwar phenomenon.

[52] Byron, *Byzantine Achievement*, 8. The more famous Lord Byron also denigrated the "travelling pedagogue, who admits the existence of the native population only to

Early in the nineteenth century, Europeans began to deploy in Hellas the narratives, methods, rules of conduct, modes of expression, and institutions of the discourse of Hellenism. These functioned as disciplinary technologies. Here I refer to systems of knowledge that regulate human bodies in their relations to society and space.[53] On the site of ruins, the disciplinary technologies of Hellenism applied their force on individual bodies by controlling access to the site and separating "safe" authorities from "dangerous" (i.e., heterogeneous to all other) populations. They furthered the ends of exploring, excavating, reconstructing, and finally enclosing the Acropolis sites.

The fields of study that overwhelmed the Acropolis with their harvest of meanings were philology and history, while the clearinghouse was archeology. Philology and history were part and parcel of a formal *paideia* offering the educated European familiarity with classical Greek and Latin literatures. They produced a collective fantasy that tended to emphasize origins at the expense of more recent events. The mode of evaluation was aesthetic, on the one hand, and positivistic, on the other hand, as we have seen. Rules of professionalism gradually, though never entirely, supplanted aesthetic experience as guides for the proper treatment of the Acropolis and the surrounding spaces. During the first half of the nineteenth century, European diplomats, dilettantes, and experts used aesthetic judgment to justify changes on the Acropolis—including the dismantling of buildings and the removal of objects to European museums or gardens where they purportedly raised the sensibilities of subjects who did not have the means or will to travel to Hellas. By the end of the century, however, archeology had acquired its own methods, terminology, techniques, standards, and institutions, including the American School of Classical Studies, the Greek Archeological Service, standing international committees of scholars and experts, and the Archeological Council. Archeology's

lament the absence of that vacuous perfection which he perceives to have been the Hellenic physiognomy" (*Lord Byron: Selected Letters and Journals* [1982], 12). See also his notes to *Childe Harold's Pilgrimage*: "Of the ancient Greeks we know more than enough. . . . Of the moderns, we are perhaps more neglectful than they deserve" (*Poetical Works* [1979], 882).

[53] See Michel Foucault, *Discipline and Punish: The Birth of the Prison* ([1975] 1979), 38. Foucault was not unaware of the importance of certain separate spaces for the successful maintenance of discipline: "Discipline sometimes requires *enclosure*, the specification of a place heterogeneous to all others and closed in upon itself" (141). Foucault discussed the relationship between space and power in "Questions on Geography" (1980) and "Space, Knowledge, and Power" (1984).

configuration of methods and institutions governed rules of entrance
and exit, systems of opening and closure, circulation of bodies within,
on, and around buildings, and, generally, the uses of the Acropolis.

One example of the changes that archeology has overseen is the construction of a major architectural addition on the site of the Acropolis
during the second half of the nineteenth century, and present-day plans
for a new addition. The Acropolis Museum was built in "a relatively
non-visible low area in the SE corner of the surface of the rock of the
Acropolis."[54] The museum became a heterotopia within a heterotopia.
Unlike the ancient ruins, the building itself was designed to be "non-
visible." Its function was to reveal itself only through its contents.
Hence the museum is not pictured anywhere in the museum catalogue,
except where its low roof and sides appear accidentally in aerial views
of the entire site. During the early 1990s, Greeks planned to build a new
Acropolis Museum at the foot of the Acropolis rather than on the site.
An international jury selected Manfredi Nikoletti and Lucio Passarelli,
two Roman architects, to design the museum, although in September
1993 the State Council of Greece declared invalid the international
architectural contest in which their plan prevailed. The chosen, deferred plan showed an unobtrusive, subterranean building. As Nikoletti informed the public at the time of his victory, "the entrance and
part of the structure are to be below ground 'so as to convey the idea of
a descent into history.' "[55]

Aesthetics and archeology combined with legal, economic, political, and other institutional considerations, including tourism, over
which the Greek government began to gain control after World War II,
and with art, over which the West has never lost control. Together
they constructed, as it were, a noninhabitable, nonutilitarian space.
They oversaw the surveillance of bodies and buildings on the site. And
they ultimately determined the matter of the Acropolis's guardianship.
Discourses of knowledge were transformed into actual relations of

[54] Dontos, *The Acropolis and Its Museum*, 18.
[55] See the newspaper article "Two Romans Have Been Chosen to Design the New
Acropolis Museum" (1990). Greek authorities are still planning to house in the new
museum, once designed and built, not only marbles currently in storage at the old
museum but also the Parthenon Marbles, although the British Museum has not yet
promised to return them. Upon learning about recent delays, the late Melina Mercouri
(d. 1994) commented: "The decision of the State Council defers our dream. . . . Besides
the Parthenon Marbles περιμένουν το σπίτι τους 'are awaiting their home'" (Τί θα
γίνει με το μουσείο της Ακρόπολης; [What will become of the Acropolis Museum?]
[1993]).

power between Europe and local authorities (government officials, museum directors, archeologists, professors of classics and archeology), travelers and local subjects, citizens of various classes, parties, interests, and places of origin. These power relations limited or at least controlled and only occasionally, again after World War II, enhanced the perceived relationship between the Acropolis and contemporary Athens.

One example of the limiting, or perhaps blinding, effects of disciplinary technologies is that they prohibited recognition of the presence upon and around the Acropolis of a local population. People had continued to use the Acropolis as a very effective *kástro* or *frúrio* 'fortress' well into the nineteenth century. Opposing parties regularly fought either to gain or to maintain protection of the Acropolis during the Greek War of Independence against the Ottoman Empire (1821–29 and again in 1833, when the Ottomans were forced finally to retreat from the Acropolis). General Yánnis Makriyánnis (1797–1864), who detailed in his memoirs the Ottoman siege of the *kástro* 'fortress' from 3 August 1826 to 24 May 1827, saw "Turks everywhere in the *patrída* 'homeland', and the Athenians' *kástro*, Hellas's hope, was in danger: if that was lost, the *patrída* would have a bad fate."[56]Both Greek-speaking rebels and Ottoman authorities recognized that to hold the Acropolis was to win Athens, a strategic site in the battle to control the Attic peninsula and to create an independent Hellas. While this was happening, Europeans continued to discuss ways of protecting the supreme values of Hellenism, which the Acropolis represented for them, from "vandalism" by the very groups who were seeking the physical protection of the Acropolis as a citadel-fortress.

It should not be assumed, however, that the Acropolis and other ancient artifacts had no other monumental value for competing local groups. Although I discuss Greek views in greater detail in the chapters that follow, it may be appropriate here to refer to one text that shows the value rebelling Greeks placed on the monuments of antiquity during their war of independence against the Ottomans. In a passage from his memoirs dated 1833, Makriyánnis offered classical artifacts to the service of his homeland, bestowing on them a value equal in some significant way to his life:

> I had two excellent statues, a woman and a prince, both solid—their veins showed, that's how perfect they were. When Poros was de-

---

[56] Yánnis Makriyánnis, Απομνημονεύματα (Memoirs) (1947), 1:298. See 1:273–325 for Makriyánnis's account of the entire siege.

stroyed, some soldiers took them and were ready to sell them to some Europeans at Arta: they wanted 1000 *tálara* [monetary unit]. I ended up there, I happened to be passing by; I grabbed the soldiers, I spoke to them. "Even if they give you 10,000 *tálara* for these, don't stoop to letting them out of your *patrída* [fatherland]; these are what we fought for (I take out and give them 350 *tálara*); and when I see the governor (since we eat together), I'll give them to him and he'll give you whatever you ask for to keep them up there in the *patrída*." And I hid them. Then through my reference I offered them to the king to make them of use to the *patrída*.[57]

From a technical point of view, Makriyánnis appreciated the two statues for their *entélia* 'perfect condition' and their realism: "their veins showed." From the viewpoint of citizen, however, he perceived their ultimate *utilitarian* function: they would serve the *patrída* as monuments of an ideal: "these are what we fought for."[58]

Regardless of the value the local population placed on ancient monuments, however, from an early stage the discourse of Hellenism served to exclude Ottoman authorities and Greek subjects not only from European debates about the processes of decision making and definitions of proper usage but also from the terms of possession of the Acropolis. One technique was to define what it meant to "appreciate" the Acropolis. Definitions of appreciation largely excluded local sentiment, as Edward Gibbon's infamously defamatory *Decline and Fall of the Roman Empire* shows. Without ever having visited Athens, Gibbon confidently observed that the "Athenians walk with supine indifference among the glorious ruins of antiquity; and such is the debasement of their character, that they are incapable of admiring the genius of their predecessors."[59] Of course, Gibbon's authority was not weaker because he had never visited Athens. To walk in the local surroundings of the Acropolis was not a prerequisite for knowing the Acropolis or appreciating its genius.

Comments like Gibbon's about the "supine indifference" of local populations bolstered claims that the local population and its authorities were in no position to protect the Acropolis, while European

[57] Makriyánnis, Ἀπομνημονεύματα (Memoirs), 2:63n.

[58] To understand their precise value, to understand what exactly Makriyánnis fought for, one would have to study the ideals Makriyánnis's memoirs repeatedly embrace.

[59] Gibbon, *Decline and Fall*, 2:1178. It should be noted that Gibbon constructed his "vision of decline," according to Stoneman, by analogy to his "experience of Rome" in 1764 (*Literary Companion*, 130).

powers like Great Britain, France, and Germany, with their showcase national museums decorating the metropolitan centers of London, Paris, and Munich, could clearly offer such protection. Thus definitions of proper appreciation were actively employed both to determine the matter of the Acropolis's proper guardianship and to increase museum acquisitions.

Romantic Expropriations: The Case of the Parthenon Marbles

One should not forget that the Acropolis is a heterotopia where the West has quite literally seized the ruins of Hellas for its own uses—namely, the collection of cultural artifacts, the provision of an aesthetic education, the expansion of historical knowledge, and the enhancement of national treasures and international prestige. The most notorious expropriation is, of course, Lord Elgin's lavish effort to "save" the best marbles of the Parthenon by "pulling down modern houses to get at buried remains" and carting the marbles home to Great Britain in 1802.[60] Even today, the argument continues to be made against Greek efforts to recover the Parthenon Marbles that the "Elgin" Marbles are "safest" in the British Museum. That the debate about the appropriate housing of the unearthed "Elgin" fragments has found no comfortable resolution is not coincidental to the functioning of the Acropolis as a space of another order. Perhaps the matter of providing appropriate housing for "misappropriated" artifacts lifted out of spaces defined by their very uninhabitability can never finally be settled.[61]

Some descriptions of Athenian reaction to the transfer of the Parthenon Marbles from the Acropolis to Piraeus—where they were placed on ships headed for Britain—actually show interest in local perceptions. Two sources refer to a popular assumption that ancient statues were animated and could be "not infrequently heard to mourn and bewail their present condition."[62] But the sources contradict one another

[60] See Hobhouse, *Journey through Albania*, 1:345n.

[61] "Misappropriation" is the term Greek officials use to describe Lord Elgin's activities on the Acropolis: "The miscreant was a diplomat and the misappropriation was covered by the authority of an official action, a permit from the Sultan. He was Thomas Bruce, Lord Elgin" (Dontos, *The Acropolis and Its Museum*, 18).

[62] As related by Stoneman, *Land of Lost Gods*, 175. The two sources are Hobhouse, *Journey through Albania*, and F. S. North Douglas, *Essay on Certain Points of Resemblance between the Ancient and Modern Greeks* (1813). A similar perception prevailed among

in their interpretation of local response. Although *he* strongly opposed the marbles' removal, John Cam Hobhouse, Baron of Broughton (1786–1869), reported some Athenians actually expressed satisfaction that Elgin had "saved" the marbles from Turkish mastery over their human souls; they mourned only the bondage of the "petrified bodies" remaining on the Acropolis: "Some Greeks, in our time, conveying a chest from Athens to Piraeus, containing part of the Elgin Marbles, threw it down, and could not for some time be prevailed upon to touch it, again affirming, they heard the Arabim [the spirit] crying out, and groaning for his fellow-spirits detained in bondage in the Acropolis. The Athenians suppose that the condition of these enchanted marbles will be bettered by a removal from the country of the tyrant Turks."[63] F. S. North Douglas, a fellow gentleman traveler, recorded a somewhat different reaction of an "illiterate servant of the Disdar of Athens." The servant actually transferred his mourning for the removal of one Caryatid onto "the five other *koritsia* (sisters)" when he heard the other Caryatids manifesting "their affliction by filling the air at the close of the evening with the most mournful sighs and lamentations."[64]

Although both authors were sympathetic to Athenian perception—indeed Douglas generously concluded that we "cannot refuse to acknowledge that the Athenians are not so indifferent as it has been sometimes represented to the wonders and monuments of their city"[65]—their descriptions quoted above do not take seriously the local population's views on the proper context of the marbles. Instead

---

Byzantine Greeks. For a remarkable account of Byzantine views, see Cyril Mango, who studied the effect of pagan statues on the Byzantine spectator, as recorded in Byzantine texts, especially the genre of *ekphrasis* 'description.' He notes both "popular" and "intellectual" reaction to the antique statuary, "superstitious" and "Christian reinterpretation." His purpose is to "set up a test case of the Byzantine attitudes towards antiquity" ("Antique Statuary and the Byzantine Beholder" [1963], 155). He is quite careful not to allow modern assumptions about the aesthetic value of classical art to predispose him negatively toward Byzantine attitudes.

[63] Hobhouse, *Journey through Albania*, 1:348.

[64] From his *Essay on Certain Points of Resemblance between the Ancient and Modern Greeks*; quoted in Stoneman, *Land of Lost Gods*, 174–75. For a contemporary Neohellenic twist on this theme, see the poem Βρετανικό Μουσείο (Ελγίνου μάρμαρα) (British Museum [Elgin Marbles]) (1956) by Kikí Dimulá. The poet sees the lonely Caryatid in the British Museum coming alive one August night along with the nearby statue of Dionysus, the two of them "passionately erecting in their memory with nostalgia's sobs and tears the Parthenons and Erechtheia deprived of them."

[65] Douglas, *Essay*; quoted in Stoneman, *Land of Lost Gods*, 175.

they promote orientalist curiosity about the strange and unfamiliar practices of the Ottoman population. Each author features local beliefs as the product of a mysterious, exotic naïveté rather than as fully developed theories about the past. Whether they draw the conclusion that Athenians are pleased to have the marbles removed or that they mourn for their loss, the descriptions work negatively by *not* fully representing local views; and in conjunction with the related discourse of orientalism, which renders these local views exotic, they act to discipline the local population.[66]

The Ottoman attitude toward Elgin's activities remains entirely undocumented. Although British authorities regularly argue that Ottomans directly authorized Lord Elgin's removal of the Acropolis marbles, the document of said "authorization" is not extant in the original. Only an Italian translation of the lost original remains—a document in which the Ottoman Porte addresses local Ottoman authorities. Here I quote a distant relative of the lost Turkish text—an excerpted English translation of the Italian translation of the original—which was said to have been given to Lord Elgin's chaplain, Philip Hunt, with directions for the local Ottoman authorities. One should take note that the letter directs itself to the appropriate "comport" not of Elgin's party but of the Ottoman authorities, whom it orders to allow Elgin and his artists to enter the Acropolis, model temples with chalk, measure fragments, erect scaffolding, dig, walk, view, contemplate, and copy pictures and buildings:

> It is our desire that on the arrival of this letter you use your dilegence to act conformably to the instances of the said Ambassador as long as the said five artists dwelling in that place shall be employed in going in and out of the citadel of Athens which is the place of observation; or in fixing scaffolding around the ancient Temple of the Idols, or in modelling with chalk or gypsum the said ornaments and visible figures; or in measuring the fragments and vestiges of other ruined buildings; or in excavating when they find it necessary the foundations in search of inscriptions among the rubbish; that they be not molested by the said Disdar nor by any other persons; nor even by you to whom this letter is addressed; and that no one meddle with their scaffolding or implements

[66] Hobhouse elsewhere appears keenly attuned to local reaction to the marbles' removal. He precisely quotes "a singular speech of a learned Greek who said to me, 'you English are carrying off the works of *the Greeks*, our forefathers—preserve them well—we Greeks will come and re-demand them'" (*Journey through Albania*, 1:347–48n).

nor hinder them from taking away any pieces of stone with inscriptions and figures. In the aforesaid manner see that you behave and comport yourselves.[67]

Among British travelers, Lord Byron expressed great sympathy for local interests. It is no coincidence that Byron fought aggressively both in words and in deeds for the modern Greek cause.[68] Although he worshipped the classical past, in *English Bards and Scotch Reviewers* Byron condemned Elgin's costly pursuit of "misshapen and maimed antiques." In his opinion, "Aberdeen and Elgin" were wasting "useless thousands on their Phidian freaks." Byron's *Curse of Minerva* was one of few British texts that dared satirize the British Crowd's divided reaction as it "admires the plunder" but "abhors the thief."

As the debate about the restoration of the Parthenon Marbles continued late in the nineteenth century, it was not unusual to find the disciplinary technologies of Hellenism buttressed by arguments from other related discourses, including orientalism, as we have seen, and, in the next example, colonialism. One interlocutor compared the prospect of restoring the "Elgin" Marbles to returning "Gibraltar, Malta, Cyprus, India." I refer to James Knowles's response in "The Joke about the Elgin Marbles" to learned scholar Frederic Harrison, who advocated the marbles' restitution in an article entitled "Give Back the Elgin Marbles."

From his own viewpoint in favor of restoration, the modernist poet of the Hellenic diaspora C. P. Cavafy (1863–1933) responded to each of Knowles's more "audacious" statements.[69] According to Cavafy, Knowles confuses the purposefulness-without-purpose of the aesthetic object with the economic and political advantages of the British colony: "[Mr Knowles] thinks that if the marbles are restored, Gibraltar, Malta, Cyprus, India must be given away also—forgetting that if those possessions are necessary to British trade and to the dignity and safety

[67] William St. Clair, *Lord Elgin and the Marbles* (1967), 90. The English version is St. Clair's translation from the Italian rendition given to Philip Hunt, which is now part of the Hunt Papers.

[68] Byron died on 19 April 1824 at Mesolonghi alongside a faction of besieged Greek rebels. He describes his motives for taking up "The Sword, the Banner, and the Field" in his poem "On this day I complete my Thirty-Sixth Year." For a carefully annotated compendium of Byron's views on Greece, see Harold Spender, *Byron and Greece* (1924).

[69] Cavafy's response appears in three articles, " 'Give Back the Elgin Marbles' " ([1891] 1963), Τα Ελγίνεια μάρμαρα (The Elgin Marbles) ([1891] 1963) and Νεώτερα περί των Ελγινείων μαρμάρων (The latest on the Elgin Marbles) ([1891] 1963).

of the British, the Elgin Marbles serve no other purpose than that of beautifying the British Museum."[70]

Although Cavafy found Knowles's argument spurious, one can be quite certain that the Englishman's interesting juxtaposition of Hellenism and colonialism did not fall on deaf ears at home in the colonial power of Britain. It is no accident that Knowles's text also refers to the Greek government as merely "transitory." Here the colonial discourse is working full force alongside Hellenism's search for pure origins to disassociate a "mixed little population which now lives upon the ruins of ancient Greece" from permanent claims.[71] Apparently for Knowles, modern Greeks could make no rightful appeal to gain possession of the marbles, any more than they could permanently govern themselves. Cavafy here reminded his English readers that the Greek government that Knowles so easily dismissed had actually "made laws prohibiting illegal traffic in Greek antiquities; and they have established several well-stocked and well-managed Museums."[72]

Cavafy's essay also informs us of Knowles's second main argumentative line, that a likely "clash of the Eastern Question" would hasten the marbles' destruction on the Acropolis. In the Greek government's defense, Cavafy, alongside Harrison, presents the counterargument that "the climate of Bloomsbury is injurious to the sculptures."[73] But the matter of environmental compatibility has more recently emerged as an argument by which enlightened Europeans *and* Greek authorities discipline the conduct of the local population. Although the modern scholar Richard Stoneman clearly appreciates the "national honour" that Greeks bestow upon their archeologists, he also welcomes the prospect of cooperation between archeologists of the American School and "the New Republic."[74] But he offers this sympathetic warning to the Greek Archeological Service concerning pollution in Athens: "The biggest issue confronting the Greek Archeologial Service is one not so much of restoration as of conservation. The pilfering lords have gone, but the hungry clouds of pollution do damage in Athens nearly as

[70] Cavafy, " 'Give Back the Elgin Marbles,' " 10.
[71] Quoted in Cavafy, " 'Give Back the Elgin Marbles,' " 11.
[72] Cavafy, " 'Give Back the Elgin Marbles,' " 11.
[73] Ibid., 10.
[74] Stoneman wrote *Land of Lost Gods* after 1973, when the military dictatorship led by Colonel George Papadopoulos deposed King Constantine and "proclaimed the creation of a 'presidential parliamentary republic' to be ratified by referendum" (Richard Clogg, *A Short History of Modern Greece* [1979], 196).

bad."[75] Stoneman then closes with guarded praise of Greece and Turkey's "responsible" behavior as "guardians of the ancient past."

Let us turn to the observation quoted at the beginning of this chapter, namely, that the Parthenon, worn down on the surface, "has disappeared into textual, visual, or photographic commentary," even as "it has been stepped upon by tourists"; "yet it can at every moment emerge again, as it does emerge, new and different, each time" we "speak about it."[76] As tenaciously as Western Hellenism has clung to the Acropolis as a *topos* of cultural ruins, its *logos* has not been able to contain the *topos* of the Acropolis, or, more broadly, the *topos* of Hellas. On the one hand, the *logos* of Hellenism itself becomes a *topos* to which European topographies persistently return to produce new interpretations. On the other hand, this same *logos*, manifested in space on the *topos* of ruins, becomes contested territory. Although a heterotopia of the West, the *topos* of Hellas is not empty space, incidentally occupied by ancient Hellenes followed by their "mixed" descendants. As the cosmopolitan sights, sounds, and physical particles of modern Athenian life rise up in the atmosphere and becloud this monument to antiquity's glory, they present the Western observer with complex juxtapositions—what Chateaubriand might still have referred to as a "confusing assemblage."[77] The simultaneity of differences in fact charges this heterotopia with social and cultural meanings. In the end, they jumble the European textbook original while they also affect the local milieu.

Literary repossessions of the Acropolis, which activate distinctions between the then and the now, here and there, recovered and lost, usu-

---

[75] Stoneman, *Land of Lost Gods*, 300.

[76] Yánnis Tsiómis, Επιστρέφοντας από την έκθεση (Returning from the exhibition) (1985), 14.

[77] In 1806, Chateaubriand discovered what he referred to as a "confused assemblage": "les chapiteaux des Propylées, les colonnes du Parthénon et du Temple d'Erechthée, les embrasures d'une muraille chargée de canons, le débris gothiques des chrétiens et les masures des musulmans" (*Itinéraire*, 177). In a postmodern setting, we find another author, Gwendolyn MacEwen, enjoying sonic juxtapositions on and around the Acropolis: "The strident notes from the *bouzoukia* of Plaka—the night-spots which form a weird, winding network of music and laughter along the lower slopes of the mountain of the Acropolis. Above, in the Parthenon, the freaky stillness of history. Below, a maze of streets full of cafés, *boîtes*, *tavernas*, each competing with the other for the right to do permanent damage to the human ear. And yet, often, hidden away in a dark corner under a roof of latticework and grapevines, the surprise: the lone *santouri* player caressing the countless strings of his instrument upon the table" (*Mermaids and Ikons*, 17).

ally serve to confirm European ties to civilization's sacred origins. Not infrequently, they also support guardianship of artifacts, the weight of which Neohellenic reality more than any other bears. And they make light of other nations' claims—most notably the Greeks'. Obversely, Greeks habitually rely on the *topos* of the Acropolis to express their anxieties about European conspiracies to disinherit them from their Hellenic heritage while they also seek to affirm the legitimacy and exclusiveness of their own ties. Their discussions of this and other Hellenic archetopias implant the ideals of a modern Panhellenic unity in the citizens of Hellas and, to some degree, in philhellenes, as we shall see in the chapters that follow.

The Acropolis might be viewed today as a symbol not of Greece's ancient glory but of its modern predicament. It might be related, too, to other abandoned building complexes, dialectical signs of eternal lastingness and inevitable ruin: to the Paris arcades of the nineteenth century, in which Walter Benjamin perceived "the utopian potential of the modern . . . and its catastrophic and barbaric present reality";[78] or to the Piazza d'Italia in New Orleans, greeted with fanfare when first designed and erected by Charles Moore (d. 1994) with the Urban Innovations Group in 1977–78, though the monument now lies in a state of deterioration. Having weathered the ravages of time and the elements—having faced the incumbent changes in economic, civic, social, and cultural practices—these buildings have also lost their use-value, only to be repossessed at a later date by architectural renovations or scholarly interest. Like Greece itself, the Acropolis is a site rich in cultural capital alone, although it also boasts of a "superb view" from its lofty height above the din of Athens.[79] Partitioned off from the here and now of modern Europe, it has been put on display for travelers seeking a bargain, verification of their distinguished origins, or the sweetness and light of the Mediterranean landscape. In this way it makes up for Greece's dearth of power and prestige, on the one hand, and lack of a cheap labor force, on the other hand, which might otherwise entice long-term investment in Greece. Having put the ruins of its history on tour, Greece thus features the culture of ruins as *its* most recognizable *modern* signature.

[78] Susan Buck-Morss, *The Dialectics of Seeing: Walter Benjamin and the Arcades Project* (1989), 251.
[79] Kazantzakis, *Report to Greco*, 137.

CHAPTER 3

Topos: From Revenant Nation
to Transcendental Territory

Hellas, language blind in Geography
Hellas, empty lot and colony.
　　　—From the song Γεννήθηκα στη Σαλονίκη
　　　(I was born in Thessaloniki), by Dionísis Savvópulos

On the map of Europe you search to find your mark, but Stelios the superb and the "Minor Mode of the Orient" confuse you. Nowhere and to no one does your heart belong. . . . And when you become anxious about the path our race is taking, you walk the tightrope on a bouzouki string, trying to find a way out of this dead end.
　　　—From the song Το αδιέξοδο (Dead end)

The nineteenth-century European encounter with the Acropolis systematically disregarded views of local residents while it created its own topography of Hellenism. On the Acropolis, a *topos* of modernity simultaneously reconstructed and dismantled through the dream of recovering lost origins, Europeans reproduced the unequal power relations played out in politics and trade. By some twisted logic, they put themselves on their maps as Hellenism's aboriginal occupants; they made themselves official curators of the classical Greek past. Greeks could assist them in their role of preserving the culture of ruins provided they did not get in their way. Yet Neohellenes did not passively accept this ancillary role. One should not forget that knowledge and power are best understood by their enabling effects. Once disciplinary technologies were deployed in Greece, venerated sites like the Acropolis became places where power was immanent for Greeks as well as Europeans, to whom Greeks now found themselves vitally tied. In the process of becoming second-class Europeans, Greeks would also become first-class entrepreneurs in the business of mapping Hellenism.

Panhellenic Contentions

If Hellenism can be viewed as a "cultural exemplar of Europe,"[1] then surely Neohellenism, the restored foundation of a Panhellenic union, has been exemplary in its simulation. Indeed Neohellenism has been tireless in its effort to present to the modern world an integrated image of Hellenism. Through persistent toil, it succeeded in instituting Hellenic identity on the geopolitical map of nations. It should be noted that Greeks achieved independence and national unification at a relatively early date (1832) even by Western standards—not only before the other Balkan countries, but also before Italy (1861), Germany (1871), and Ireland (1922). In addition, Greeks, former subjects of a powerful Eastern empire, may be said to have gained the status of modern independent nation-state without having passed through administrative colonialization by the West.[2] This accomplished, they were invaded by a Bavarian king and his court of scholars and administrators, who were instrumental in establishing ancestor worship as the norm in the Greek Kingdom.

Hellenism, like the Acropolis, has generated numerous struggles of interpretation and confrontations about its control. To this day, these interpretive battles ceaselessly haunt Greeks; they continue to affect the way Greeks view their state, circumscribe their nation, define their present unity, even count their friends and enemies. One important

---

[1] Michael Herzfeld, *Ours Once More: Folklore, Ideology, and the Making of Modern Greece* (1982), 5.

[2] This statement holds true only if one ignores the fact that the Ionian islands and the Dodecanese were colonized first by the Venetians and then by Great Britain, while Crete was colonized by the Venetians; in addition, the Greek peninsula for four hundred years prior to the foundation of the Greek state was part of the Ottoman Empire, which had its own policy of expansion and incorporation. It is odd that many Greeks maintain that the culture of the Eptánisa (Seven Ionian Islands) presents the purest expression of "Hellenicity"—meaning that it shows the least signs of Ottoman influence. Why is British and Venetian colonization so invisible? Why does Western influence sit so well with Greeks, who continually focus their attention on sorting through Ottoman cultural deposits? It could really be argued that modern Greece endured a "colonialization of the mind" (see Onwuchekwa Jemi Chinweizu and Ihechukwu Madubuike, *Decolonising the African Mind* [1987]), given that its system of education was imported directly from Germany.

battle seized upon the shape and size of a Hellenic *topos*. Greeks have endlessly debated the precise boundaries of their *topos*. Indeed, tracing an imaginary *topos* of Hellenism over the political map of the world has been a permanent obsession, a *topos* in its own right. Hellas is a classical *topos*, Greeks commonly assert, with all the ambiguity this statement contains. Caught between *logos* and *topos*, discourse and geography, Greeks have frequently found themselves fighting battles in which the prestige of Hellenism, on the one hand, and the land of Hellas, on the other, are the coveted prizes. Geopolitical territory has set off numerous cultural battles in the land of politics. Culture, in turn, has played a major role in shaping the politics of land.

Greeks therefore have devoted political speeches, linguistic studies, and literary and critical texts to the mapping of their homeland. And, on a narrowly circumscribed plane, they have succeeded in conferring on the heterogeneous populations of the southern Balkan peninsula and on several Greek diasporas a sense of shared space. They have resolved, to some degree at least, matters of coexistence and succession. They have consolidated a single milieu for Neohellenism from the scattered and separate milieus of distant communities, diverse ethnic groups, neighborhoods, cosmopolitan centers, churches, monasteries, and the countryside that once constituted Ottoman Hellenism. They have also standardized a modern language, produced a national narrative, and created a literary canon—all crucial to achieving their Panhellenic union.

Fundamental to their ongoing topographical project is a discussion of *topos* itself. Indeed, the negotiation of *topos* has been basic to Greek history, politics, and culture for the past two hundred years. Perceived as a cornerstone of the nation, alongside people and history, a shared *topos* becomes a precondition for the restoration of Hellenism: Hellenism can develop naturally and find self-fulfillment only within its self-evident geography—so the *logos* goes. A genealogy of the Greek usage of *topos* shows that the term receives its deceptively transparent referentiality during this century. Under certain conditions, *topos* becomes the preferred term—competing with *éthnos* 'nation', *yénos* 'nation, people, race' (Latin *genus*), *fíli* 'race, nation', *laós* 'people', and *patrída* 'fatherland, homeland'—for invoking the self-presence of Hellenism. In its literary usage, *topos* is almost formulaic. It designates a space physically inhabited by Hellenes in either the past or the present. This century's invocations of *topos* claim greater familiarity and possessiveness—ο τόπος μας 'our *topos*'—as if the Hellenic *topos* had become more intimate and narrow.[3] In contrast to the intimate twentieth-century tone, one finds one hundred years earlier a more neutral usage that just identifies a particular geographical space with its historical inhabitants: ο τόπος όπου το παλαιόν εκατοικούσαν οι Έλληνες 'the territory where Hellenes dwelled in ancient times."[4] Especially after World War I, *topos* becomes an organism with a *pnévma* 'spirit'.[5] It acquires real *sinesthímata* 'feelings', which bad times tan deprive.[6] And it develops an independent *zoí* 'life'.[7] As the century progresses, usage becomes more and more figurative. *Topos* develops attributes that transport it above the din of everyday life. It becomes *iperuránios* 'transcendental'.[8] It becomes "haunted and magical, a verdant *topos*, an *atopic topos*."[9]

Certainly the present-day, self-evident referentiality of *topos* raises questions about the topographical enterprise that preceded, particularly in the tumultuous first half of this century. When, how, and why did Greeks conceive the southernmost peninsula of the Balkans to be the site of origin, the place of homecoming for Hellenism? How did authors line up their conceptual maps of Hellenism with the existing political map of Hellas at various stages? How did they relate their topographies to more expansive delineations of the nation—as opposed to the state—that rendered this the authentic plane of Hellenism's development?[10] How did they adapt Greek culture to their

[3] Τούτος ο μικρούτσικος τόπος 'this tiny little *topos*' (Yánnis Psiháris, Το ταξίδι μου [My journey] [(1888) 1979], 86); ο τόπος μας ο κλειστός 'our closed-off *topos*' (George Seferis, *Mythistorema* 1.1, in Ποιήματα [Poems] [1974], 43); ο μικροσκοπικός τόπος 'the microscopic *topos*' (Zísimos Lorentzátos, Δοκίμιο 1 [Essay 1] [1947], 17).

[4] Grigórios Konstandás and Daniíl Filippídis, Νεωτερική γεωγραφία (Neoteric geography) (n.d.), 71.

[5] Το πνεύμα του τόπου μας 'the spirit of our *topos*' (Dimítris Pikiónis, Το πρόβλημα της μορφής [The problem of form] [(1946) 1985], 8).

[6] Ο τόπος μας έζησε χωρίς γενναία και ευγενικά συναισθήματα 'our *topos* lived without brave and noble feelings' (Yórgos Theotokás, Ελεύθερο πνεύμα [Free spirit] [(1929) 1988], 63).

[7] Είναι καλό και χρήσιμο να μελετούμε τη ζωή του τόπου μας 'it is a good and useful thing to study the life of our *topos*' (Theotokás, Ελεύθερο πνεύμα [Free spirit], 19).

[8] Τόπος υπερουράνιος (Transcendental topos) is the title of a book by Greek philosopher Stélios Rámfos ([1975] 1983).

[9] Jimmy Panúsis, from a radio broadcast of 27 August 1988, in Η ζάλη των τάξεων (Class muddle) (1989).

[10] The nation and the state are not the same. The nation is the "imagined community" conceived when a heterogeneous group consents to three basic assertions about the identity of its constituent parts: that there exists a social body with an explicit and

discursively constructed space? How did contemporary cultural movements, in turn, map their homeland? What role, finally, did Neohellenic topographies assign to a Hellenic tradition?

Greek texts from the late nineteenth to the mid-twentieth century
offer a wealth of material for understanding the changing topogra-
phics of Hellenism. Viewed chronologically, Neohellenic discussions
of *topos* reveal ways in which Greeks revised their maps of the homeland as a foreign policy of irredentism gradually gave way to one of
consolidation and containment. In the discussion that follows, I make
my way, patiently and slowly, through several important Greek texts
in order to establish a genealogy of *topos* in Greek literary history. That
is to say, I give interpretive readings of carefully selected passages as a
way of tracing the uses of *topos*, while I also advance a rather complex
argument about Neohellenic topographies.

The thread of my argument is this. Throughout their modern
history, Greeks have fought intellectual battles over conflicting conceptions of their *topos*. Ideas of ethos and ethnos, tradition and modernity, autochthony and their own secondariness in relation to both
Europe and the ancients, find a visual symbol in the physically limited
but culturally expansive *topos* of Hellenism. During the period of the
state's formation and expansion, Greeks devised foreign policy to
make the Kingdom of Hellas fit a Byzantine-inspired map of the
Hellenic nation extending into the recesses of Asia Minor. Later they
revised the map to accommodate losses that proved the impossibility
of the project. They then raised the standard of high culture to signal the boundaries between what was Hellenic and what was non-
Hellenic.

In the texts I study, certain trends are recurrent. Throughout a
period of some one hundred years, Neohellenes have relied on argu-

---

peculiar character; that the interests and values of this social body take priority over all
other interests and values; and that this social body must be as independent as possible
and usually requires at least the attainment of political sovereignty. The state is the
apparatus that legitimizes, organizes, manages, and operates the affairs of a sovereign
body. In the modern world, the state is designated as "the possessor of sovereignty over
a given territory" (Breuilly, *Nationalism and the State*, 355), with the qualification that it
should exercise sovereignty directly only in the public sphere (given that a distinction
between the public and private spheres is maintained). The sovereign nation-state, a
peculiarly modern institution, is the apparatus adopted by nationalist movements that
have achieved autonomy within a given territory. On the tension between the claims of
the state and the rights of the individuals that constitute the nation, see Breuilly, 353–
65; and Adamantia Polis, "Notes on Nationalism and Human Rights in Greece" (1988).

ments of their temporal continuity from the archaic through the classical and the Byzantine into the modern world. They have used the argument of continuity to stake out a desired territory, even though they have stood to lose a great deal when their achievements are compared to those of their esteemed ancestors, particularly the ancient Greeks. The disciplines of philology, archeology, and philosophy all spotlight classical Hellas as the brightest hour of Hellenism, while Neohellenism operates de facto in the darkness of the present, that is to say, outside the power and prestige of its past. Thus many authors whose work I discuss felt compelled to respond, whether directly or indirectly, to "the European debate about whether or not we Greeks were the true descendants of the ancient Greeks."[11] Their answer was frequently a restatement of Hellenism's present-day conundrum: to be a cultural *topos* "blind in geography"—existing wherever Hellenic values prevail—*and* to be a modern geopolitical entity, an "empty lot and colony" occupying the smallest, poorest spot on the map of Western Europe.[12] How was this possible? Could one really have it both ways? Was there any other way? Everywhere one also finds a stubborn contrast between the desired *topos* of Hellenism and the political map of Hellas. Always distinguishing between Hellenism and Hellas, the *éthnos* 'nation' and the *krátos* 'state', Neohellenic authors cleared a plateau for Hellenism above and beyond mainland Greece. Whether more east- or westwardly oriented, Byzantine- or ancient-inspired, inclusive or exalted, politically, geographically, or culturally resonant, their *topos* of Hellenism always assumed its fullest glory.

One may also note perceptible changes in Neohellenic topographies, the most important of which is a sweeping historical movement from the ideal of a revenant nation to the vision of a transcendental *topos*. The first major transition comes at the turn of the twentieth century. Three major intellectual figures, Yánnis Psiháris (1854–1929), Íon Dragúmis (1878–1920), and Periklís Yannópulos (1869–1910), give expression to the theme of transcendence. Supplementing the parliamentary project of the Megáli Idéa 'Great Idea', the neo-Byzantinist irredentist vision that emphasized history, geography, and politics, Psiháris and Dragúmis, who were not adverse to the Megáli Idéa, explored the resources of a Greek vernacular culture as an important

[11] Zísimos Lorentzátos, "The Lost Center" ([1961] 1980), 91.
[12] See Dionísis Savvópulos, Γεννήθηκα στη Σαλονίκη (I was born in Thessaloniki) (1979).

instrument of expansion.[13] In contrast, Yannópulos, the idiosyncratic philosopher of art, delineated the horizon of a specifically Attic *topío* 'landscape' against which he measured an autochthonous but capacious artistic tradition of Hellenism.

A second important transition in the direction of transcendence occurs mid-century, most markedly from December 1944 to October 1949, the years of the bloody Greek civil war. At this time, a certain view of *topos* acquired its *deontología* 'logos explaining its moral necessity'.[14] Now the cultural mission of conveying the superiority of Neohellenism as a preserver of certain Western values completely superseded the moribund foreign policy of expanding state boundaries so as to contain the territory of the nation. As Greeks surrendered their plan to recover areas in the southern Balkans and western Asia where Greek-speaking Orthodox people had once been in the majority, they drew a different map of Hellenism. Under banners of their own making—Hellenic Hellenism, Neohellenism, and Hellenicity—intellectuals and poets of the 1930s and 1940s, including Yórgos Theotokás, Zísimos Lorentzátos (b. 1915), and Dimítris Nikolareízis, synthesized the projects of Psiháris and Dragúmis, the prophets of vernacularism, and, most important, Yannópulos, clairvoyant of the Hellenic landscape and author of aesthetic nationalism.

Transformations of the *Megáli Idéa*

Many documents evince that Neohellenes tirelessly devoted themselves to delineating Hellenism's full expanse. Their topographical enterprise involved both defining the symbolic significance of place *and* affirming Neohellenism's historical connection to a particular territory. Some topographies gave geographical markers to an ideal *topos*,

[13] The Megáli Idéa, which dominated Greek foreign and military policy from 1843 to 1922, set its sights on a unified Hellenic Kingdom representing some map of Byzantium, with Constantinople as its capital. The expanded Kingdom was to include areas Greeks had settled in the Balkans, around the Hellespont, in Asia Minor, and along the western and southern shores of the Black Sea. In this context, Psiháris's opening chapter makes sense. "For a nation to become a nation, it needs two things: to expand its borders and to produce its own literature. . . . It must expand not only its physical but also its intellectual borders. It is for these borders that I am now fighting" (To ταξίδι μου [My journey], 37).

[14] See Theodorakópulos, To πνεύμα του νεοελληνισμού (The spirit of Neohellenism), 137.

though they may have remained vague about actual frontiers. In others, geographical space recedes like a Platonic shadow, while the ideal *topos* becomes illuminated. The first kind of geographic mapping appears in Ioánnis Koléttis's famous speech on the Megáli Idéa given before the Constituent Assembly (1844). Psiháris and Yannópulos practice the second, imaginative kind of geography, which places culture at the heart of Hellenism. Dragúmis, as politician and author, brings together discussions of actual and conceptual space, proposals for social-political as well as cultural reconstruction.

In his fateful speech of 1844, Koléttis (d. 1847), a Hellenized Vlach, powerful politician, and influential member of Parliament in the independent Hellenic Kingdom, argued for the expansion of political boundaries to fit a territory he associated with Byzantine Hellenism and its capital city, Constantinople: "The Kingdom of Greece is not Greece. [Greece] constitutes only one part, the smallest and poorest. A Greek is not only a man who lives within this kingdom, but also one who lives in Jannina, in Salonica, in Serres, in Adrianople, in Constantinople, in Smyrna, in Trebizond, in Crete, in Samos, and in any land associated with Greek history or the Greek race. . . . There are two main centres of Hellenism: Athens, the capital of the Greek kingdom, [and] 'The City' [Constantinople], the dream and hope of all Greeks."[15] Given Western topographies of Hellenism, which place Athens at their center, it is defamiliarizing to find Athens figuring only negatively as a limiting factor in this speech. Yet this is standard practice in nineteenth-century Neohellenic topographies. Athens, the Acropolis, and other classical sites, symbols of European receptiveness to Hellenism, constituted only one rubric of identity markers for Neohellenes. Constantinople, capital of the Eastern Roman Empire, was a more important landmark for Greek-speaking Orthodox Christians who lived scattered throughout the Balkans, in the Danubian provinces, Asia Minor, Anatolia, and along the shores of the Black Sea. In the period under discussion, Constantinople became the symbol of an imaginary Panhellenic union organized on the common ground of the Greek language and the Orthodox faith, juxtaposed to a

[15] Trans. Clogg, in *Short History*, 76. Brackets are Clogg's. The entire speech appears in the "Proceedings of the National Assembly of the Third of September in Athens" (1844). On the history of the text, see K. Th. Dimarás, Ελληνικός ρωμαντισμός (Greek romanticism) (1982). See Éli Skopetéa, Το πρότυπο βασίλειο και η Μεγάλη Ιδέα (The model kingdom and the Megáli Idéa) (1988), for a powerful discussion of the ideology of the Megáli Idéa.

rival Western (Latin) Christianity. Even today, η Πόλη 'The City', as Greeks still refer to it, remains a Neohellenic topographical signpost. Moreover, it is coveted territory, 'space to which identity is attached by a distinctive group who hold or covet that territory and who desire to have full control over it for the group's benefit."[16] Athens and Constantinople together are emblematic of prior unification in the nationalist argument "that Greeks constituted a nation, and they had done so before."[17] During the nineteenth and early twentieth centuries, the recovery of both ancient and Byzantine Hellenism remained for Greeks a precondition for the rebirth and development of their modern nation. Greeks repeatedly argued that their civilization could develop naturally and find self-fulfillment only within the historical expanse emanating from these two points of origin.[18] And so they repeatedly retraced the boundaries of a Hellenic *topos* around these two cardinal points.

The key to the irredentist vision appears in the formula that the real Greece spans not only places where contemporary Greeks reside or land legally under their administration but "any land associated with Greek history or the Greek race," as Koléttis stated.[19] The *vasílio* 'kingdom' and the *éthnos* 'nation' are nonidentical, as are the Helladic and the Hellenic, the actual and the ideal, Athens and Constantinople. Hellenism becomes a unique social organism extending across space and into time past, present, and future. Constantinople, Hellenism's territorial center, resonates alongside the bureaucratic center of the state, Athens. The ideal city, capital of Byzantine Hellenism, signifies the homogeneity and distinctiveness of an unfinished Hellenism, while it leans uncomfortably against the self-enclosed legal entity of the Helladic Kingdom symbolized by its capital, Athens.

There is something teleological in Koléttis's irredentist vision of *topos*. The speech suggests that the revenant nation, unfinished and in the process of becoming, is moving in the direction of a specific *telos*,

---

[16] Knight, "Identity and Territory," 526.

[17] Herzfeld, *Ours Once More*, 16.

[18] See Ion Dragúmis, Ελληνικός πολιτισμός (Hellenic civilization) ([1914] 1927), 233–34.

[19] At the time of Koléttis's speech, the Kingdom controlled the Peloponnese, Attica and the central mainland including the southern part of Thessaly, and the islands of Euboea, Hydra, Spetses, Andros, and the Cyclades. It incorporated "none of the great centres of Greek commerce in the Ottoman Empire, Smyrna, Salonica, Alexandria, and Constantinople" (Clogg, *Short History*, 70) nor other important towns such as Arta, Ioannina, and Volos.

the unification of all Greeks living "in any land associated with Greek history or the Greek race." As the *topos* expands in space, it also connects Neohellenes to their past: to Greeks of the Turkokratía 'Turkish occupation' and, prior to them, Greeks of the Byzantine era.[20] Furthermore, it places those who inhabit the Kingdom of Greece, "the smallest and poorest" of places, on the same plane as those living "in Jannina, in Salonica, in Serres, in Adrianople, in Constantinople, in Smyrna, in Trebizond, in Crete, in Samos, and in any land associated with Greek history or the Greek race." The vision of an enlarged Hellenic *topos* finally serves to transcend local, regional, and supranational allegiances. Around the ideologically charged center of Constantinople, Hellenes living within and outside Hellas find their ideal homeland.

The general context of Koléttis's speech is the ideology of nationalism, which generated successive visions of a restored *topos* of Hellenism. I use nationalism in the strong sense of a cultural and political ideology appearing in the late eighteenth century and continuing to the present day. Nationalism assembles a group of people whom it discovers as sharing a language and ethos. It encourages this group to assert the uniqueness of its identity, to claim political sovereignty on the basis of this cultural uniqueness, and to acquire a territory, a *topos* reflecting the natural boundaries that would contain all the sharers of the common culture. The paradox of what John Plamenatz calls "Eastern nationalism," a rubric under which one should include Greek nationalism, is that "to retain their nationality, their separate cultural identity, they had in many ways to imitate the foreigners with whom they refused to identify themselves. And in so doing, they could not help but loosen the hold over themselves of ancestral ways."[21]

The Neohellenic nationalist argument in each of its many forms moves simultaneously in two directions. In one direction Greeks are pulled closer to Ευρώπη 'Europe' or the Δύση 'West' (but never to the

[20] Turkokratía 'Turkish occupation' refers to the four centuries (1453–1821) during which the Ottoman Empire controlled the Greek peninsula. Neohellenes recall Ottoman rule as a repressive, foreign occupation, a period of *sklaviá* 'enslavement.'

[21] John Plamenatz, "Two Types of Nationalism" (1973), 31. "Eastern nationalism" is a purposeful misnomer. It refers to the nationalism of peoples from Eastern Europe, including Greece, but also from the continents of Asia, Africa, and Latin America. It is "Eastern" only in the sense that it is secondary to "Western" nationalism. And it is secondary in this sense: that a non-Western people assert their own civilization as an equal if separate partner *within* a "Western civilization," which ultimately precludes their equal participation.

Φράγκοι 'Franks, Crusaders') that rediscovered Hellenism. This pole buttresses claims of cultural distinction. In the other, they are pushed toward the antithesis of the West—symbolized by Βυζάντιο 'Byzantium' or the Ανατολή 'East'. Here Greeks felt, and to a great extent continue to feel, they could assert their difference from the West.[22] The East presented both the most serious threat to the nation and its salvation. For in the East lay the nation's greatest enemy but also its spiritual center, "The City." And in the heart of that city, as far as possible from European reconstructions of the classical world, stood the Orthodox patriarchate. Once the nationalist argument attached Hellenic ethnicity to this religious *katafígio* 'place of refuge' from the Muslim host, the patriarchate became an ideologically charged center around which an expansive *topos* of Hellenism—rather than of Orthodoxy, as before—was seen to radiate.

"Who can look at the Patriarchate and the Patriarch without feeling shaken?" Psiháris asked rhetorically in Το ταξίδι μου (My journey) (1888), his now canonical manifesto of cultural "demoticism."[23] In this

[22] For contemporary views on the topic "Hellenes or Europeans?" from a Neo Orthodox perspective, see the Greek periodical Σύναξη 34 (April-June 1990). Perhaps the most influential anti-Western manifesto from the postwar era is Lorentzátos's "The Lost Center." See Artemis Leontis, "'The Lost Center' and the Promised Land of Greek Criticism" (1987), and Stathis Gourgouris, "The Simulations of the *Center*: Lorentzátos's Neohellenism against the Modernist Phantom" (1990), for critiques of Lorentzátos's arguments.

[23] "Demoticism," a cultural movement that took shape in the late nineteenth and early twentieth centuries, covered education, linguistics, history, and literature. The goal of demoticists was to standardize vernacular dialects and to adopt these (over the archaizing "purist" language officially in place until 1977) as the language of both culture and the state. Demoticism's proponents, among whom linguist Yánnis Psiháris was initially the most visible, argued that the Greek vernacular was more clear, intelligible, and natural, and that it was closer to life and speech. They claimed that the state revival of ancient Greek (institutionalized with the foundation of the state in 1830) falsified the noble spirit of the Greek people, interfered with the natural development of the language, and isolated the learned minority from the unschooled majority. Demoticists defended the vernacular, first, in the name of Homer, Dante, Shakespeare, and Racine, all of whom wrote in the language of their times, with its mixed and "corrupt" forms and foreign words; second, in the name of the people, who expressed themselves naturally, consistently, and directly; third, in the name of nature, which directed the evolution of things according to the inner laws of their noble (de)generation; and, fourth, in the name of tradition. According to Dragúmis, another of demoticism's powerful proponents, "for nations, memory is tradition. . . . Tradition is the link between the individuals of a single race, both present and past, which makes them a nation. History is the consciousness of that link" (Ελληνικός πολιτισμός [Hellenic civilization], 203).

fictional account of a Greek intellectual's journey through Hellenism, Constantinople and, more specifically, the patriarchate appear as the soul of a besieged nation both prior to and after the creation of the state. "For four hundred years this tiny *topos* stood alone, a wooden house, a little old house, our only refuge, our only homeland. It was here that the nation clung."[24] Psiháris shows interest in the patriarchate not merely for its deliverance of local populations during four hundred years of Ottoman rule; the patriarchate's contribution is also its present-day symbolic value and its promise of regained control in the future. The *topos* of the patriarchate has the synecdochic power to evoke a neo-Byzantinist fantasy in which the whole of Byzantine Hellenism survives Ottoman repression intact. It becomes tinder for rekindling the passion of Greek ethnicity in its submerged Eastern territories.

In the demoticist revision of the Megáli Idéa, which comes to supplant Koléttis's rearward vision of a wholesale return to Byzantium, Athens figures positively, as Greek nationalism feels its cultural pull to the West.[25] Athens represents another coordinate of expansion. It is the intellectual and spiritual origin of Europe, home of poetry and philosophy. In Athens, the Hellenic world must find its point of attachment to the ancestral line of European civilization. Here it can reactivate its literary tradition. "This small *topos*," although not exactly operational in the machinery of civilized modernity, is the European's energy source, as Psiháris attests:

> Even if I die tomorrow, I will have had my fill of life now that I have seen Athens. This is where the world was born. It is here and in Rome that Europe received its education. This small *topos* filled the earth. From here we derived mind and thought and ideas. It made us into human beings. The place is called Athens, and never did another name with so few syllables mean so much in the world. For the name says it all. Whoever comes to such a place treads reverently over its earth; the sky which you look at is the one that great men looked at in their time; the horizon which you observe today with such joy is the one that their eyes observed every day. In this atmosphere lucid ideas were born,

[24] Psiháris, Το ταξίδι μου (My journey), 86.

[25] It should be noted that the authors of demoticism were very clearly Western-oriented thinkers. Psiháris, the founding father, held a professorial chair in linguistics in Paris, where he lived permanently. Like many Greek intellectuals living and working in the United States today, he visited Hellas sporadically; like their work, his, too, initially met with suspicion.

poetry and philosophy were created. And when the bold ones climbed up to the Acropolis, they made out the same sea which you now make out.[26]

Here the liturgical invocation of the place-name reduces the complex history of Greece's modern capital to the imaginary moment when "Europe received its education" and Neohellenes rediscovered theirs. Athens, once a vibrant city, later a beleaguered village, site of sometimes radically participatory, sometimes tyrannically exclusive governments, host to friendly and hostile occupying powers, fuses past and present through the immediacy of experience. It becomes one and the same place where ancients and moderns alike observe the same earth, sky, horizon, atmosphere, and sea—tags that unify the *topos* of Hellenism as they conflate nearly three thousand years of history. The fetishized name of Athens "says it all," reducing to a single breath the distinguished history, cultural contribution, and spiritual continuity of what Psiháris refers to as the national soul.

"The City" and Athens are not demoticism's only discovery points. Psiháris's topography reveals other markers at every narrative and expository turn. We find new dimensions of the Neohellenic identity, character, and fate in each corner of the Hellenic *topos* revisited: on Greek islands, in villages, towns, cities, and neighborhoods, in any of the narrator's fictional conversations with unschooled individuals whose speech indicates for him the natural pattern of the Greek vernacular. Even the island of Chios induces the self-discovery of nationhood; it inspires the following observation on the part of Psiháris about "the Greek's fortune . . . in Greece and Europe": "He hasn't yet found firm ground, but keeps on moving. He doesn't know today what will happen tomorrow, and asks himself: 'Will everything suddenly collapse on me, or will I enjoy the light of day again tomorrow morning?'"[27] Chios paradoxically becomes a reference point for this transitory aspect of Greek identity, as defined by Psiháris, since Chios produced a figure incarnating the temporal and spatial constancy of national identity in flux: "Homer," who is for Psiháris the sign of the social organism at work weaving disparate tales from various villages into a unified if sometimes contradictory poetic *logos*.[28]

[26] Psiháris, Το ταξίδι μου (My journey), 158.

[27] Ibid., 115.

[28] I discuss Psiháris's answer to Homeric questions about authorship and composition in Chapter 6.

Demoticists like Psiháris consistently argued that virtue and knowledge reside in the simple people, who are the overwhelming majority, and in their collective traditions. Place-names such as Constantinople, Athens, Chios, and Piraeus mark the vitality and persistence, expanse and uniformity, of the Greek people. Key geographical points in the *topos* of the homeland represent the immanent power of a solid community without reference to official state boundaries.[29] While demoticism suggested that the nation had legitimate claims of sovereignty over a space greater than that controlled by the Greek Kingdom, the map it drew acquired symbolic rather than pragmatic value. Instead of serving as a geographic guidepost for the expansion of the Kingdom, demoticist topography indicated the cultural expansiveness of Neohellenism. Furthermore, it subordinated the multiplicity of elements and diversity of manners found in the populations that inhabited the Greek world to a uniformly solid community of demotic speakers. Finally, it sought to extend the intellectual horizons of Neohellenism to include older layers of the Greek vernacular.

Demoticists' battle to redefine Neohellenism's horizons represents only one of many efforts to circumscribe the *topos* of Hellenism by regulating culture. Intellectuals like Psiháris enforced the Megáli Idéa in their scheme to extend Hellenism from Homer to Romiosíni,[30] from Athens to Constantinople. They supported the politics of aggressive military expansion (1880–1921) and gave it legitimacy, because they nourished the assumption that there was a disjunction between the actuality of the state and the ideal of the nation. Within

---

[29] Benedict Anderson describes the historical self-conception of the nation in relation to time; it is "a sociological organism moving calendrically through homogeneous, empty time"; "a solid community moving down (or up) history" (*Imagined Communities*, 31). Certainly one should also add a spatial dimension; the nation also imagines itself as a solid community moving back and forth in homogeneous, empty space. This is why the presence of nonintegrated groups in one's land appears so intrusive.

[30] *Romiosíni* is very nearly impossible to translate into English. It is the nominalized form of the adjective *romiós*, a Greek vernacularization of the adjective *romaios* 'Roman'. This name attaches itself to the occupants of the Greek peninsula at some unspecified time after the Romans destroyed Corinth (146 B.C.). *Romiosíni* is a vernacular coinage of the late nineteenth century. It signifies the national-popular body and its Byzantine-Ottoman-Christian popular heritage, the traditions and language of the *Volk*. A commonplace citation for the distinction between Hellenism and Romiosíni in everyday Greek discourse is Patrick Leigh Fermor, *Roumeli: Travels in Modern Greece* ([1966] 1983), 96–147 ("The Helleno-Romaic Dilemma"), where *Romiosíni* is glossed as "the Romaic World, Romaic-hood" (99). See also Herzfeld, *Ours Once More*, 18–23. I discuss Romiosíni extensively in Chapter 6.

this gap they created a niche for themselves, where they became the homeland's most important mapmakers.

The interrelation of politics and culture appears most visibly in the work of Dragúmis, politician and man of letters. Crucial to his demoticist vision is a careful distinction, again, between the "natural" borders of the Hellenic nation and the "artificial" boundaries of the Helladic state:

> The Hellenes of Hellas, let us call them the Helladics, identified in their minds the Hellenic state, the Hellenic kingdom, the tiny Hellas, with the Hellenic nation. They forgot about the Hellenic nation, Romiosíni, Hellenism. They forgot that the state, the kingdom, is temporary, and they imagined what it would be like if it were perfect. And their conception of perfection consists in any other state in Europe that has succeeded. . . . But these gentlemen, these Hellenes, the Helladics, do not see that England lives naturally, because it has its natural boundaries, has English earth as its center, is a finished state and so spreads out into all the world. Whereas Hellas (liberated Hellas, that is, the state) does not live naturally, because it is the artificial ruse of foreign diplomats; it doesn't have its natural borders, it is a temporary, moribund organism with an artificial center, and not a finished state.[31]

By characterizing the state as a temporary and imperfect solution, a "moribund organism," an "artificial ruse of foreign diplomats," this text offers contrasting signs of distinction. Opposed to tiny Hellas is the vast "Hellenic nation, Romiosíni, Hellenism." Once again we find the nation opposed to the state—that monstrous creation of Western diplomats. The nation can naturally fulfill Hellenism's wish for self-government. It can connect an integrated patchwork of simple, organic communities. In other words, the nation comprises social groupings of the kind that Max Weber and Otto Bauer labeled *Gemeinschaft*, in which association is based on the feeling of members that they belong together as a distinct group with a subjectively and collectively held identity and a sentiment of solidarity. These groupings are unlike the impersonal associations formed for specific political purposes, or *Gesellschaft*.[32] Loyalty to the group derives from loyalty to a

---

[31] Dragúmis, Ο ελληνισμός μου και οι Έλληνες (My Hellenism and the Greeks) (1903–9), 108.

[32] In "Nationalist Ideology and Territory," James Anderson draws on this Weberian distinction between two types of social groupings. He argues that the nation is originally conceived as a kind of *Gemeinschaft*, whereas the state is a kind of *Gesellschaft*.

place—*topikismós* 'localism' is a term Dragúmis frequently uses—and a common *filí* 'race'. Regionally shared codes of honor and ancestral traditions—*ta pátria* 'things from our fathers'—rather than an abstract, "Frankish system" control behavior. Under no circumstances can anything, let alone a foreign system of governance, abolish loyalty to time and place: "*topos* and time cannot be undone in the human world."[33]

Here we find evident in yet another Neohellenic topography the Eastern nationalist's opposition to Western systems. This communitarian vision upholds the value of regional communities over the state, indigenous roots over Western influence, traditions, manners, codes, and a local base over institutions, systems, centralized government, and uniform overcoding of an abstract sovereignty.[34] In this way it promotes a kind of premodern archaism, and so appears to fend off the onrush of Western modernity. Its political project is to strengthen local influence and boost grass-roots participation so as to stay the tide of migration from village to Athens, Greece to the West. To this end, it engages culture to redraw the map of Hellas so as to feature a spatially expansive, loosely organized union of autonomous, individually coded communities. Its *logos* subordinates the state to the nation: "The entire nation is the creator of the state, and the nation fashions the state for the purposes of the nation so that it may produce its civilization in one body, undisturbed and securely—so that it may blossom."[35] There was no better reason for the state's coming into existence—so Dragúmis argues. The state, therefore, "does not have the right to confine itself to its narrow political borders and to forget parts of the nation which remain outside its borders."[36] Like both Koléttis and Psiháris before him, Dragúmis does not confine *topos* to existing state boundaries but extends it beyond the physical borders of

[33] Dragúmis, Ελληνικός πολιτισμός (Hellenic civilization), 184.

[34] According to Deleuze and Guattari, "primitive societies operate essentially by codes and territorialities. . . . Modern, or State societies, on the other hand, have replaced the declining codes with univocal overcoding, and the lost territory with a specific reterritorialization (which takes place in an overcoded geometrical space)" (*A Thousand Plateaus*, 212–13).

[35] Dragúmis, Ελληνικός πολιτισμός (Hellenic civilization), 183. In the same essay, Dragúmis also asserts: "Let there be no state if it hinders or disfigures the national spirit. If the state cramps the nation, it must necessarily change shape or disappear. For the state which hinders the nation is superfluous and harmful. What is needed for the birth of a Hellenic culture is an independent, that is, a Hellenic political life" (231).

[36] Dragúmis, Ελληνικός πολιτισμός (Hellenic civilization), 183.

Hellas. *Topos* becomes fluid and negotiable, specified by ethnic, historical, and cultural rather than constitutional markers, yet capable of
taking the shape of a "very substantial, material, measurable, and
concrete entity" when the obligations and interests of the state are
attached to it.[37]

In the shaping of *topos*, the nation and, logically and institutionally
prior to it, communities of Hellenes hold ultimate authority. Paradoxically, however, Dragúmis's communitarian nationalism reterritorial-
izes Hellenism in what becomes a *state* policy; it is the state that must
rebuild the nation and, ultimately, spread its civilization. This pattern
of reterritorialization is not peculiar to Greek nationalism. Frequently
nationalism will construct a nation-state (in this case, Hellas) on the
imaginary site of the national body (Hellenism, the community of
Hellenes) and, through the state, proceed to define the nation's history,
language, and geography.[38] Frequently, too, it may announce that its
"final purpose, destiny, mission, call it necessity of nations," is to
produce a distinct *politismós* 'culture, 'civilization'.[39] "This is a task
worthy of nations—a humanistic, a truly human project. . . . This is
how nations can surpass their borders, overflow and become broader,
higher, fuller, and conquer the earth. . . . At the same time, it does not
suffice for a nation merely to be civilized; it must be civilized with its
own civilization."[40] Although *politismós* appears to be an *entópios kar-
pós* 'fruit that grows from within *topos*',[41] it cannot be reduced to a
single locality. Every indigenous effort is part of a "humanistic" project that seeks to overcome, through the particularity and distinctiveness of native contributors, the limits of local contingencies, to surpass
the borders of the state, to become universally accessible and admi-
rable. Territorial ethos and local roots become buried in the modern
teleology of global civilization, which adopts the region, the nation,
and, beyond that, the human race as its transcendental signifier. To

[37] Gottman, *Significance of Territory*, 15.

[38] Portugali has studied the Israeli-Palestinian case. Based on this example, he
describes a core doctrine of nationalism: "Nations can only be fulfilled in their own
territory, with their own state and government"; "the nation-state—the unity of
people, territory, and government—is the genuine unit within and through which
people conduct their social, economic and cultural affairs" ("Nationalism, Social Theory, and the Israeli/Palestinian Case," 55).

[39] Dragúmis, Ελληνικός πολιτισμός (Hellenic civilization), 181.

[40] Ibid., 181–82.

[41] Ibid., 183. On the adjective *entópios* or *ntópios*, see my discussion of entopia in
Chapter 4.

highlight the immanent validity and inner pattern of growth in a particular nation therefore finally serves to achieve transcendence—to produce a civilized, Hellenized, enlightened, modern humanity.

Cultural demoticists like Dragúmis and Psiháris, both Western-influenced thinkers, found license to reterritorialize local community interests in the expansive, imaginary community of the nation, with its unique civilizing mission. Their project took shape at a time when the state policy of irredentism was aggressively pushing to expand the borders of Hellas to include Hellenism's "unredeemed" territories.[42] But theirs was not the only reterritorialization of Hellenism offered during Greece's period of expansion. In the idiosyncratic but influential work of Yannópulos we find what may have been the first aesthetic approach to *topos*. Its imaginary alignment of nation and state focuses on the color and line of a particular Greek *topío* 'landscape'. With this focus, it offers little resistance to European formulations of a Hellenic aesthetic. Indeed, its philosophical debt is to German texts. Yet its message is ultimately that Hellas belongs to Neohellenes. And its ambivalent proposal proved especially attractive to the writers who came of age in the 1920s and 1930s.

Aesthetic nationalism identifies the *topos* of Hellenism not with the unredeemed nation but with the *topío* 'landscape' of the Greek peninsula: the geography and climate identified most readily with the Attic sun and Aegean Sea. Located at the intersection of East and West, North and South, this *topío* is seen to remove itself from these axes' influence. It exists in itself and for itself. Here Hellenism is made to work for Neohellenes, as it becomes a *national* category. The *topío* radiates with light, in contrast to the northern landscape, and generates energy, in contrast to the lethargic south, in Yannópulos's eyes. It finds its own artistic building blocks, the καμπύλη *kambíli* 'curved line' and transparent φως *fos* 'light', everywhere reflected in the color κυανούν *kianún* 'cyan blue'—elements that comprise Neohellenism's national individuality. Their sphere of operation is neither the artwork nor the appreciating subject but *topos*, which becomes the self-evident category of Hellenism.

---

[42] The theological metaphor of an "unredeemed" nation appears in the Italian word *irredenta* from which irredentism derives. The same metaphor is found in the Greek phrase *alítrotos Ellinismós* 'unredeemed Hellenism', which refers to ethnic Greeks living outside Hellas. Irredentism is the state policy of redeeming the "irredenta," hence expanding borders to include "the settlement area of the nation—where compatriots live under foreign rule" (Mellor, *Nation, State, and the Territory*, 58).

The standard work of aesthetic nationalism is Yannópulos's Η σύγ-χρονος ζωγραφική (Contemporary painting) (1902). This essay begins by describing the Neohellene's "single responsibility to this *topos*: that we ourselves study ourselves, our past and our present, so that we can learn who we are, what we are capable of doing, what paths we should follow, in what direction tomorrow, what near and distant future; that we study and analyze our surrounding reality, the people and their works, so that we can know what they mean and what we are saying."[43] Although Yannópulos is alluding here to the primary responsibility of the enlightened European, the need to study oneself—to analyze, that is, one's present in the light of the past so as to recognize who one is and what one might become—this text gives clear territorial boundaries to the subject and object of analysis. There is always a limit around the human subject; there is always a root beneath, which connects one to a particular place and people. For Neohellenes, this limit is the *topos* of Hellenism, with its distinct natural landscape. Nature and tradition are its two constituent elements; they shape the physical environment; they regulate the activities of Hellenes. Tradition, with its mythological, heroic, classical, Byzantine, religious, and folk *cosmos*, links a group to its genealogical substratum and defines its authentic expression, while nature, earth, and soil continually nourish and channel its creative energy.

If the responsibility of the individual emanates from a particular substratum, then to study oneself is not to satisfy one's curiosity about the nature of a free-floating citizen of the world, a universal soul, but to participate in "creating a homeland."[44] The artist enjoys no exception to this rule. Artist without homeland, artistic expression without borders, works of art that belong generally to all of humanity—all these are undesirable and useless for aesthetic nationalism. To make art is to build a homeland, the highest calling of artist, critic, and layperson alike. And to build a homeland in turn requires that one recognize the unique signs of one's *topos*, which one must describe or depict. The responsibility of the critic is to discover signs of Hellenism's "so very narrow and so highly illuminated *topos*."[45] The task of the artist is to use them. The purpose of every work of art should

[43] Periklís Yannópulos, Η σύγχρονος ζωγραφική (Contemporary painting) ([1902] 1988), 7.
[44] Ibid., 65.
[45] Ibid., 22.

therefore be to express Hellenism's geoclimatic particularity. This is essential work in building a homeland: "The homeland signifies nothing without its own painting, sculpture, architecture, literature, music, and so many other things."[46] Within the homeland, artists must feel, comprehend, and recreate the natural color and line of the Hellenic *topos*, as reflected in the Helladic *topío*. Furthermore, they must submit their every artistic expression to the determining forces of the landscape, which connects their work to the cultural continuum and racial substratum of Hellenism. This is the bottom line for Yannópulos. Without total immersion in the *topío* 'landscape' of Attica and the Aegean, with their clear lines and color, without careful study of the Hellenic *cosmos* on all levels, including the natural, the mythological, the heroic, the folk, the religious, the Byzantine, art cannot become "the highest expression of human energy." Conversely the artist becomes "the highest priest of the human community" when she or he "creates each line, each color, each echo, from blood."[47]

It is important again to stress that this theory of *topos*, which relies on German aesthetic theories to make its point, proffers the *topío* of Hellas as a *national* landscape and the aesthetic of Hellenism as a *national* aesthetic. The *topío* is Neohellenic, as is the aesthetic. Indeed these two categories are closely tied. To restrict access to Hellenism, Yannópulos's essay does not seize the East—"The City," the patriarchate, Orthodoxy—as a counterbalance; instead it ties Hellenism organically to the Helladic *topío*; it suggests that Hellas, the major ideal of Western thought, can find its real expression only in works produced by real Hellenes—the Hellenes of Hellas. A major presupposition of this theory, found in another essay, Η ελληνική γραμμή, το ελληνικό χρώμα (Hellenic line, Hellenic color) (1904), is that the human spirit is organically tied to its place of origin on earth. A unique "aesthetic of each people" expresses the integrity of inner and outer worlds.[48] Conversely, when a people derive their representations from things that have little to do with their own natural environment, they create false images—as do Europeans when they imitate the Hellenic ideal, or Neohellenes when they adopt a European line as their *aféndi* 'master'.

---

[46] Ibid., 65.

[47] Ibid., 22.

[48] Periklís Yannópulos, Η ελληνική γραμμή, το ελληνικό χρώμα (Hellenic line, Hellenic color) ([1904] 1988), 142.

Of course, the interdiction against adopting a foreign master does not prevent aesthetic nationalism from borrowing its conception of Hellenism's *olótita* 'wholeness' almost wholesale from German aesthetic paganism, as I have already suggested. Not unlike Weimar classicism, Yannópulos's theory of art finds Hellenism's essential integrity in the fragments of classical Greek sculpture, the "natural and miraculous blossom" of Hellas.[49] Here one finds a bold appropriation of terms used by Johann Joachim Winckelmann, who detected in ancient sculpture and architecture a "noble simplicity and tranquil grandeur" ("eine edle Einfalt und eine stille Größe") that was the unique product of a particular climate, age, and culture. Neohellenic aesthetic nationalism makes out *safínia* 'clarity', transparency of light and air, purity of line, symmetry, eurythmia, grace, gaiety, and Socratic irony to be the primary characteristics of classical art.

Unique to the Neohellenic rendition, however, is the declaration of autochthony: the proclamation that characteristics deriving from the natural and unchangeable line of the Hellenic *topío*—the curve and the absolute presence of light, with its clarity and brightness, unity and singleness, lightness of color—appear in their purest form, albeit with endless variation, in the simplicity, order, harmony, nobility, fineness, not only of all ancient architecture but also of some Byzantine churches, a few common shacks, and the best examples of Neohellenic art, which seem to grow out of the Hellenic landscape. Where everything is light and nobility, the color of cyan blue prevails, as it does in the Aegean and Attic summer landscape, with its hot sun, clear sky, barrenness, and pure blue color: "The most beautiful Hellenic season, the Attic season, is the summer, when ethereal barrenness reaches perfection. . . . You will see with your eyes a thousand times the sea —with its most cyan blue, open, glassy, metallic color."[50] This is the ideal *topío* of contemporary art. Here light passes through everything and reveals the truth of things: the "pleasure" of the color itself and the "clarity" of the line.[51]

What is prescient in this nationalist appropriation of Winckelmann's aesthetic theory is the argument that the pleasure of the *topío*, the aboriginal call of the "Mother Earth," is so powerful that it can pull the Hellenic nation, even in its diasporic odyssey, toward a single center,

[49] Ibid., 97.
[50] Ibid., 121.
[51] See ibid., 138.

an emerging homeland. The centripetal force of Hellenism may also extend its pull to the imagination of other national groups, however. There is, in fact, a major contradiction in Yannópulos's work that reveals the ideology of his aesthetic. This contradiction appears in the text's tendency to slip back and forth between claiming for Hellenism a universality and a particularity. In a rare ecumenical mood, for example, it features the Attic and Aegean landscape as the "natural" *topos*, the "temple" or workshop not only of Hellenic but of all art. Yannópulos imagines that, under ideal conditions, "Attica will eternally be the natural *topos* of the artist, the natural temple of art."[52] When this happens, "each Rembrandt" who approaches the temple of Hellenism will move

> in the direction of light, to a *cosmos* which one desires, imagines, but cannot see, to approach with a shiver of reverence and lay the hands on your green grasses with passion as if touching the golden gates of an entrance which suddenly opens a path into a beautiful and absolutely brilliant *cosmos*, the dreamlike *cosmos* of every poet, which you have before your eyes and belongs to you, your own real *cosmos*, your earth, your mother, whom you love in the depths of your heart, by whatever you say, by whatever you do, you love in your depths as the Hellene you are.[53]

It is significant that this reverie on the approach to Hellenism's golden gates closes with an apostrophe to the compatriot "Hellene." With its rhetorical shift away from just any repentant Rembrandt to a fellow "Hellene" who loves "your earth, your mother, . . . in the depths of your heart," the text makes a special case for Neohellenes to take the *topos* to be their own. Obversely, it denies the non-Hellene equal power to approach the *cosmos* of dreams. Only indigenous occupants of the Balkan's southernmost exposure possess the right of direct access to what are in fact the temples to *local* gods. Indeed, the text argues systematically throughout this and other essays that non-Hellenes are incapable of giving authentic expression to Hellenism. They inevitably create false images when they adopt the Hellenic aesthetic.

What becomes apparent through the alternating claim of particu-

[52] Yannópulos, Η σύγχρονος ζωγραφική (Contemporary painting), 35.
[53] Ibid., 40–41.

larity and universality is that aesthetic nationalism benefits from linking itself to *both* a geographically specific *and* a transcendent *topos*. In its geographically limited circumscription, Hellenism remains the possession of a particular group, provided this group firmly anchors itself in its *topío* 'landscape'. The landscape regulates a national aesthetic. In its transcendental scope, however—that is to say, as the "Mother Earth" of all art—Hellenism can produce the best art in the world. The universalized aesthetic functions finally to transform the *topos* of Hellas into a continent of creativity transcending actual geography. Yet aesthetic nationalism offers a fundamentally ethnocentric message to contemporary Greek artists—a powerful mythology of resistance that served poets and artists well especially after the military expansion of Greece's geopolitical boundaries proved impossible.

The Transcendence of Hellenicity

The Greek army's military defeat in the Greco-Turkish War (1920–22) was so stunning and had so many long-term repercussions that Greeks to this day refer to the event as η καταστροφή της Μικράς Ασίας 'the Asia Minor disaster' or simply η καταστροφή 'the Disaster'.[54] "The Disaster" made the dream policy of militarily expanding the state to fit the Hellenic nation effectively moribund. Poets and critics now began feeling the pressing need to reconcile themselves to the idea of a geographically limited state. Some sought reconciliation by developing a cosmopolitan vision of culture that broke out of nationalist prescriptions. Theotokás (1906–66), a preeminent spokesman of cosmopolitanism, studied Neohellenism in the light of not only its own "intellectual heritage" but also the artistic potential

[54] On 16 August 1922, an invading Greek army with its sights on Ankara was routed by a Turkish attack in the region of Afyonkarahisar and forced to retreat first to Smyrna, then to the coast of Asia Minor. In the aftermath of the Greek army's evacuation of Smyrna (8 September 1922), there followed a "full-scale massacre of the Christian population, in which the Armenians suffered the greatest casualties. . . . A quarter of a million people fled to the waterfront to escape the inferno. . . . Within a few days . . . a 2500 year presence on the western littoral of Asia Minor had been abruptly terminated in conditions of total disaster" (Clogg, *Short History*, 118). Over a million and a half refugees from the uprooted Greek and Armenian populations of Asia Minor arrived in Greece. For more on the social effects of this vast population movement, see Renée Hirschon, *Heirs of the Greek Catastrophe: The Social Life of Asia Minor Refugees in Piraeus* (1989).

of *modernismós* 'modernism'.[55] He undertook to chart from what he called his "airborne" perspective the position of Neohellenism in relation to contemporary European movements.

With his liberal manifesto Ελεύθερο πνεύμα (Free spirit) (1929), Theotokás addressed Greek authors seeking to gain international recognition as (Western) European artists. To help broaden their intellectual horizons, he described the options available to a *topos* caught "in the confusion of the modern world, beaten by the great winds of postwar Europe."[56] The text declares the choice between tradition and modernity passé. Artists are compelled now to discover ways of synthesizing local color and Western sophistication, faith and nihilism, tradition and modernity. Its message to compatriots is that they seize the moment—"broken, withered, and lost in the mire of contemporary life" though they might be—and free their imaginations.[57] They should ask not *whether* but *how* to assist in the progress of "a small and narrow-minded, self-absorbed provincial community" now making unmanageable strides to keep up with the uncontrollable "development of its *topos*."[58] An essential ingredient of success is the overcoming of prescribed limits on artistic expression. Thus the liberal corrective to the ills of parochial thinking is to stride in "a garden of Neohellenic letters . . . [without] limits": "We can wander all paths, but we will not find the outer boundaries of the garden anywhere. The hopes that it offers at every step are infinite. Its earth, which has not yet given birth to tall trees because it has not been tilled enough, hides rich and inexhaustible resources. For it is possible to express the limits of nations which have come to an end, but the genius of a living people knows no bounds in its breadth or depth."[59]

As the decade of the 1930s progressed, however, artists and critics increasingly attended to background material in Theotokás's earlier stride through the Neohellenic "garden."[60] They reclaimed the in-

---

[55] Theotokás wrote essays, novels, and plays. His best-known plays are *Argo* (1936) and *Leonis* (1940). He was director of the National Theater of Athens 1945–46 and 1950–52. For a critical analysis of his response to European modernity, see Martha E. Klironomos, "George Theotokas' *Free Spirit*: Reconfiguring Greece's Path towards Modernity?" (1992).

[56] Theotokas, Ελεύθερο πνεύμα (Free spirit), 61.

[57] Ibid., 63.

[58] Ibid., 62.

[59] Ibid., 72.

[60] I am referring here to Theotokás and his contemporaries—Odysseus Elytis, Andréas Embiríkos, Dimítris Kapetánakis, Andréas Karandónis, Níkos Nikoláu, Di-

tellectual heritage of a specifically Ellinikós Ellinismós 'Hellenic Hel
lenism', Neoellinismós 'Neohellenism', Ellinismós 'Hellenism', or
Ellinikótita 'Hellenicity'.[61] This became the special condition for the
Neohellenic, albeit cosmopolitan work of art—a condition named by
aesthetic nationalism: that manner of artistic expression be authentically and autochthonously Hellenic. Of course, the artistic phenomenon of aesthetically upgrading traditional art forms to create a native
aesthetic should be viewed in the light of comparable aesthetic theories
found elsewhere during the same period. In Fascist Italy, for example,
the neo-Hegelian and self-styled "philosopher of fascism" Giovanni
Gentile, minister of education in Mussolini's first cabinet, defined
an aesthetic of *italianita* 'Italian ness'. Spanish intellectuals, too, imposed a requirement that Spanish literature and art reflect its *hispanidad*
'Spanish-ness'.[62]

In Greece, the Hellenic ideal became a touchstone of both modernist
and antimodernist artistic expression in the 1940s and 1950s.[63] As
Greek intellectuals lost all hope of increasing the physical expanse of
their state, recovering an "unredeemed" nation, or politically unifying
themselves, they also either abandoned the state of Greece for a transcendent Hellenism or rendered with metaphysical hues the physical
and cultural landscape contained within their "microscopic *topos*."[64]

mítris Pikiónis, Nikítas Rántos, George Seferis, and Yórgos Sarandáris, some of whom
achieved international recognition. For more on this topic, see Chapter 4.

[61] Seferis coined "Hellenic Hellenism" in 1938 in his Διάλογος πάνω στην ποίηση
(Dialogue on poetry). I discuss this essay in Chapter 5.

[62] See Mario Vitti, Η γενιά του τριάντα· Ιδεολογία και μορφή (The generation of
the Thirties: Ideology and form) (1979), 200. The conservative dogma of Hellenicity
required that contemporary writers and artists should draw from types authentically
Greek (see Ioánnis Metaxás, Το προσωπικό του ημερολόγιο [Private journal] [1960],
passim)—whereas liberals, who were not untouched by the conservative dogma, *suggested* they study traditional forms. Vitti argues that the dogma of Hellenicity derives
from General Ioánnis Metaxás's Fascist intervention in art (1936–41).

[63] The precondition that contemporary artistic expression should strive to achieve a
"Hellenic ideal" is assumed in a discussion orchestrated by the art journal Ζυγός (May
1956). The journal posed the question, "Are there common points of contact between
modern art and the ideal of Hellenic art?" to the artists Spíros Vasilíu, Váso Katráki,
Periklís Byzántios, Níkos Engonópulos, Lázaros Laméras, and Konstandínos Lukó-
pulos. None of the artists questioned the existence of such an ideal. More recently,
however, "Hellenicity" and the Hellenic ideal were subject to both criticism (see Ánna
Kafétsi, Ελληνικότητα και εικαστική δημιουργία [Hellenicity and artistic creation]
[1986]) and historical study (see Eléni Vakaló, Ο μύθος της ελληνικότητας· Η φυσιογνωμία της μεταπολεμικής τέχνης στην Ελλάδα [The myth of Hellenicity: The
physiognomy of postwar art in Greece] [1983]) in the visual arts.

[64] Lorentzátos, Δοκίμιο 1 (Essay 1), 17.

In either case, their topographies situated Hellenism in a place that transcended time and place while also remaining deeply rooted in the soil of the Greek peninsula. They placed tradition, a corpus of literature and art that best expressed the autochthonous aesthetic, along the horizon of the natural landscape. This "hardly perceptible preexisting framework" finally became the *topos* of Hellenism from which contemporary culture was to draw its nourishment.

Hence, when critic and poet Lorentzátos urged his readers not to "expect anything from the geographical size of our country," he was advising not that they form a truly internationalist movement but that they recover Hellenism's authentic, if underground, artistic tradition.[65] What beckoned was "a low-voiced *super flumina Babilonis* whispering through the most secret cells of the nation: in the folk tales, the dirges, or the songs of our people, of our poets and prose-writers. . . . An indefinite tone of spiritual anguish, a sense of catastrophe harking back to some lost paradise; the deep awareness of some great tribal longing which remains unanswered through the ages."[66] Lorentzátos projected this aesthetic ideal over and above the map of a war-torn Hellas as a shield against uncontrolled foreign invasions. The ultimate agent of preservation was *topografikí mními* 'topographical memory',[67] a method of recalling the persistence of Hellenism despite changes in history and transformations in geography. On the national, rather than on a broadly cultural, horizon, artists could find the properly Hellenic alternative to what were for Lorentzátos two equally "monotonous," foreign solutions: "the modernization of Hellenism, or the Hellenization of Modernism."[68]

The discovery of an "uneven *topos* existing much more in time than in space" made *topos* an emblem not of physical expanse but of cultural continuity and metaphysical well-being.[69] Furthermore, *topos* came to signify the "spiritual and intellectual potential" of a people both fiercely grounded in local communities and perennially scattered across the world. This people could not be "rooted in" an administratively de-

[65] Ibid. Lorentzátos's first published article, "Edgar Allan Poe and the Philosophy of Composition," appeared in the journal *Elliniká grámmata* in 1936. His first major publication is the remarkable monograph discussed here.

[66] Lorentzátos, Δοκίμιο 1 (Essay 1), 34; see the English translation hereafter referred to as "Solomos," 19.

[67] Lorentzátos, Δοκίμιο 1 (Essay 1), 16.

[68] Lorentzátos, "The Lost Center," 127.

[69] Lorentzátos, Δοκίμιο 1 (Essay 1), 17.

fined space—especially the modern state—as the following remarkable passage argues:

> We reconcile the localism [*topikismós*] of the Hellene and the Diaspora of the Jew. We are perpetuating the name of an uneven *topos* which exists much more in time than in space. For this reason our fate remains incompatible with the fate of peoples rooted in space, but is continuously woven around the insoluble problem of the two dimensions. We are the suitors of time, and the outcasts of space. . . . Today more than ever before, we must not expect anything from the geographical size of our country. Today more than ever before, we must ask ourselves whether we can offer the coming ages anything else but our spiritual and intellectual potential. That is, if we are to keep alive the name of this microscopic *topos* with its marble ruins and constant conflicts, bright history and troubles, shining sky and poverty, bony mountains and islands, Euclid and Odysseus, intelligent people and isolated chapels, wise men and charlatans, Alexander the Great and seafarers, places of recluse and taverns—in this age-old cradle of the Mediterranean where, as our grandparents and old ladies used to say, once upon a time the *cosmos* was born.[70]

Here the state appears temporally secondary, ideologically nonessential, to the survival of Hellenism—with its "marble ruins and constant conflicts, bright history and troubles." The symbolic markers of Lorentzátos's "microscopic *topos*" are neither the geographical boundaries nor the constitutional limits of Hellas but the high and low expressions of an "intelligent people's" bright but troubled spirit.

The effort to extend national horizons over a transcendental plane by defining the themes and styles of a Hellenic tradition was certainly no aberration for postwar Neohellenes. Rather it was most symptomatic—one exemplary contribution to a self-perpetuating cultural project that took hold during the years of the Greek civil war. Those four years in Greek intellectual and literary history paradoxically created a movement toward consolidation. Certain interpretations of the tumultuous events that occurred during the first half of the twentieth century became codified into what is today the dominant narrative of Hellenism's evolving fate. As evidence of this consolidation, one can point to the numerous thematically related essays published between 1944 and 1950 by artists and critics who had made their appearance in

---

[70] Ibid., 16–17.

Greek letters one decade earlier.[71] Significant points of contact between these essays are their searching inwardness, studied repression of contemporary events, and strict recoding of earlier cataclysmic moments in Greek history into a story of national self-discovery. They all narrate how Neohellenism managed to recover its deepest cultural roots during the previous decade, just after the nation had become geographically contained within the island-scattered, sun-bathed, sea-contained Kingdom of Hellas. And they baptize this space of containment and recovery "our *topos.*"

To explain the positive aspects of containment within this *topos*, some authors reinvoked the year 1922, or "the Disaster," as a privileged signifier of collective upheaval and recovery. Certainly this was the first important historical memory for individuals who had come of age in the 1920s and 1930s. For this generation, 1922 marked the greatest turning point in Greece's modern history. Within a decade after its occurrence, "the Disaster" had come to represent the moment when Neohellenes ceased to expect anything from the geographical size of Hellas.

An important article by the critic Nikolareízis, however, indicates that a symbolic rewriting of "the Disaster" was also taking place during the Greek civil war. Η παρουσία του Ομήρου στη νέα ελληνική ποίηση (The presence of Homer in modern Greek poetry) (1947) uses "the Disaster" metonymically to represent the flow of Neohellenism home to Greece from the foreign shores of Asia Minor, and the

---

[71] A list of related works from this period would have to include the following: scholar and literary historian K. Th. Dimarás's Ιστορία της νεοελληνικής λογοτεχνίας (History of Neohellenic literature) (1948); poet Odysseus Elytis's Η αισθητική και συναισθηματική καταγωγή του Θεοφίλου Χατζημιχαήλ (The aesthetic and emotional origin of Theófilos Hadzimihaíl) (1947) and Η σύγχρονη ελληνική τέχνη και ο ζωγράφος Ν. Χατζηκυριάκος Γκίκας (Contemporary Greek art and the painter N. Hadzikiriákos Gíkas) (1947); art critic Manólis Hadzidákis's review of the artist Níkos Nikoláu's exhibition of new paintings Έκθεσις Νικολάου (The Nikoláu exhibit) (1948); folklorist Stílpon Kiriakídis's "Language and Folk Culture of Modern Greek" (1946); poet and critic Zísimos Lorentzátos's Δοκίμιο I (Essay I) (1947); critic Dimítris Nikolareízis's Η παρουσία του Ομήρου στη νέα ελληνική ποίηση (The presence of Homer in modern Greek poetry) (1947); architect and theorist Dimítris Pikiónis's Το πρόβλημα της μορφής (The problem of form) (1946); poet, critic, and diplomat George Seferis's poem Κίχλη (Thrush) (1946) and his essays Θεόφιλος (Theofilos) (1947), Γράμμα σ' έναν ξένο φίλο (Letter to a foreign friend) (1948); Δεύτερος πρόλογος στο βιβλίο μου Θ. Σ. Έλιοτ· Η Έρημη Χώρα και άλλα ποιήματα (Second prologue to My Book T. S. Eliot, *The Wasteland and Other Poems*) (1949); and philosopher and humanist Ioánnis Theodorakópulos's Το πνεύμα του νεοελληνισμού (The spirit of Neohellenism) (1945).

recovery of an undercurrent of a Hellenic tradition that continues "its flow in other underground cradles in the earth," even against the tide of "historical conditions against the nation":[72]

> In 1922, the great Greek army, which had proceeded to the heart of Anatolia, returned in defeat to the shores of Asia Minor and set sail for a λυγρός νόστος [Homer: lūgros nostos 'pitiful homecoming']; it traveled in the same direction as the Homeric Achaeans after the fall of Troy. This time, however, a wave of the uprooted Hellenic population followed the army, returning to its land of origin. The provinces along the shore of Asia Minor, from the plain of Troy to the delta of the Maeander—where for years immemorial a singular Hellenic civilization flourished—were being abandoned by the Hellenic language and emptied of everything Hellenic; the entire geographical region of Asia, sanctified by the birth of the Homeric epic, would now be left out of the bright cycle of Hellenic history.[73]

What is striking in this passage is the subtle shifts in subject away from "the presence of Homer in Neohellenic poetry" to the presence of Homer in recent Greek history, which is only then reflected in poetry. The critical text itself incorporates the Homeric epic into the events of 1922. In fact, it uses Homer to reinstate Neohellenism's historical and geographical links with Greek antiquity, even while describing the most disruptive event of Greek modernity—the rupture of significant ties with "the entire geographical region of Asia," the region of the unfree world.

The rhetoric of the passage is so remarkable and at the same time so representative of literary expression during this period that it deserves careful analysis. A distinctive feature is its skillful movement back and forth between ancient myth and historical present. In the first sentence, the Homeric phrase λυγρός νόστος (lūgros nostos 'pitiful homecoming', Odyssey 1.327) appears with reference to the defeated army's return to Greece.[74] The face of the victorious Achaeans then merges

---

[72] Nikolareízis, Η παρουσία του Ομήρου (The presence of Homer), 211. A summary of this article appeared in the American journal Portofoglio, which devoted an issue to contemporary cultural life in Greece; the entire essay was printed in the Greek journal Néa estía (December 1947).

[73] Nikolareízis, Η παρουσία του Ομήρου (The presence of Homer), 209.

[74] In the Odyssey, the Achaeans faced a λυγρός νόστος 'pitiful homecoming' not because they lost but because they paid for unsanctimonious victory with disharmony at home and disfavor with the gods. Thus λυγρός νόστος 'pitiful homecoming' refers not to the humiliation of defeat in war but to such postwar tragedies as domestic violence (Agamemnon), suicide (Ajax), and belated homecoming (Odysseus).

with that of the defeated modern army, as ancient Ionian colonies (together with names such as Ilios, Troy, Maeander) silence contemporary Turkish claims to the region. The western shore of Asia Minor, long governed by Ottomans, becomes a place "sanctified by the birth of the Homeric epic" but finally lost to Hellenism.

One concludes that this text uses the Homeric epic to manipulate parallels between ancient myth and modern history—and to elide major differences between the archaic and modern worlds. This device will be recognized as the "mythical method," the modernist literary technique described by T. S. Eliot in his review article "Ulysses, Order, and Myth" (1923). Here it is employed to account for cataclysmic change in the topography of the Hellenic diaspora along the eastern Mediterranean basin: the uprooting of the Greek population in Asia Minor, the containment of Greeks within the Greek peninsula and the surrounding islands. Nikolareízis gives figurative prominence to similarities between the mythical and modern destinies of the Achaean army and the Greek soldiers in 1922.

At the same time, Nikolareízis's text suppresses two major points of difference. First, the Achaeans were victorious, whereas the modern force lost to Kemal Atatürk's rebel forces near Ankara. Second and more significant, although both Homeric heroes and modern Greeks "set sail for a λυγρός νόστος [lūgros nostos 'pitiful homecoming']" in the direction of the Greek mainland, the "uprooted Hellenic population" was actually forced to leave its homeland. Yet, by manipulating present history in terms of the mythical past, the essay represents this forced transplantation of a large Greek-speaking population from Asia Minor to the modern Kingdom of Greece as a return to the "land of origin."

One should note, then, that a particular literary technique, the "mythical method," is being used here to interpret Greek history and geography. Through the Homeric theme of the lūgros nostos 'pitiful homecoming', mainland Greece is made to appear as the original home of a population of refugees; and Hellenism, decentered after the loss of access to the space of Byzantium, now modern Turkey, finds itself reassembled within the geographical territory of Hellas, where, one assumes, the "bright cycle of Hellenic history" can now replay itself. It is this last point that I wish to stress, since the rhetorical sleight of hand that places the territory of Greece at the historical and cultural center of Hellenism is so dexterously executed that it may escape one's attention. While the author seems merely to be transferring fragments from one cultural milieu to another for the purpose of embellishing modern history, he is in fact redrawing the map of the Hellenic world.

One should also stress the double movement of cataclysmic loss and remarkable persistence that marks this discussion of history. The same theme appears in the treatment of poetry. In language very similar to that of Lorentzátos, Nikolareízis observes: "When historical circumstances challenged the survival of a nation, the river of Greek tradition continued to flow in some other subterranean cradle of the earth"[75]— specifically in the small "stream" of references to Homer found today in the works of Dionísios Solomós (1798–1857), Ángelos Sikelianós (1884–1951), Nikos Kazantzakis (1885–1957), George Seferis, and Odysseus Elytis, Greek authors whom Nikolareízis quotes.

Nikolareízis argues that poetry that represents the actual ungluing of the nation from its past offers the most successful relocation of Homer in the modern world. The essay's point of reference is Seferis, whose poetry historically presupposes and lyrically represents the containment of Hellenism "approximately within the area covered by classical Hellas."[76] Into a literary world of fading heroism and broken artifacts, Seferis introduces "mutilated" Homeric myths and figures and accommodates the grandeur of the past to the narrow limits of Hellenism, "not only in the dimension of space, but also of time and on the level of culture, on which it projected its deepest meaning."[77] Because his accommodation is appropriate to narrow times, Seferis can provide a proper homecoming for Homer in the modern world. His simple "unrhetorical poetry . . . sustained the standards of another life."[78]

Simple language aside, however, this important essay invokes powerful geographical and climatic forces as virtual assurance that antiquity continues to pervade the contemporary world, even where political and historical factors conspire to erase Hellenism's presence. This is the point that I wish finally to emphasize. One observes the text slipping into a mild form of territorial determinism—a theory much in the air in the late 1930s and 1940s.[79] It concludes that a specifically

[75] Nikolareízis, Η παρουσία του Ομήρου (The presence of Homer), 211.

[76] Ibid., 227.

[77] Ibid., 226.

[78] Ibid., 233.

[79] The belief that race, land, and climate are primordial determinants of cultural diversity has roots in certain strands of German and Italian idealist philosophy. In Greek letters, this view first appeared in the work of Yannópulos, as we saw above. A few decades later, Nikos Kazantzakis also expressed this view.

Neohellenic modernist such as Seferis is finely positioned to continue directly the tradition of the ancients—despite the destruction in 1922 of geographical and political ties with Ionia and Asia Minor—precisely because he possesses roots in the physical origins of that civilization and draws life from its deepest source.

A significant change is evident in Hellenism's topography. Poetry itself has become a geographical marker. Its affiliation with classical texts derives not from the pure blood or enduring spirit of the author— arguments that appear under other circumstances in Greek literary history. Now antiquity is luminously present in the poet's experience of the *topío* 'landscape' of Hellas. The present-day poet's ability to conjure up Homeric heroes in an ailing modern world is one effect of the poet's own, as well as Homer's, apparently unmediated relationship to this *topío*. This new literary *topos* functions to erase differences in space and time: "If the Greek poet observes around him the islands and the shore of his fatherland, and the sea, that same sea which was so tied to the fate of his *topos*, it is *impossible* for him *not* to hear the echo of some Homeric lines or visualize images from the *Odyssey*, the epic that was watered by the brine of the Aegean."[80] Obversely, Homer, "the first painter of the Hellenic soul and the Hellenic *topío*,"[81] is of infinite importance to the Neohellenic tradition. Viewed as the first to draw directly from the resources of Hellas's *topío*, Homer becomes the aboriginal poet of Hellas, ancient and modern, as his epic poems "seem to encapsulate the mysteries of a primordial aesthetic success which remained exemplary through the centuries."[82] Here we discover the cultural logic that affiliates modern poets with Homer by viewing their poetry as expressions of the same primordial aesthetic and as products of the same Greek soil.

The logic of this argument, though evident in a range of literary essays and imaginative works appearing in Greece after the rise of the Metaxás dictatorship and throughout the cold war, is not self-explanatory. Indeed it requires further investigation and analysis. There are larger contextual matters that give it reason. These involve major transformations in the ways a Western vanguard came to view Hellenism during the first half of our century, as well as changes in the ways Neohellenism came to view—and to present—itself. A confluence of changing

[80] Nikolareízis, Η παρουσία του Ομήρου (The presence of Homer), 236 (my emphasis).
[81] Ibid., 235.
[82] Ibid., 236.

attitudes gives sense to the Neohellenic *modernist* impulse to sublimate major historical breaks by depicting antiquity's sometimes muted, sometimes bright physical illumination in the Hellenic *topío* 'landscape'. The next step is to follow the contrapuntal play between Western and Neohellenic modernist revisions of Hellenism during the first half of this century. While the more familiar British modernist voice reveals skepticism about *its* ethnocentric investment in Hellenism, particularly in the outright dismissal of present-day Greeks, the Neohellenic voice rehearses the aesthetic nationalism of Yannópulos, whom it adopts as a kind of cult hero. Incidentally, the contrapuntal interplay between these two voices develops so intricately that the one sometimes seems to speak for the other. Even the American modernist Henry Miller, a self-avowed philhellene, can be found praising Yannópulos's views, as if in Yannópulos's work Miller had discovered his *American* brand of Hellenism. After the analysis that follows of modernist transpositions from 1900 to 1950, both European and Neohellenic, we will turn to some postwar Greek texts, examining them in detail, to understand how they give modernist form to the argument found in Nikolareízis's text. How do they express the opposing trends of rupture and continuity of Hellenism? In the more specialized vocabulary of this book, the question is this: how does their modernist *logos* evince a Homeric *nostos* in the transcendental *topos* of Hellas?

PART II

RETERRITORIALIZING HIGH MODERNISM

Entopia: Modernist
Transpositions of the Native

And so sinking and surging like the flight of an eagle through mid-air
it dropped at last upon the tough old riddle of the modern Greek and
his position in the world today.
> —Virginia Woolf, "A Dialogue upon Mount Pentelicus"

You never heard of Yannopoulos either, did you? Yannopoulos was
greater than your Walt Whitman and all the American poets combined. . . . He became so intoxicated with the Greek language, the
Greek philosophy, the Greek sky, the Greek mountains, the Greek
sea, the Greek islands, the Greek vegetables, even, that he killed
himself. . . . Are there any French writers or German writers or
English writers who feel that way about their country, their race,
their soil? . . . You can't know what a rock is until you've heard what
Yannopoulos has written.
> —Henry Miller, *The Colossus of Maroussi*

The essence of cultural life is indivisible from the earth and the
history of the people where it belongs. . . . One must define what
that earth is and what its cultural meaning is, since this fundamentally predefines authentic art and essential thought and even history
as a unity conceived from spirit. . . . Before any valuable influence
comes an intelligible sense of the Hellenic earth and Hellenic history.
> —Konstandínos Tsátsos, Πριν από το ξεκίνημα ΙΙ
> (Before setting out II)

Literary and artistic responses to Hellenism during the first half of
the twentieth century were not everywhere the same. Indeed, the first
four decades of the century witnessed many contradictory reactions to
the great tradition of the classics. One can point first to the artistic

avant-garde in the West, which repudiated academic imitation, particularly imitation of the Greek ideal. For some versions of modernism "the dethroning of the Greek ideal amounts to a straight inversion. It is understood as turning the table in favor of something like a 'nonclassical tradition' built out of a range of 'submerged' sources and artworks now brought to the surface—not least from non-Western, exotic systems of art."[1] Some experimental artists, most conspicuously Pablo Picasso (1881–1973), Fernand Léger (1881–1955), and Juan Gris (1887–1927), then defected gradually from a position of outright rejection at the beginning of the century to one of renewed interest in the classical tradition around 1915 and continuing into the 1930s and 1940s. They joined the ranks of Giorgio De Chirico (1888–1978) and others who from the beginning of their careers had "absorbed the German romantic vision of the classical world."[2] Like dancer Isadora Duncan (1877–1927)—who, mounting "with prayerful feet toward the Parthenon," tried to discover an anatomically grounded form of dance "to express the feeling of the human body in relation to the Doric column"[3]—they sought to replace the older romantic idea of Hellenism with a newer, paradoxically more *primitive* vision of Hellenism. Their " 'classical revival', 'the call to order', 'the return to order' . . . gathered momentum during the First World War in France and Italy, and spread rapidly after peace was declared."[4]

Revisions of Hellenism

Imitation of the Hellenic and Roman sculptural ideal still comprised the better part of training in the visual arts around 1900, just as memorization of Greek and Latin texts remained a staple of a good European education. To rebel against rote learning of the classics, and at the same time to draw on their endless resources, literary modernists developed innovative techniques such as the elliptical quotation.[5]

[1] Sarat Maharaj, "The Congo Is Flooding the Acropolis: Art in Britain of the Immigrations" (1991), 88.

[2] Elizabeth Cowling and Jennifer Mundy, "On Classic Ground: Picasso, Leger, de Chirico, and the New Classicism, 1910–1930" (1990), 71.

[3] See Isadora Duncan's essay "The Parthenon" (1903 or 1904), written on the occasion of her dance on the Acropolis, in *The Art of the Dance* (1969), 64.

[4] Cowling and Mundy, "On Classic Ground," 11.

[5] Examples are Paul A. Valéry (1871–1945), Rainer Maria Rilke (1875–1926), James Joyce (1882–1941), Ezra Pound (1885–1972), Hilda Doolittle (H. D.) (1886–1961),

In dense, sometimes inscrutable clusters of allusion, they recycled
more or less obscure mythological and literary references, place-
names, even extensive passages from ancient sources.[6] It seems that
the fragmentary, often ironic use of *koinoi topoi* 'commonplace topics
of learning' better expressed the state of Hellenism in a troubled
modern world.

Some travelers to Greece remained fully possessed by a romantic
vision of Hellenism, and many remain so even to the present day. For
them, the *topos* of Hellas is the site of myth: a noninhabitable space to
which they may return to reflect on their own lost origins. To study
the color of the Parthenon; to contemplate the apocalyptic rubble of
the Acropolis; to peruse the naked beauty of the Attic landscape,
stripped in the mind's eye of its native occupants; to dismantle buildings, or carry away statues, marble stones, and potsherds;[7] to do all

---

T. S. Eliot (1888–1965), Paul Éluard (1895–1952), and W. H. Auden (1907–73), to
name only a few. Peter Hutchinson, in *Games Authors Play* (1983), 107, notes that
quotation from Latin sources became a prominent literary device during the Middle
Ages. He might also have mentioned its extensive use in Hellenistic and Augustan
poetry. Like Hellenistic poetry, modernist quotation represents a "competitive" form
of "game" (Hutchinson's terminology) that challenges the learned reader to catch the
reference. We should be careful to distinguish this literary device from the modernist
thematic treatment of ancient myths in dramatic revivals of Greek tragedies. Some of
the best-known are Jean Anouilh, *Antigone* (1942); Guillaume Apollinaire, *Les mamelles
de Tirésias* (1903, produced as an opera with Poulenc's music in 1947); Jean Cocteau,
Antigone (1922) and *Orphée* (1926); H. D., *Helen in Egypt* (posthumously published in
1961); André Gide, *King Kandaules* (1901); Jean Giraudoux, *Amphitryon 38* (1929) and
La guerre de Troie n'aura pas lieu (1935); Eugene O'Neill, *Mourning Becomes Electra*
(1931); Rainer Maria Rilke, *Sonnets to Orpheus* (1923); Jean-Paul Sartre, *Les mouches*
(1943); Carl Spitteler, *Olympian Spring* (1910); Paul A. Valéry, *The Pythian Prophetess*
(1922); Hugo von Hofmannsthal, *Elektra* (1903), and Richard Strauss's operatic adap-
tation of that play; and Franz Werfel, *Trojan Women* (1914). In each case the author relies
on an audience's familiarity with a basic story to manipulate audience expectations in
the story's retelling, or alludes to the plot incidentally to give depth to certain material
or create an ironic distance. C. P. Cavafy's best historical poems also achieve ironic
distance. See Gregory Jusdanis, *The Poetics of Cavafy: Textuality, Eroticism, History*
(1987).

[6] Pound's "Papyrus" (in the collection *Lustra*) is a typical example. It uses the odd
detail, a word from Sappho's papyrus fragments that Egypt's dry desert sands have
preserved, to represent a string of incidental details: "Spring . . . / Too long . . . /
Gongula." Here Gongula is a woman's name in Sappho's poetry; the lacunae are
Pound's. Taken together, these form a condensed but luminous image of longing, itself
reminiscent of Sappho's poetry.

[7] Emily Vermeule mentions that "buildings from periods of Slavic, Arabic, Cru-
sader, Venetian, and Ottoman rule, or influence, intervening between the ancient
Greeks and the modern Germans, were systematically eradicated—so that contact

these things is to recollect modern humanity's now severed identity, while also affirming one's pure lineage.[8] Yet for other travelers to Greece, the sight of Hellas did not prohibit more discomfiting reflection, even beyond the self-contemplation that might jumble the normative experience of time and space. Particularly during the first two decades of the twentieth century, when visions of transcendence had just appeared in Neohellenic topographies, a tour of Hellas came to generate skepticism in some European travelers about their own *ethnic* or *national* investment in Hellenism.

The skeptical mode of reflection may not be fully evident in the romantic accounts already examined in Chapter 2. Yet travelers increasingly reported in their topographies of Hellenism "disturbances of memory," as Freud puts it, affecting their perception of ethnic and national affiliation. It should be noted here that Freud interpreted his own experience of "derealization" as a displacement of his anxiety of assimilation. In his view, the question "Can it be that the Acropolis *really* exists?" repressed the son's "sense of guilt or inferiority" that the child of a ghetto-born, uneducated, ethnically unassimilated Jewish businessman could become so Hellenized as to tread on the Acropolis.[9] The real questions that it displaced were How is it "that I should 'go such a long way'?" and "What would *Monsieur notre Père* have said to this, if he could have been here to-day?"[10]

It was this anxious experience of a modernity too quickly realized— one that increasingly brought about a transvaluation of values, in some cases, "high Modernism's own drive to overthrow 'the tyranny

---

between the intellectual present and the fifth-century Greek past should find no barrier" ("The World Turned Upside Down" [1992], 40). Among these was a Frankish tower from the late fourteenth century, which archeologists decided to tear down in 1875, setting off a public uproar. R. A. MacNeal's "Archaeology and the Destruction of the Later Athenian Acropolis" (1991) discusses the archeological principles used to justify major changes on the Acropolis during the 1800s, including the wholesale destruction of entire historical layers.

[8] See, for example, Stoneman's description of the lure of Greece: "Greece, somehow, for better or for worse, will not go away. It is the seeking for our own roots, our own reflection, in that landscape of spectacular beauty and fierce nakedness, that draws us back. . . . Those of us who can travel can see all these things . . . without needing to uproot the buildings and statues from their surroundings. The totality of landscape that gave birth to the Greek gods, to Western art, philosophy and politics, to our dreams and passions and our incurable nostalgia, will always lure us on to discovery and reflection" (*Land of Lost Gods*, 301).

[9] Freud, "Disturbance of Memory on the Acropolis," 242.

[10] Ibid., 246 and 247.

of the Greek ideal' "[11]—that also seemed to disturb the mythic wish of physically rediscovering in Hellas a *topos* of authentic origins. Against the tendency of travelers to describe a *topos* where they could discover their venerable past, there evolved a skeptical modernist *logos*, a counter-*logos* or -discourse. This counterdiscourse raised serious questions about both the eternity of Hellas and the universality of Hellenism, which seemed rooted finally in national interests. As it interrogated the terms of national identity, it also extended its diagnostic logic in another direction. Following the very sensitive compass of its skepticism, it faced a conundrum when it reached the Greek present. Who were the modern Greeks? Did they or did they not rightly belong in the Hellenic world? Were they or were they not the more legitimate descendants of the ancient Greeks? Didn't the Hellenic world rightly belong to them? Wasn't the tendency to dismiss them as a mixed, barbarian race a symptom of narrow-mindedness, the reaction of prejudiced Europeans whose political and economic interests were ultimately at stake?

These questions, at least, are faced head-on in a very unusual short story, "A Dialogue upon Mount Pentelicus," by Virginia Woolf.[12] Woolf's story offers an ironic, polyphonic rewriting of the familiar travel narrative. Its *logos* is of special interest here because it records a British modernist's revaluation of the *topos* of Hellenism. It generates skepticism about both the sentimental Victorian claim to command the values of Hellenism and the tendency to berate the "barbarian" Neohellenes for their mixed genealogy. The two issues are, in fact, closely linked, as the story shows. On Mount Pentelicus, site of a marble quarry in modern as well as ancient times, the pendulum of the six English tourists' sentiments swings back and forth between two contrary positions. It moves from the unquestioning identification of the English with real Greeks, and the modern Greeks with "barbarians," to a self-reflexive skepticism about the values of Englishness and a thoughtful identification of the modern Greeks with real Greeks. And even the most sentimental of the dialogue's interlocutors, who at first contemptuously dismisses the entire modern Greek race, discovers his real "Greek" self upon Mount Pentelicus only when he quite unexpectedly meets a Greek monk face to face.

[11] Maharaj, "The Congo Is Flooding the Acropolis," 88.

[12] The story was written at an unspecified time after Woolf's first visit to Greece in 1906 and posthumously published in 1987. Aris Berlis published his Greek translation in 1991.

From the opening paragraph, the narrative voice casts doubt, through the techniques of irony and detachment, on the travelers' confident sense of their souls' perfect lodging in Hellas:

> It so happened not many weeks ago that a party of English tourists was descending the slopes of Mount Pentelicus. Now they would have been the first to correct that sentence and to point out how much inaccuracy and indeed injustice was contained in such a description of themselves. For to call a man a tourist when you meet him abroad is to define not only his circumstance but his soul; and their souls they would have said—but the donkeys stumble so on the stones—were subject to no such limitation. Germans are tourists and Frenchmen are tourists but Englishmen are Greeks. Such was the sense of their discourse, and we must take their word for it that it was very good sense indeed.

The message here is not only that one must *not* take the six friends' "word for it" that they are not tourists (as Germans and Frenchmen are) but honorary citizens of the slopes of Mount Pentelicus; more radically, one must not "take their word" *literally* for anything regarding their "circumstance" and their "soul" in Hellas. One is led to question the very "sense of their discourse," which allows them to believe they are "subject to no . . . limitation," as the Germans or the Frenchmen, on the other hand, are. One wonders what it is that sutures their bodies to that infelicitous belief that *they* naturally belong in the rocky Greek landscape where, anyway, "the donkeys stumble so on the stones."

The group's shared views on a range of issues related to Hellas reach outward from Mount Pentelicus in two geographical directions, as our previous analysis of heterotopia would lead us to anticipate: they relate their sojourn in Hellas to home abroad and to the local surroundings—to Britain and to Greece. On the Greek language, the tourists collectively hold that Cambridge Greek is the ultimate Greek; conversely, "the fact that Greek words spoken on Greek soil were misunderstood by Greeks destroyed at one blow the whole population of Greece, both men and women and children." Concerning manners and style, "Greeks . . . were a still people, significant of gesture and of speech, and when they sat by the stream beneath the plane tree they disposed themselves as the vase painter would have chosen to depict them," not unlike the English party. The contemporary Greeks are rendered "spurious" by their contrasting "garrulous" manner and "barbarian antics, rolling and singing, pulling each other by the sleeve and chattering of the vintage that now hung purple in the fields."

As report of dialogue between members of the party begins, however, the narrator's detached, ironic voice breaks up into divergent, passionately held positions. Group opinion appears especially split on the position of the modern Greek in the world today: "Some of optimistic nature claimed for him a present, some less credulous but still sanguine expected a future, and others with generous imagination recalled a past." True to the form of the dialogue, the narrative voice divides into two conflicting views. These two views, represented by two interlocutors, stand stubbornly opposed in their assessment of how well the British can be something that the contemporary Greeks are not.

The first interlocutor, ever faithful to the discourse of Hellenism, expresses the opinion that ancient Greeks, "fixed . . . upon the beautiful and the good, . . . died as the day dies here in Greece, completely." Furthermore, they left nothing "for us but to worship in silence or, if we choose, to churn the empty air." His closing comments bring discussion back to the role of the British: one cannot fill the emptiness of Hellenism's disappearance by turning to English summaries of its achievement such as those found in Peacock, he mourns. Here the fictional young man focuses only on the conservative message of Peacock's *Gryll Grange* and misses the satirical tone sustained in that work's summaries of Greek aphorisms on the good life.

The second interlocutor is a schismatic scholar "whose character was already spotted with a dangerous heresy: for only a year ago he had made use of his brand new vote to affirm that Greek should cease" to be compulsory at Cambridge.[13] Several counterdiscourses inform this scholar's views about Hellas: a metacolonial reaction against British self-promotion as a world standard of value, manners, style, and knowledge; a growing anti-Victorian skepticism of the "sentimentalist and sloven" belief that Hellenism represents all that is "noble in art and true in philosophy"; a scholarly critique of obfuscations that hinder etymological understanding and suppress genuine archeological dispute; a political awareness of the national interests that motivate the English to identify themselves with the Greeks rather than with "the Italians or the French or the Germans, or . . . the name of any people indeed who can build bigger fleets than ours or talk a language that we can understand"; and a visceral reaction to the berating of a living

[13] Editor S. P. Rosenbaum informs readers that Woolf's older brother, Thoby, the details of whose life seem to show through in the story, had received an M. A. from Cambridge, "which entitled him to a vote against compulsory Greek at Cambridge." Rosenbaum offers no further explanation.

people. "So," he concludes, "while you read your Greek on the slopes of Pentelicus, you deny that her children exist any longer." This second voice concludes that "Greek" finally functions as a sign around which English society can organize itself: its high culture, educational system, and rhetoric of superiority over other nations. Furthermore, the adoption of a Greek identity conceals Britain's ultimately parochial motives. The "Greek" does not exist except to affirm the English. Thus the most skeptical member of the party seeks to expose the ideology that governs the equation of the Greek with the English and so nearly dispenses with the British discourse of Hellenism altogether.

The narrator's stance from the beginning of the story, however, has borne a distrust of all the characters' thought and speech. As we have seen, the story begins with the travelers' denying entirely a place for the Neohellene on the "solid and continuous avenue" of Hellas. At a second stage, dialogue begins on the topic of the Greek's and the Briton's respective positions in the modern world. The neophyte returns to his original dismissal of the Greek population on the grounds of genealogy, while the scholar takes that dismissal as an opportunity to reflect negatively on the English invention of the Greeks. Then, at the point of absolute disagreement, what would be a most ungentlemanly conclusion, dialogue comes to a sudden halt as events in the story take over.

Here the narrative triggers a broader revaluation of Englishness and Hellenism through the modernist technique of epiphany, a sudden encounter that interrupts discussion and transforms beliefs. Its focal point is an exchange of words in modern Greek. Oddly, perhaps appropriately, Woolf left the content of this exchange blank in her unpublished manuscript, whereas the editor of the text has confidently filled it in. When a native "brown monk . . . large and finely made" with "the nose and brow of a Greek statue" appears suddenly before them, "the English could not have told at the moment at which point they stood, for the avenue was as smooth as a ring of gold." The monk gives his greeting—"[καλησπέρα] which is good evening, and it was odd that he addressed the gentleman who had been the first to proclaim the doom of his race."[14]

When thinking about the story's end, one should keep in mind the part "A Dialogue on Mount Pentelicus" plays in revaluating a standard

[14] The editor acknowledges that he "inserted the Greek into a blank in the typescript."

British *logos* on the *topos* of Hellenism. Here the Greek monk's greeting in Greek extends the limits of Hellenism into the present, which
then circles round again to the past. It also alters the meanings of both
Englishness and Hellenism in the once passionately closed mind of the
neophyte, so that both find their fulfillment in the present. "The
conviction was his that he now spoke as a Greek to a Greek." Full of
significance, the contemporary landscape mystically confirms the actuality of this exchange, against the disavowal of a lifelong education:
"and if Cambridge disavowed the relationship the slopes of Pentelicus
and the olive groves of Mendeli confirmed it." As in the Neohellenic
logos of aesthetic nationalism described in the previous chapter, in this
modernist *logos*, too, we find Hellas's natural environment playing an
active role in confirming what is Hellenic and dispensing with what is
not. What nature confirms—and this *is* an inversion of the *logos* of
Hellenism examined in Chapter 2—is that the modern Greek offers
the traveler real access to Hellenism. The Neohellene is naturally
Hellenic.

I would argue that Woolf's brief story precociously transposes two
important components of British Hellenism, the once-excluded Neohellenic and the once-revered British. The effect of the story is to
move the *neo-* element of Neohellenism from the marginal branch of
bastard son to a distinguished place in the genealogy of Hellenism,
even as it dislocates "Cambridge" (or Englishness) from a point on this
end of Hellenism's most direct line of descent to the branch of a distant
relative by marriage of ideas. In topographical terms, "A Dialogue
upon Mount Pentelicus" places Hellas squarely within Neohellenic
territory, previously seen to lie somewhere in Hellenism's backwaters.
The epiphany of Woolf's story also opens a chasm between the ancient
Greek and the loyal British subject, once viewed as successive inhabitants on high culture's imaginary plane. The modern subject experiences the erosion of crucial links between himself and antiquity. After
suffering a loss of confidence in the truth of Hellenism, this subject
recovers a certain sense of belonging in the Hellenic world (though one
written through with irony) only through identification with the
native, *modern* Greek.

By challenging the unquestioning identification of Englishness with
Hellenism, and, at the same time, identifying modern Greeks with
"real" Greeks, Woolf's story not only raises questions about the values
of Englishness; it also seeks a more authentic, native, perhaps exotic
origin for the truth and beauty of Hellenism. It turns to the Neohellene

to mediate once seemingly unproblematic relations with the Greeks. If this represents a Western modernist impulse, we may find ourselves wondering where modernism in Greece turns *its* innovative eye during the early twentieth century. Might we comprehend the changes in Neohellenic topographies referred to in the last chapter in the light of the modernist transposition just described? Does the decentering of a powerful value like "English" and the concomitant annexing of *neo-* to Hellenism line up in some way with Neohellenism's *recentering* of Hellenism within the peninsula of Hellas? To put it more speculatively, might one understand Neohellenic reterritorializations as Greece's own very interesting deterritorialization of Western Hellenism? To answer these questions, I shall have to follow another thread in Neohellenic discussions about culture. This intellectual quest will lead through some texts already discussed, some not. The common topic is the Neohellenic aesthetic: the theory of art that relates the making of modern art in Greece to a return to Hellenic roots, a recovery of native forms, and a repositioning of the artist in Hellas entopia, as I shall presently explain.

Hellas Entopia: Art for Natives' Sake

It might be said that Western Europeans, even in their more skeptical mode, have felt largely confident of their modern identity, including its classical component. In the twentieth century, they have shown a propensity for revising endlessly stories of their origins. In the arts and in everyday life, they have appropriated apparently primitive practices of other cultures as a means of discovering their own more authentic roots. On the other end of history, whenever they have questioned their belonging in the modern world, what they have doubted is not that they reached the modern era fraudulently or belatedly but that they achieved a modernity to their liking. Whether their present world is good and its history is told right—these things are up for grabs. But there is no question that modernity is of their own making. *Its* history is *theirs*. These things are given.

Neohellenes, in contrast, have from their modern beginnings remained self-conscious of an inherent disparity between themselves and their Hellenic selves, an identity itself divided between its modern and ancient/traditional elements. From their modern institution, they have encountered the heterotopia of Hellas as a daily challenge to their present-day integrity and purity of origins. The insecurity created by their dislocation, spatial and temporal, has generated several compensatory impulses. The most interesting is Greeks' tendency to exoticize themselves. Greeks have regularly sought to recover the primitive element in themselves. To compensate for what others perceived as backward behavior or bad blood, they have defined their homeland, Hellas, as their native entopia, their coffeehouse, if you will, in which they are the aboriginal customers.

The term *entopia*, another Greek derivative of *topos*, exists in Greek in the adjective *ntópios* (*entópios* in the purist idiom) 'local, native, indigenous'.[15] In English, Constantine A. Doxiadis, the world-renowned architect and urban planner who held major positions in the Ministry of Public Works in Athens from 1937 to 1951, coined the noun *entopia* by analogy to *utopia* sometime in the 1960s.[16] Entopia describes the community that approaches perfection not by its dissociation from real space/time, what we call utopia, which, as Doxiadis observed, quickly becomes dystopia, but by its physical embodiment *en-* 'in' *topos* 'place'. According to Doxiadis, entopia begins in nature and moves through the "subsystems" of anthropos and society, all of which constitute "the whole system of social organization also expressed physically."[17] An entopia's goal is to "lead humans back to the harmony they badly need."[18]

Although the English coinage of entopia may be Doxiadis's own, we find in mid-twentieth-century Greece both the popular idea of a native community living in harmony with its natural surroundings and the linguistic tendency to combine *topos* with various prefixes and suffixes, including (*e*)*n-*. Both these trends were highly fashionable from the late 1930s to the mid-1960s. From the years of the Metaxás dictatorship (1936–41) through Greece's cold war reconstruction (1950–60), in the official sphere of government administration, in high culture, and in everyday life, Greeks sought to verify their natural be-

[15] Vernacular forms drop the initial unstressed epsilon, while learned forms try to tack it on again, so there is a continuous tension between the two forms, and both remain in circulation. On the competition of forms in the development of a national Greek language, see Robert Browning, *Medieval and Modern Greek* (1969).

[16] Doxiadis served as chief town planning officer for Greater Athens in 1937, head of the Department of Regional and Town Planning from 1939 to 1944, during World War II and Greece's occupation by the Germans, and became permanent secretary of housing reconstruction in the postwar period.

[17] Constantine A. Doxiadis, *Building Entopia* (1975), 305.

[18] Ibid., 308.

longing to the *topos* of Hellas. One might refer, for example, to the geoclimatic messianism of Ioánnis Metaxás, the populist leader who became Greece's dictator in 1936, gained absolute power in 1938, and then "set about his long-cherished ambition of reshaping the Greek character and remoulding Greek society."[19] Two features of Metaxás's conservative "Third Civilization" are of special relevance to modernist Ellinikótita. The first is its cultural *ethnismós* 'nationism': the idea that culture, especially folk culture, is the bearer of the nation, the conduit through which the nation maintains its identity, enters into dialogue with other nations, and finally distinguishes itself.[20] The second feature is its racial and geographical determinism: the view that *filí* 'race' and *topos* 'place' are determining factors in a people's cultural or spiritual development.[21] A more liberal example is critic Andréas Karandónis's eagerness to highlight the "onrush" of "a natural, native [*ntópia*] power" in Greek poetry composed after 1930.[22] This native power Karandónis contrasts with the inertia he discovers in Greek poetry that openly imitated Western forms. Of course his dichotomizing rhetoric, though potent, is not historically accurate. Seferis and Elytis, the poets whom Karandónis praises, wished to escape the inertia of their predecessors while also continuing to stand directly in the line of Western influences.

Yet it is the power of nativist rhetoric that is of interest here. Surely a nagging native-Western, traditional-modern dichotomy has effectively defined not only Greece's but many nondominant societies' entrance into modernity. And, I would argue, it is the continuous

---

[19] Clogg, *Short History*, 133.

[20] Dimítrios Tzióvas translates *ethnismós* with the coinage 'nationism' in order to distinguish it from *ethnikismós* 'nationalism'. On the meaning of nationism, see Tzióvas, *The Nationism of the Demoticists and Its Impact on Their Literary Theory (1885–1930)* (1986): "Nationism (*ethnismós*) . . . operates on a system of 'rarefaction,' that is a process of exclusion, which determines the difference of the national group from other groups and establishes its 'otherness' " (2–3).

[21] This latter view is expressed quite succinctly by G. Z. Mantzúfas, who wrote regularly in *Néon krátos* (New state), the cultural journal of the Metaxás regime: "The Hellenic ψυχή 'soul', we discover, is in harmonious relation with the Hellenic φυλή [*filí* 'race']. . . . The fact that we have been born in a certain *topos* where that *filí* 'race' once lived which gave to humanity classical civilization—this is not a mere coincidence" (Ιδεολογία και κατευθύνσεις εις το νέον κράτος [Ideology and directions in the new state] [1938], 1327–29; quoted in Dimítrios Tzióvas, Οι μεταμορφώσεις του εθνισμού και το ιδεολόγημα της Ελληνικότητας στο μεσοπόλεμο [The transformations of nationism and the ideologeme of Hellenicity during the interwar period] [1989], 143).

[22] Karandónis, Η ελληνική αίσθηση (Hellenic feeling), 66.

negotiation rather than the final resolution of these opposing terms that propels the making of culture in societies that perceive themselves overshadowed by the West. In Greece, even modernism thrived on playing native, traditional forms against internationalist, modernizing tendencies, as we shall see.[23] Much of Greek modernism presented itself as a native product, despite foreign influences. Like high modernism elsewhere, it cultivated an ambiguous relationship to modernism by declaring its opposition to technology and mass consumer culture. Unlike the modernist standard, however, which explored the primitive roots of exoticized *others* in its tireless search to reinvent the new, Neohellenic modernism insisted on its *own* native authenticity. It restored interest in *its* local forms. It planted *its* modernized *logos* firmly in the *topos* of Hellas. It reaffirmed *its* indigenous ties with a *Hellenic* Hellenic tradition. In effect, it resorted to tautology as a way of claiming to resist external interventions, even those it may have subconsciously courted.

Entopia represents the specifically aesthetic principle of mainstream Neohellenic modernism. It is the aesthetic principle of autochthony. It is the principle of native authenticity. It is the principle that culture is native, that culture is nature, that culture is autochthonous: *auto* 'of itself', *chthon* 'sprung from the land'. Briefly described, the principle of autochthony assigns the origin of beauty to indigenous forces, thus rendering artistic form dependent on geographical and climatic determinants. Indeed, when Neohellenes imagine their art sprouting from Hellas, when they harvest it as a *ntópio* 'native' fruit of the Hellenic *topos*, they produce a powerful image of culture whose compensatory function is not only to make up for disappointments in the dream turned nightmare of territorial expansion but also to negotiate tensions between traditionalist and modernizing, nativist and Westernizing tendencies.[24] The claim of entopia is that the *logos* of a people is mythically grounded in *topos*, even as the people themselves are rooted in the land. The requirement of entopia is that art derive directly from the landscape of Greece, rather than from foreign fashions. The aesthetic must be autochthonous. It must submit its form to the shaping forces of

[23] For a range of articles on the existence and scope of modernism in Greece and its relation both to peripheral and to dominant modernist movements, see the collection of essays entitled *Modernism in Greece? Essays on the Critical and Literary Margins of a Movement* (1990), edited by Mary N. Layoun.

[24] On the compensatory function of the aesthetic in Greece, see Jusdanis, *Belated Modernity and Aesthetic Culture*.

Greece's geography and climate, and it must give voice to native occupants. The mission, finally, of entopia is to fight with the autochthonous sword foreigners' powerful word, particularly the Western aesthetic principle of autonomy, which assigns to art a universalizing self-validation, creates a system of forms, ideas, and sentiments that purportedly give no account to any other system, and shapes customs and habits without displaying its power. Against the aesthetic of autonomy, Neohellenic modernism arrayed the aesthetic of autochthony, sometimes under the banner of Ellinikótita 'Hellenicity'.

The principle of autochthony was not modernists' invention in Greece. Rather it took shape gradually. It should be noted here that autochthony was also a criterion of value for other peripheral modernist movements, for example, the *novela de la tierra* of Spanish America, including the gaucho bildungsroman of Ricardo Güiraldes, the jungle novel of José Eustasio Rivera, and the Venezuelan plains regional tale of Romulo Gallegos.[25] Others, too, upheld the native authenticity as well as the contemporaneity of their literary or artistic experimentations. Precisely when Neohellenes came to view Hellas as their entopia, precisely when they claimed the peninsula of Hellas with its classical sites to be their native workshop, precisely when they began to study Hellas's contours in order to discover an indigenous aesthetic—this is hard to say. Certainly there are numerous beginnings. The administrative campaign to gain control over Hellenism's classical sites forms an important backdrop to literary efforts to secure a special status for Neohellenic art.

Perhaps, then, we might locate the earliest beginnings in 1834, the year after Ottomans abandoned the Acropolis's defense to the Bavarian Otto, king of Hellas, when Otto moved the capital of his new Greek kingdom from Náfplion to Athens. Conjecturing that the ancient citadel was somehow crucial to the reconstruction of a free and aboriginal Hellas, Otto and his classically trained German administrators took up the task of restoring the Acropolis. "The ruins were cleared, the Turkish fortification of the Propylaia was dismantled, the Nike temple was reerected, some restoration work was undertaken on the monuments, especially the Parthenon and the Erechtheion."[26] This building project made antiquity, as well as archeology, a physical cornerstone of Neohellenism: upon the rock of antiquity Neohellenes

---

[25] See Carlos J. Alonso, *The Spanish American Regional Novel: Modernity and Autochthony* (1990).
[26] Dontos, *The Acropolis and Its Museum*, 18.

would assemble their transhistorical Panhellenic union. The Acropolis would play the important role of making up for lost time and bad blood.[27] It would compensate for intrinsic weaknesses. Here, in marked contrast to the mixed population scattered in the surrounding area, human perfection was effectively achieved. Situated at the high panoptic center of its modern capital, it would represent order where there was chaos, pleasure where there was anxiety, purity where there was only a "mixed race," and beauty, integrity, and perfection where there was only the recurrent call for reconstruction.

Another important beginning of Hellas's nativization is found in Yannópulos's work, written during the same decade when Woolf was touring Hellas and Duncan was auditioning native Greek boys for chorus parts in her productions of ancient tragedies. Yannópulos's idea that Hellenic art must subject itself to the determining lines of the Hellenic *topos* reappeared not only in politically conservative but also in modernist manifestos from 1938 to 1948. One cannot stress enough the tremendous influence Yannópulos had on Neohellenism after the rise of General Metaxás. In 1938, two very eminent literary journals, *Ta néa grámmata* and *Neoelliniká grámmata*, devoted entire issues to reprinting and commenting on Yannópulos's work. One critic recently called 1938 "the year of Periklís Yannópulos."[28] By 1941, even the American expatriate Henry Miller, enthusiastic acolyte of George Seferis and Yórgos Katsímbalis, was waxing poetic about Yannópulos's intoxication "with the Greek language, the Greek philosophy, the Greek sky, the Greek mountains, the Greek sea, the Greek islands, the Greek vegetabes" and his description of a Greek "rock," a description so powerful that it made "you . . . know what a rock is."[29]

[27] The now infamous German journalist Jacob Phillipp Fallmerayer published a series of articles beginning in 1836, based on his *Geschichte der Halbinsel Morea während des Mittelalters* (History of the Morea peninsula during the Middle Ages) (1835), where he made the racial argument that Peloponnesian Greeks inherited no Hellenic blood, since their genealogical origin was Slavic. So traumatic was the impact of Fallmerayer's argument on the national unconscious that it generated a current of folklore studies. See Línos Polítis, Ιστορία της νεοελληνικής λογοτεχνίας (History of Neohellenic literature) (1979), 190. In his Εισαγωγή (Introduction) to his Greek translation of Fallmerayer's work, Konstandínos Romanós predicts that "one day Fallmerayer will be recognized not as a general enemy of Hellenism but as a particular historical case of an idealist philhellene" (Jacob Phillipp Fallmerayer, Περί της καταγωγής των σημερινών Ελλήνων [Concerning the origin of contemporary Hellenes] [(1935) 1984], 9).

[28] Tzióvas, Οι μεταμορφώσεις του εθνισμού (The transformations of nationism), 73.

[29] Miller, *Colossus of Maroussi*, 71.

In considering how entopia, with its principle of autochthony, became the rule of a Greek modernist aesthetic, we are called upon to return to Yannópulos's aesthetic theories. We should compare these, briefly at least, to theories that promoted aesthetic autonomy. And we should touch upon this very difficult question—one so broad that it deserves a monograph of its own: what ideology of the aesthetic in Greece subjects art to the demands of climate and geography, thus making *topos* the workshop of a specifically modern art?

As my earlier discussion of aesthetic nationalism has shown, Yannópulos's work translated Hellenism into a national aesthetic, understood as the natural line and color deriving directly from the *topío* 'landscape'. This was his obsessive concern. He caustically criticized contemporary Greek artists for not opening their eyes to the qualities of their surrounding world, instead imitating foreign works. He called for a return to *topos*, to Hellas, to the Μητέρα γή 'Mother Earth', with its indigenous traditions, natural forms, and eternal essence. It is important to recall the centrality of *topos* in Yannópulos's aesthetic theory. Yannópulos assigned the task of expressing artistic distinction neither to the aesthetic artifact nor to the appreciating subject, something we find in the German and Anglóphone aesthetic theories that Terry Eagleton discusses in his *Ideology of the Aesthetic*. Instead *topos* becomes the self-evident category of this aesthetic, the ground of being that precedes both artwork and observer. *Topos* is a law unto itself. It is that which embodies Hellenism's unique individuality. It is the sign of Hellenism's pure presence. One should further recall that Yannópulos found the qualities of the Hellenic *topos* in the Hellenic *topío* 'landscape', the geography and climate most readily identifiable with the Attic sun and the Aegean Sea. By arguing that *topos* directly regulated the aesthetic properties of art, Yannópulos assembled not only Hellenism but also the category of the aesthetic within the *topío* 'landscape' of Hellas.

One is right to anticipate that the Neohellenic aesthetic differs in important ways from the aesthetic of autonomy. It is significant that in Greece the emergence of the aesthetic as a domain of practice and judgment was *not* "closely bound up with the material process by which cultural production becomes autonomous," as Eagleton claims it was in Great Britain and Germany.[30] The aesthetic became a force in Greece without artists' ever disassociating their activity entirely from

[30] Terry Eagleton, *The Ideology of the Aesthetic* (1990), 8–9.

other domains, including the political and social. The emergence of
the aesthetic may be traced to that period of transition outlined in
Chapter 3, when the Neohellenic *logos* about *topos* acquired its aura of
transcendence. Art began to *supplement* though not to supersede politics entirely as the force that potentially infused Hellas, including its
classical sites, with a specifically Neohellenic identity. Yet art never
constructed a self-sufficient domain in Greece, not even today. One
may be tempted to explain this Neohellenic difference by arguing that
Greece has lagged behind others in modernizing itself; the other side of
this explanation is the patronizing assurance that Greeks may learn to
create a self-validating, nonreferential art, given time. But I have
already expressed my reservations about comparative criticism that
relies on an image of culture's moving belatedly from more to less
intense power zones. It might be more fruitful to consider the Neohellenic aesthetic of autochthony in light of changing European views
of Hellenism.

Let us take a closer look at the Neohellenic assumption that while
Hellenism is a universal value it requires a native expression. Yannópulos's aesthetic nationalism proposed that while Hellenism might
be universally appreciated it could be achieved only locally. To appreciate Hellenism, one might be anywhere situated; but to express it, one
had to be native, born of its soil—so Yannópulos declared. It is this assumption that allowed him and his diverse followers to argue that Neohellenes could embody in their work the values of Hellenism, whereas
non-Hellenes could not. Certainly the European traveler might pass
through the beauty of ancient sites to arrive at freedom; but this was
only the freedom of appreciation. Autonomy was the reward of the
disengaged traveler. Autochthony, in contrast, was the responsibility
of the native—so Yannópulos asserted. From this avowal came the
declaration that the Neohellene could find no freedom in Hellas; he
only faced the immense responsibility of *topos*. Of all Europeans, the
Neohellene alone remained subject always to the internal laws of
his *topos*. His *national* responsibility was to give Hellenism a native
artistic expression—to create art for natives' sake. Since non-Hellenes
were not native to the *topos* of Hellas, since the Hellenic aesthetic was
not *ntópio* to them, Yannópulos argued, they inevitably created false
images of Hellenism when they imitated Hellenism in their work.
Through an alternating claim of universality and particularity, this
creative thinker linked the category of the aesthetic both to a transcendental and to a geographically specific signifier of *topos*. Whether he

defined the Hellenic aesthetic for a particular people or for the world, however, he always assembled Hellenism within the geopolitical territory of the Hellas. In this national territory, he claimed that the Neohellenic artist would become the "highest priest" not just of the *national* community but of "the *human* community."[31]

The view that the Neohellenic artist is responsible to the human community for rebuilding a Hellas entopia is certainly not just a side effect of Yannópulos's excessive "intoxication," as Henry Miller put it, with the Hellenic *topos*. It involves a masterful, highly original, and broadly influential conflation of two important ideals of modernity, the national and the aesthetic. The two ideals are quite analogous in their modern conceptualizations. Both the aesthetic and the national are subject to the rule of autonomy, both emphasize their own liberating potential, and both feature the unity, integrity, and distinctiveness of their product, the artwork and the nation respectively. Finally, I would add that it is not only theories of the aesthetic that cover "a varied span of preoccupations: freedom and legality, spontaneity and necessity, self-determination, autonomy, particularity and universality."[32] Theories of the nation do as well. Thus the discourse on beauty and the discourse on the nation converge on many important points. In addition, both of these ideals are coincidentally represented by the term *Hellenism—but only for Greeks*. It is no coincidence, therefore, that Neohellenic aesthetic theories should conflate the aesthetic and the national. We should not be surprised to find in aesthetic nationalism a structural homology between the concept of the Neohellene as grounded in the national context and the idea of the Hellenic artwork as responding directly to the earth and soil. Neither the Hellenic person nor the Hellenic artwork is self-determining or self-regulating. There are no "free particulars" in Greece—whereas Eagleton discovers free artistic and individual particulars in the British and German essays he reads.

Aesthetic nationalism not only conflated the national and the aesthetic ideal; it also played on the reciprocal interdependence of geographic and discursive conceptions of *topos*. It conceived of Hellas as both place and ideal. It capitalized, too, on the dual signification of "Hellenism": its reference to the cultural identity of a politically sov-

[31] Yannópulos, Η σύγχρονος ζωγραφική (Contemporary painting), 22 (my emphasis).
[32] Eagleton, *Ideology of the Aesthetic*, 3.

ereign people living within a territorially delineated space (the political *topos* of the nation-state) and to the coherent, luminous, and brilliant artistic heritage of the classical past (the aesthetic *topos* for perfection). It depended, finally, on a European conception of the Hellenic aesthetic, to which it gave a Neohellenic twist. Despite its devastating critique of Eurocentrism, it relied especially on a German image of Hellenism, the aesthetic signification of which it adapted to Neohellenic ends.

An important side effect of this nativist revision of Western Hellenism was that it rendered the Greek state (Hellas) rightful protector of art's original site (Hellas). Its articulation of the Neohellenic difference granted to Neohellenes not only special access to Hellenism but also special protective rights over the *topos* of Hellas, including its classical sites. Neohellenes might not only nativize Hellas's sites; they might also nationalize these—provided, of course, they made them the workshop of artistic creativity.

The Neohellenic Modernist Turn

We can now examine the modernist contribution to nativizing Hellenism, with its many interesting contradictions. Perhaps it should be noted first that although Greek letters boast of formal innovation early in the twentieth century in the Greek diaspora, with Cavafy a conspicuous example, a coherent modernist movement appeared in Greece only after World War I.[33] Modernist literature reached a broader audience in the late 1930s and achieved power as the language of high culture only after World War II. Indeed, I would argue that the postwar reconstruction from 1945 to 1960 comprises the period of modernism's consolidation in Greece. In making this claim, I am moderately challenging a commonplace assumption of Greek criticism that modernism, to the extent that it did develop in Greece, took shape in the 1930s and continued along the same course in the 1940s and 1950s. It

[33] Greeks used the term *neoterikós* 'neoteric', alongside *protoporiakós* 'pioneering' and *sínhronos* 'contemporary', to signify progressive writing styles. *Neoterikós* was the adjective mainstream modernists preferred to refer to their own stylistic innovations. The term *modernismós*, which first appeared in Greece as early as 1921 with reference to Italian futurist poetry, had a pejorative connotation. For a history of the terms *neoterikós* and *modernismós* and their usage in Greece, see Tziovas, Οι μεταμορφώσεις του εθνισμού (The transformations of nationism), 19ff.

seems to me that modernism's consolidation in Greece coincided historically not with the interwar period but with the beginning of the cold war. It was then that the potential of a radical intervention in the arts, let us call it an avant-garde, which had indeed gathered energy in the 1930s, dissipated. It was then that many of the artists and writers whose work had appeared in the 1930s rallied their thoughts in a unilateral direction, one defined in large part by theories of aesthetic nationalism.[34]

We should recall that the postwar years were a time when antagonistic Eastern and Western superpowers drew lethal battle lines through Hellas.[35] In the period between two dictatorships—the rule of Metaxás, at one end, and the military junta of General Geórgios Papadópulos (1967–74), at the other—Greeks endured war against an invading Italian army on the Albanian front (1940); German occupation (1941–44); civil war, first with British, then with American intervention under the Truman Doctrine (1944–49), leading to the death of 7 to 8 percent of the population, the forced evacuation of some 25,000 children to countries of the Eastern bloc, and the political exile of thousands of adults; reconstruction, the intensified development efforts (with all the political complications of such a capitalist neocolonialist strategy) made under the Marshall Plan (1948–51); and the Turkish occupation of northern Cyprus (1974–present).[36]

It makes sense that in an era of continuous insecurity, Greek culture would return to a key issue raised by Yannópulos at the beginning of

[34] I am not referring here to the first postwar generation, the poets and artists whose work began to appear after 1945. For an analysis of their poetry's topographical and political orientation, see Vangelis Calotychos, "Realizing and Resisting 'Self-Colonization': Ideology and Form in Modern Greek Poetics (1790–1960)" (1993), chap. 5.

[35] This is quite literally the case, since the cold war effected one of the last major changes in Greece's borders. In 1947, Greece lost claims to northern Epirus—a region of southern Albania occupied by ethnic Greeks and sought by Greece as war reparation—in exchange for the Dodecanese islands, occupied by Italy since 1911. January of 1991 witnessed yet another complex side effect of the recent cold war thaw, the "return" of ethnic Greeks (alongside fleeing Muslims and Roman Catholics) from the same region of Albania to northwestern Greece. This newest arrival of refugees has met with little favor in Greece, where government officials cling to statistical information about the presence of a large Greek minority in northern Epirus in support of their continuing claim to this region.

[36] George C. Marshall, U.S. secretary of state, urged U.S. financial support of European recovery on 5 June 1947. The U.S. Economic Cooperation Administration financed the plan for three years beginning in 1948.

this tumultuous century, which had announced itself with the *megáli itta* 'great defeat' of the Greek army by Turkish troops in Thessaly (1897) and then witnessed the territorial expansions that followed the Cretan declaration of *énosis* 'unification' with Greece in 1908 (Crete officially joined Greece in 1913) and two Balkan wars (1912–13), World War I, the uprooting of Orthodox Christian populations from Eastern Thrace and Anatolia (1922), the ensuing social, economic, and political crisis in Greece, World War II, and, finally, Greece's civil war. The greatest problem Greek culture faced was "the problem of difference (or *Ellinikótita*): how to distinguish . . . 'Hellenic Hellenism' from 'European Hellenism' and to highlight its strategic role in Western civilization."[37] It seemed that the greatest challenge Neohellenes faced mid-century was to discover a Hellenic form that could survive the turmoil the nation had been facing for some fifty years. Thus while European modernists skeptically surveyed their own investment in Hellenism—at first rejecting it, then revising it, then primitivizing it—Greeks endlessly discussed *their* native identity, their cultural output, the nature of their *topos*, and their investment in Hellenism, as we have seen, even as they tried to incorporate within Hellas the diverse communities of newly acquired territories, displaced diaspora populations, homeless refugees, venerated and vilified veterans. And critics and artists masterfully succeeded in standardizing a vernacular literary language, creating a canon of Neohellenic masterpieces, and, most important, adapting Western Hellenism to some very powerful signifiers, all hybrids of the Hellenic.

It should be noted here that Neohellenism is unusual among nondominant cultures in that both its traditionalists and its Westernizers, the two opposing parties that took shape as Greece shifted its orientation to the West, have taken Hellenism to be the sign of privilege.[38] Each side has competed for the authority to control the semiosis of Hellenism. To this day Neohellenism continues producing interesting new hybrids: Byzantine Hellenism, Eastern Hellenism, Helladic Hel-

---

[37] Tzióvas, Οι μεταμορφώσεις του εθνισμού (The transformations of nationism), 51–52.

[38] One might consider any number of contrasting cases: modern Iran, for example, where the Westernizing Pahlavi dynasty attempted to revive a Persian identity to the exclusion of the traditionalist Muslim identity—at the cost of support from the Muslim majority. Here the two opposing terms had different signs, also perceived to be mutually exclusive. On the cultural politics of the Pahlavi dynasty and the conflict of the "modernizing" state with the "traditionalist" hierarchy in Iran before 1979, see Said Amir Arjomand, *The Turban for the Crown: The Islamic Revolution in Iran* (1988), 75–87.

lenism, anti-Helladic Hellenism, Roméic Hellenism, Hellenic Hellenism, Macedonian Hellenism, Marxist Hellenism, Neo-Orthodox
Hellenism, and Neo-Orthodox Marxist Hellenism are but a few examples. Greek modernism, a rather complex amalgam of Westernizing traditionalists and traditionalizing Westernizers, combined Western Hellenism with a nativizing Roméic Hellenism in the principle of
Ellinikótita 'Hellenicity'. With this aesthetic principle, a liberal humanist gloss for *parádosi* 'tradition', modernists subsumed the modern
in the traditional, the Western in the native.

I note here that the term *Ellinikótita* 'Hellenicity' did not acquire
currency before the 1930s, when a group of European-educated, most-
ly liberal, anti-Marxist poets and critics, the "Generation of the Thirties,"[39] tried its hand at steering the difficult course between traditionalist and modernizing forces. To navigate between "the clashing
rocks of vulgar populism of the past and menacing socialism of the
present,"[40] they turned to the native aesthetic, to Ellinikótita. This
would become the emblem of a new brand of humanism that would
feature the Neohellenic difference *within* European Hellenism.

In actuality, the modernist turn in Greece in the 1930s involved no
real revolution at all. Instead modernism moderately restated the demoticist position. It brought together the positions of cultural vernacularism, on the one hand, and aesthetic nationalism, on the other
hand. In the best book to date on Greece's cultural movements between the 1930s and early 1940s, Dimítris Tzióvas argues that modernists' recurrent interest in Ellinikótita is symptomatic of Greece's
institutional instability and political, cultural, and geographical mar-
ginalization in Europe after 1930.[41] Modernists' attachment to Ellinikótita must therefore be viewed in the broader context of Neohellenes'
sense of dislocation within the modernized West, something that may
have reached both its greatest crisis and its most powerful sublimation,
I would add, when Greece became annexed to the Western alliance
through bloody cold war politics.

As the cultural movement of the 1930s "prepared itself for a new

[39] For a critique of the term "Generation of the Thirties" and, more generally, the
filiative representation of literary succession, see Artemis Leontis, "Modernist Criticism: Greek and American Defenses of the Autonomous Literary Text in the 1930s"
(1990).

[40] Tzióvas, Οι μεταμορφώσεις του εθνισμού (The transformations of nationism),
39.

[41] Ibid., 40.

humanism which would smooth the horns of the Neohellenic dilemma" and "find a new cultural balance with Europe," its "representatives tried to reconcile demoticism with cosmopolitanism, Makriyannismós with modernism, everyday speech with well-wrought
writerliness."[42] Like Yannópulos and Dragúmis before them, modernists located Neohellenic literary production within the *topos* of Hellas.
Like their precursors, they made culture and geography reciprocally
interdependent. Theirs was an aesthetic of autochthony, an "aesthetic
of native authenticity,"[43] an aesthetic that mystically idealized the
native, worshipped the Aegean landscape, and liturgically invoked the
Greek light. At the intersection of the Hellenic ideal and its racial/geo-
climatic reification, somewhere on the coordinate plane where the
modern, the national, the traditional, and the classical might be said to
meet, modernists staked out their native, transcendental *topos*. Here
they would plant Neohellenism's local garden. Modernists bracketed,
however, the question of determinism—or so they claimed. Just how
Neohellenism was to cultivate its *topos*, to harvest its fruits, just what
form its art should take as it absorbed nutrients from the recycled
classical pagan, Byzantine Orthodox, Ottoman folk past that nourished the modern present—these things could not be determined be-
forehand. What mattered was not how Neohellenic art revealed its
Hellenicity but the mere fact that it would be situated harmoniously,
intelligently, perhaps syncretically, but squarely within the *topos* of
Hellas.

This measured and contradictory argument appeared in 1938 just
before the outbreak of World War II in an essay that seemed conservative at the time but would become the model of thinking within a
decade. I refer to Konstandínos Tsátsos's Πριν από το ξεκίνημα
(Before setting out), which was published in two installments and was

[42] Ibid., 53. Makriyannismós might be described as the populist insertion of revolutionary hero Yánnis Makriyánnis's semiliterate memoirs into the Neohellenic literary
canon. See Stathis Gourgouris, "Writing the National Imaginary: The Memory of
Makriyannis and the Miracles of Neohellenism" (1989), for an insightful analysis of this
phenomenon. Postwar critical essays that promoted Makriyánnis's works include the
following essays on General Makriyánnis: J. Th. Kakridís, Στρατηγός Μακρυγιάννης·
Μια ελληνική καρδιά (General Makriyánnis: A Greek heart) ([1964] 1972); George
Seferis, Ένας Έλληνας—ο Μακρυγιάννης (A Hellene—Makriyánnis) ([1943] 1981);
Yórgos Theotokás, Ο Στρατηγός Μακρυγιάννης (General Makriyánnis) ([1945]
1961).

[43] Tzióvas, Οι μεταμορφώσεις του ενθισμού (The transformations of nationism),
73.

followed up in the same year by a response to George Seferis entitled Ένας διάλογος για την ποίηση (A dialogue on poetry).[44] Tsátsos's side of the discussion comprises the lesser-known half of a "dialogue" with Seferis, a commonplace citation in Greek criticism.[45] Tsátsos, the moderate, Western-oriented philosopher, critic, and public intellectual who became president of the Greek Republic in 1975, provided a line of thought that would bridge Yannópulos's aesthetic nationalism with a modernist aesthetic and find a formal correlative in Greek poetry and art during the 1940s and 1950s.

Tsátsos's essay steps cautiously at first, then gradually lets down its guard as it falls into some pervasive traps of deterministic thinking. The essay begins by calling attention to the importance of proper *topothétisis* 'positioning' or 'placement' in the creative act. *Topothétisis* is the guarantor of an individual's autonomy. To take a *thesis* in one's *topos* is to assert one's unique particularity without trespassing the heteronomous eternal laws that apply a priori to the general case: "Depending on *topothétisis*, every meaning of life (which is entirely personal) changes, without the eternity of law that governs the general case being affected."[46] Although Tsátsos's essay begins with this very interesting argument about the variable nature of *topothétisis* in any creative act, including politics, it eventually reduces *topothétisis* to a precondition for aesthetic creativity in a particular *topos*, the nation-state, Hellas. It characterizes "the essence of cultural life" as "indivisible from the earth and the history of the people where one belongs" and maintains that "one must define what that earth is and what its cultural meaning is, since this fundamentally predefines authentic art and essential thought and even history, as a unity conceived from spirit." "Especially in Hellas," Tsátsos goes on to say, "we must become aware of the internal coherence of each historical period and its common meaning. . . . Before any valuable influence (from abroad)

[44] For the purposes of citation, I refer to the two installments of Tsátsos's essay as I and II.

[45] Seferis's side of the discussion, entitled Διάλογος πάνω στην ποίηση (Dialogue on poetry), is reprinted in Greek and English collections of his critical essays. Neohellenists frequently refer to this essay. I discuss it in Chapter 5.

[46] Konstandínos Tsátsos, Πριν από το ξεκίνημα (Before setting out) (1938), I:51. In 1935–36, just three years before Tsátsos published this essay, Martin Heidegger wrote his groundbreaking philosophical essay "The Origin of the Work of Art," signaling his turn from politics to the arts. In "The Origin of the Work of Art: Addendum" (1956), Heidegger attempted to clarify his earlier comments on "fixing in place of truth" (82); like Tsátsos after him, Heidegger referred to this creative act by its Greek name, *thesis*.

comes an intelligible sense of the Hellenic earth and Hellenic history."[47] Here *topothétisis* becomes a defense against both historical (Marxist) determinism, on the one hand—since engagement with *topos* is a personal matter—and sophistic (internationalist) relativism in the arts, on the other hand—since *topos* binds one's loyalties to a particular place: "Depending on *topothétisis*, every meaning of life (which is entirely personal) changes, without the eternity of law that governs the general case being affected. Thus even the Parthenon is a composite of the realization of general aesthetic rules, while at the same time it is an absolutely singular work."[48]

The direction of the argument finally crystallizes when Tsátsos compares finding one's Archimedean point in creative activity to realizing the proper placement of an ancient temple such as the Parthenon. It is not the architectural analogy so much as the specifically *Hellenic* analogy of the ancient temple—resting on the earth, emerging out of the earth, and rising in itself and in all things—that determines the course Tsátsos's argument will finally take. As in Yannópulos's essays on art, here, too, we find a conflation of the aesthetic and the national ideal, the two dimensions of Hellenism. I might add that the idea of ancient temples' deriving their religious authority from their location in the Hellenic *topos* appears elsewhere, for example in the aesthetic theories of Hrístos Karúzos and Dimítris Pikiónis; indeed it is found repeatedly in Neohellenic criticism from the 1940s to the 1970s. The idea also appears in Martin Heidegger's "Origin of the Work of Art," which describes the ancient Greek "temple work" "standing there, open[ing] up a world and at the same time set[ting] this world back again on earth, which itself only thus emerges as native ground."[49]

For Tsátsos, *topothétisis* finally means finding one's proper place not in an international scene but within the *topos* of Hellas. In this case, too, the *topos* of Hellas is incarnated in the Hellenic *topío*, and, by analogy, in all that it produces, including Neohellenic art. To fine one's place in *topos* means to dig one's roots so deeply into the Hellenic "earth and in the chthonic spirit" that one's artistic expression sprouts naturally from "the very sources of Hellenic life, defined each time from the original placement of a consciousness that lives the only possible authentic life."[50] The author warns that finding an "objective

---

[47] Tsátsos, Πριν από το ξεκίνημα (Before setting out), II:98.
[48] Ibid., I:56.
[49] Heidegger, "Origin of the Work of Art," 42.
[50] Tsátsos, Πριν από το ξεκίνημα (Before setting out), II:100.

form" does not mean fitting one's work into a prepared mold: "*topos* must be common for every aesthetic consciousness without being commonplace."[51] Yet Tsátsos does not hesitate to describe the traits of Ellinikótita. When he proclaims certain features to be a priori criteria for aesthetic practice and judgment, he ends up where Yannópulos began:

> Some people approach the idea of Ellinikótita from the path of nature, others from the path of history; still others approach it through poetry and art or from the succession of its religions. For this reason we may differ among ourselves on many points. Isn't its internal unity so impossible to shatter, however, that we may agree on certain crucial points? A virtue of light that dispels shadows, dullness, and mystery, that gives clarity to lines and contours. A virtue of measure that cannot bear exaggerated size, that sacrifices the titanic and the gigantic for the Olympic and the human, that gives the soul limits for each outburst. . . . A measure that is steadfast but supple.[52]

The parallels between Tsátsos's Ellinikótita and Yannópulos's description of the Hellenic *topío* are obvious. Both stress the "virtue of light," the "clarity" of "lines and contours," the "virtue of measure." Both find virtues native to the Hellenic *topos*. Tsátsos's Ellinikótita is an indigenous aesthetic. It is a plain description of the aesthetic of autochthony.

Paganlike worship of the Hellenic landscape became commonplace during the next decade. Even the modernist Seferis, who in 1938 had come into conflict with Tsátsos presumably because of Tsátsos's propensity for dictating the traits of Ellinikótita, ten years later did not resist ascribing a "humanizing function" to the "light" of "the principally Hellenic *topío*."[53] This light would make visible "lines that are drawn and erased; bodies and personalities, the tragic silence of the *persona*."[54] It would finally merge with the living force that ran through not only "the blood of man" but all of Hellenism from Homer to the present. As debates about literature's national affiliation took shape in the 1940s, even liberal exponents of modernism responded to the conservative

---

[51] Konstandínos Tsátsos, Ἕνας διάλογος γιὰ τὴν ποίηση (A dialogue on poetry) (1938), 254.

[52] Ibid., 258.

[53] George Seferis, Μιὰ σκηνοθεσία γιὰ τὴν Κίχλη (Stage directions for *Thrush*) ([1949] 1981), 55.

[54] Ibid.

turn in politics. Authors who, in the early 1930s, had featured culture as the Hellenic contribution to a Western civilization with an international scope took a distinctly nationalist turn after 1938. While they resisted blatantly racial conceptions of Hellenism, they yielded to arguments about the influence of climate and geography on cultural orientation—even against their own former protests.

With the aesthetic of autochthony in mind, modernists reterritorialized the classical tradition, broadly appropriated by others for nearly two centuries, for their own minor dominion of the post-Byzantine, post-Ottoman, modern state. Thus, while cold war reconstruction precipitated Greece's particularly rapid economic, industrial, and social modernization, Seferis and Elytis, alongside others of the same cultural milieu, entered into a literary dialogue with the Hellenic *topos* of tradition. They made this *topos* of tradition the signature of their modernizing *logos*, something that seemed to please both a national and an international audience. Their work is one important instance of postwar unification/reconstruction efforts in the Western bloc. Their stated intent was to cross the limits of parochialism, to transcend narrowly national (or political) concerns, while they also sought to overcome the rupture with tradition and the fragmentation of time that followed from the country's sudden, violent entrance into modernity.[55] And so they attempted to bring Greece culturally into alignment with the modern world while they also struggled to recover the true origins and real cultural potential of *Hellenic* Hellenism.

They either incorporated modernist techniques into the emergent myth of Hellenicity or renounced them for their irrelevance to Hellenism. Their recontextualization of classical authors took the form of the elliptical quotation—the same technique T. S. Eliot, Éluard, H. D., Joyce, Pound, Rilke, and others employed to express their fragmented ties with the Hellenic past. In Neohellenic revisions of Hellenism, the elliptical quotation became the ultimate modernizing innovation made in the name of a Hellenic *native* tradition. Here the learned quotation somehow registered the concrete sociopolitical needs of a besieged, war-torn, and shrunken modern state. More to the point, when they reassembled the fragments of Hellenism in their literary texts, they recoded Hellenism. Turning away from the territory of the nation, the

---

[55] The attack on parochialism began as early as 1929 with Theotokás's manifesto of liberalism, Ελεύθερο πνεύμα (Free spirit). At that time, however, Theotokás had not sought a reconciliation of the modern with the traditional, the European with the local.

vision of the integrated community, and the geographical expanse of the state, they focused attention on the disengaged domain of culture. Unlike their Western European and American counterparts, however, who did not seek a territorial return on their investment in Hellenic culture, Neohellenic authors tested the capacity of the unincorporated literary quotation to annex Neohellenism to Hellenism. Their literary texts themselves became a privileged *topos* that preserved while it also modernized the language and spirit of the Greek people.

Seferis and Elytis, internationally the best-known poets of this group, were especially effective in recontextualizing Hellenism in their work. Their strange juxtaposition of antiquity and modernity, eternity and immediacy, universality and particularity, triggered a national-cultural remembrance of things past. It gave poetic form to a spiritual landscape that was on the collective mind. It was to depict Hellenism's immemorial embodiment in place, its entopia, as well as its perennial displacement, its atopia, in the contemporary world order. In their poetry, both Seferis and Elytis combined diverse notions: the modern political ideal of an autonomous territory, a *topos* containing the national body (national territory); the rhetorical figure of a common-place site of return, a *topos* cultivated to reassure an expectant audience of its collective vision (the literary citation); and the wish image of an excavated, reconstructed ancient site, a *topos* set apart from normative space where one could recover the intrinsic value of beauty, truth, and reason (the archeological site). They cited Hellas as always ours, yet never entirely possessed. And they updated the state of a Hellenic entopia. Hellas would not become the ambiguous but powerful sign of an authentic, native, and naïve place of origin, on the one hand, and of its modern, sentimental, belated reconstruction, on the other. Finally, they subjected their poetics both to the determining forces of the landscape and to the rule of aesthetic autonomy.

The literary outcome combines Western and non-Western features for an international and national audience, as we shall presently see. Typical of a peripheral modernism is its conscious displacement of European cosmopolitanism by a nostalgic appeal to indigenous traditions. Typical, too, is the drive to appeal to a national audience's sense of outrage at the appropriation of its past by others. In contrast to much European and American high modernist art, which features an urban setting, international flight, and the theme of spiritual exile, one finds the nationist orientation of Neohellenic modernism, with its recurrent theme of a cultural return to the light of the national *topos*.

The landscape is bucolic, the rhetoric populist. The native language promises organic union with the natural surroundings. Fragmentation of form becomes the banner of resistance to foreign intervention. And the image of a home resurrected within a shipwrecked homeland becomes the nostalgically recalled center of civilization. In the next two chapters, I shall explore just how the poets Seferis and Elytis reconstructed their postwar Hellenic homeland. I shall also try to show how they used their poetry to urge the Greek native, long displaced by foreign occupations, economic forces, and an uninterrupted state of war, as well as by the European traveler, to return home to a Hellenic entopia.

CHAPTER 5

Nostos:
Hellenism's Suspended Homecoming

I was seeking, without being precisely aware of it, the road to Rome. Ever since my first visit the city had become for me, not only on all its historical levels but rather in its spiritual essence, in other words in a sense that transcended history, the holy city; yet withal one not chosen but discovered, an ancestral homeland and a goal of pilgrimage. Every fresh sojourn in Rome strengthened this relation to my life. I knew myself bound to the *Roma aeterna*. In the course of years and decades I realized that this bond contained a secret with many layers of symbolic meaning.
                    —E. R. Curtius, *Essays on European Literature*

Noon at the archaeological museum. They unearth now—some in crates, some bare to the flesh in the earth—the statues. In one of the big old galleries, familiar from our student years, with the dull facade that somewhat resembled the dreary public library, the workmen excavate with shovels and pickaxes. If you didn't look at the roof, the floor, the windows, and the walls with inscriptions in gold, this could be any excavation. Statues, still sunken in the earth, appeared naked from the waist up, planted at random. . . . It was a chorus of the resurrected, a second coming of bodies that gave you a crazy joy. . . . Emotion from this sudden familiarity. The bronze Zeus, or Poseidon, lying on a crate like an ordinary tired laborer. I touched him on the chest, where the arm joins the shoulder, on the belly, on his hair. It seemed that I touched my own body. . . . Crazy about the [*topos*]. Every day carried away more and more by this drunkenness. The sea, the mountains that dance motionless. I found them the same in these rippled chitons: water turned into marble around the chests and the sides of headless fragments.
                    —George Seferis, *A Poet's Journal*

Crisis, sometimes represented by the *topos* of the lost center, is a salient feature of discussions about culture in Europe beginning in the late eighteenth century. Romantic writers lamented literature's loss of a naïve disposition. Significantly, they also attributed to the bards of ancient Hellas a purity lost to them. They measured their own senti- mental and self-conscious attitude against the harmony of experience and utterance native to their cultural ancestors.[1] The opposition Hel- lenic versus modern remained intact throughout the nineteenth and into the twentieth century. The Victorian critic Matthew Arnold, for instance, facing the threat of social anarchy, called for bold reforms to rediscover "sweetness and light," which, he observed, "evidently have to do with the bent or side in humanity which we call Hellenic. . . . To say we work for sweetness and light, then, is only another way of saying that we work for Hellenism."[2] With the turn of the century, some heralds of modernity, finding themselves on this side of history, announced a conscious and deliberate break with the classical past and a search for new forms of expression.[3] Reckoning as their ambiguous gain the loss of central authority provided by ancient prototypes such as the Hellenic, they hastened a crisis of dissolution.[4]

The Crisis of Tradition: Hellenism's Second Coming

In Greece things developed in a different way, as I have already indicated. The first articulation of a threatening crisis in literature and

[1] In his letter to Wilhelm von Humboldt dated 26 October 1795, Schiller asked a series of plagued questions about his own circumstances as a modern poet: "Given my distance from the spirit of Greek literature, to what extent can I still be a poet and indeed a better poet than the extent of my distance seems to allow? . . . I am not a naive writer. How is it then that I can still be good?" (quoted in the introduction to Friedrich Schiller, *On the Naïve and Sentimental in Literature* [(1795–96) 1981], 12).

[2] Matthew Arnold, *Culture and Anarchy: An Essay in Political and Social Criticism* ([1868] 1971), 123.

[3] For a brief survey of modernist attitudes toward the past, see Stephen Watson, "Criticism and the Closure of 'Modernism'" (1983), 16–17.

[4] Malcolm Bradbury and James McFarlane describe the modernist view of history as "crisis-centered" ("The Name and Nature of Modernism" [1976], 20) and point to a "Great Divide between past and present, art before and art now" (21): "Indeed Mod- ernism would seem to be the point at which the idea of the radical and innovating arts . . . that had been growing forward from Romanticism, reaches formal crisis—in which myth, structure and organization in a traditional sense collapse, and not only for

the arts corresponded chronologically not with the beginning but with the end of the European debate, when modernists elsewhere either espoused a break with tradition or reinterpreted the past. The "Asia Minor disaster," in 1922, first incited serious talk about a crisis of tradition. With this disaster, Greek intellectuals felt that the figure of the lost center had found its literal fulfillment in their *topos* and so had become history. The topography of Hellenism had lost a major historical center. Wouldn't the *topos* of Hellas, too, become decentralized? Wouldn't Hellenism become secondary, self-conscious, sentimental, hence unequivocally modern? Greeks sensed that they might now have to forfeit their theoretically privileged position, which they had once translated into a dream of restoring past civilizations intact.

The second articulation of crisis in Greek letters came in the mid-1940s, when a ruthless civil war superseded celebrations of a victorious resistance to German occupation. Inevitably, Greece's mid-century crisis has been read against "1922," since the modernists of consolidation, with George Seferis a leading figure, kept returning to this event as they tried to find a symbol to deflect attention from the present agony. No matter how hard they tried, however, they could not completely repress the details of their circumstances; their point of reference remained the Greek civil war, an ominous sign of the emergent cold war. Thus, even as they sought to distance themselves from present-day party politics, even as they returned to older layers of history to render their present meaningful, even as they tried to recover an ancestral homeland, a "goal of pilgrimage" where they could transcend the unpleasantries of history, they played their part in marketing Hellas to the free cold world. Their cultural politics nicely supplemented anti-Communist policies of a forged unification, since their works organized themselves neatly into a national literary canon that could be consumed by individuals widely divided from one another in class origin and political affiliation.

In Greek literary history, 1922, the first scene of loss to which all histories would inevitably return, acquired both its antihero and its hero in the late 1920s. The antihero, poet and satirist Kóstas Kariotákis (1896–1928), inevitably stood in juxtaposition to the hero, George

---

formal reasons. The crisis is a crisis of culture; it often involves an unhappy view of history—so that the Modernist writer is not simply the artist set free, but the artist under specific, apparently historical strain. If Modernism is the imaginative power in the chamber of consciousness . . . it is also often an awareness of contingency as a disaster in the world of time: Yeats's 'Things fall apart; the centre cannot hold' " (26).

Seferis. When Kariotákis committed suicide in 1928, intellectuals pub-
licly denounced this notorious act as a violation of faith in the constancy of poetic value. Within three years, Seferis published his first
collection of poetry, Στροφή (Turning point) (1931). In the codifica-
tion of literary history that would take place during the 1940s, Seferis's
appearance on the literary scene would come to signal the *strofí* 'turn'
away from Kariotákis's nihilistic, lethal satire, and the return to the
living *parádosi* 'tradition' of the homeland.

Seferis's role was to moderate crisis, reclaim tradition, and, by his
own metaphor, effect a cultural *nostos* 'homecoming, return to light'.[5]
His intervention began in the 1930s and continues posthumously even
to the present day. Seferis was one of a small but influential group who
in the 1930s came to understand that modernism would leave behind
the Greek poets who did not assimilate it. This was an interregnum
period of rehabilitation, when European modernists retreated from
the "role of violence-inciting artistic provocateurs whose aim was to
startle the culture out of lethargy."[6] They now sought to legitimize
new cultural forms, often by revisiting tradition and reinterpreting it.
The spirit of rehabilitation nicely suited a Greek poet who was not by
nature a provocateur. In deference to a modernistically reactivated
tradition, Seferis sought to extend the boundaries of Neohellenic literature, previously defined by more narrowly national interests, in the
direction of European aesthetics; at the same time, he linked the
problematic of the autonomous artwork to the permanent values of his
Ellinikós Ellinismós 'Hellenic Hellenism'. This, in sum, was his win-
ning formula.

Early in his career, Seferis began surveying the site of homecoming,
that ever-receding *topos* of lost origins. He cautiously asserted that
Neohellenes might regain access to this vanishing center through
Hellenic tradition. As early as 1938, when he was still defending poetic
experimentation, Seferis assuaged fears of crisis by "carefully grafting
some concepts and practices of European modernism onto the legacy
of Greek tradition."[7] Noteworthy in the Διάλογος πάνω στην

[5] *Nostos* 'homecoming, return to light and life' is the Homeric word referring to the
Achaean heroes' homecoming after their war against Troy. We encountered the Ho-
meric phrase *lūgros nostos* 'pitiful homecoming' in Nikolareízis's text, discussed in
Chapter 3.

[6] Michael H. Levenson, *A Genealogy of Modernism: A Study of English Literary
Doctrine, 1908–1922* (1984), 40.

[7] Dimítris Dimirúlis, "The 'Humble Art' and the Exquisite Rhetoric: Tropes in the
Manner of George Seferis" (1985), 59.

ποίηση (Dialogue on poetry), his polemical response to the articles by
Tsátsos discussed in the previous chapter, is Seferis's studied equivocation on the subject of Neohellenism's orientation to the modern. I shall
analyze this equivocation before moving on to discuss Seferis's postwar work, which presupposes the earlier conflation of the modern
with the Hellenic.

What incited Seferis was Tsátsos's questioning the relevance of the
modernist experiment: how "Hellenic" could its subject, form, and
language be, given that it refused to position itself properly within the
topos of Hellas? Tsátsos asked. Although he announced the Kantian
origins of his critique of judgment, Tsátsos failed to mention the
discursive source for his term of perfection, European modernity's
nostalgic delineation of the Hellenic.[8] What eluded him was how
directly his fear that Neohellenism might forfeit the integrity of its
Hellenic past depended on romantic laments of a lost innocence and
communality—the very stuff of Western Hellenism. He promoted a
venture into genuinely Hellenic sources. He envisioned a subterranean
navigation through Hellenic history. He called for a rooting of Neohellenic works in Greek soil without foreign intervention—as if the
search for the Hellenic were unmediated by other European intellectual concerns.

In response to Tsátsos, Seferis identified Neohellenism both with
modernity and with its own homonymous other, the "Hellenic,"
terms antithetical in Western schemes of thought. He even suggested
that Neohellenism might return home to Hellenism through a modernist aesthetic. With this equivocation on the Hellenic potential of
modernism and the modern implications of Neohellenism, he entangled modernism in what was still a conservative-dominated debate
on the Hellenicity of contemporary values.[9] Of course, Seferis cau-
tioned that although "it is a great and beautiful thing for one to speak
about the 'Hellenicity' of a work," the term must not be too closely
defined.[10] Furthermore, he disavowed the censorial function of criti-

---

[8] Kant analyzed a faculty of judgment independent of the faculty of cognition, with
its objective a priori. Of the faculty of judgment, he felt "we may reasonably presume
by analogy that it may likewise contain, if not a special authority to prescribe laws, still
a principle peculiar to itself upon which laws are sought, although one merely subjec-
tive *a priori*" (Immanuel Kant, *The Critique of Judgment* [(1790) 1982], 15).

[9] Although Seferis claimed that Tsátsos introduced Hellenicity as an a priori criterion of artistic value, Seferis was actually the one who interposed the term in order to
reject it.

[10] Seferis, Διάλογος πάνω στην ποίηση (Dialogue on poetry), 98.

cism in Greece. Critics should give no prescriptive criteria predetermining what form an artwork should take. This was not their job. Their work was to describe artistic perfection already achieved. Seferis thus subordinated national content to aesthetic form. Yet he also made the Hellenic and the aesthetic synonymous, as Yannópulos and others had done before him. Hellenic values consisted of and at the same time constituted whatever was aesthetically legitimate.

In his topography of Hellenism, Seferis traced the spread of Hellenic values from the ancient Greek world to modern Europe. Like demoticists before him, he distinguished the Helladic from the Hellenic, which he favored. Hellenism extended its power over a vast, fertile territory where culture sprouted, matured, scattered, and spread freely, while mainland Hellas suffocated the native Greek population.[11] To qualify further the semantic field of Hellenism, Seferis grafted a synonymous adjective to the noun and coined the term *Ellinikós Ellinismós* 'Hellenic Hellenism'. He gave historical content to this linguistic innovation by way of a narrative. He told of Hellenism's march through ancient, Hellenistic, and Byzantine Greek civilizations into the European Renaissance, which was propelled, he claimed, by displaced Byzantine scholars who left Constantinople after its fall to the Ottomans (1453). The plot thickens as the Helladic world becomes institutionally divided from the Hellenic. With the establishment of the modern state in 1831, Neohellenes regained the potential of assembling Hellenism within a marked geographic space. They might have stationed Hellenism in Hellas and thus made Hellas Hellenic. Hellas remained undeveloped, however, because politicians did not under-

---

[11] Seferis's poem *Mythistorema* (Myth-history or Novel) (10.1–2, 12–17) complains that "our *topos*" has become altogether

> sequestered all mountains
> whose roof is a low sky, day and night.
> . . . .
>   It is shut off
> by the two Symplegades. At the harbors
> where we go on Sundays to breathe freely
> we see under the sun's light
> broken planks from unfinished voyages
> bodies that have forgotten how to love.

Andréas Karandónis first suggested that the sequestering of *topos* here refers to the "Asia Minor disaster," which closed off Neohellenism's physical and imaginary access to Anatolia (Ο ποιητής Γιώργος Σεφέρης [The poet George Seferis] [1963], 111–12).

stand that to establish a Hellenic presence was not only to relocate an actual group in a *topos* but also to develop an entire cultural milieu. Instead they imported a set of foreign values that "had nothing to do with our *topos* at all."[12] Much of what appeared Hellenic to the burgeoning state was in fact foreign to the *topos* of Hellenism.

Yet, according to Seferis's interwar topography, Hellenism continued to exist and spread as an exiled force, as it had in ancient times. By situating Hellenic letters temporarily outside Hellas, Seferis was able to define the conditions for Hellenism's homecoming. From classical times to the present, the "scattering" of "Hellenism far and wide" Hellenized people round the world.[13] It was to Western Europe that Neohellenes would now have to turn for inspiration, according to Seferis. To achieve their *nostos*, they would have to realign their culture with "our *topos*." They could transform the geographic plane of their state into a homeland by developing a genuinely *Hellenic* Hellenic culture: by cultivating a properly Hellenic attitude toward tradition, discovering an artistic form, style, and language appropriate to Hellenism, and so producing an authentically Hellenic product. "Hellenism will show its face when the Greece of today has acquired its own real intellectual character and features. And its characteristics will be the synthesis of all the characteristics of all true works of art which have ever been produced by Greeks."[14]

It is noteworthy that Seferis, a Greek from Asia Minor, typically discovered the characteristics of Hellenic Hellenism in works produced by Greeks of the diaspora—Greeks, that is, who spent much if not all of their life outside Hellas and learned Greek alongside another language. He identified as Hellenic "the deepest features of Calvos, the verses of Solomos, the agony of Palamas, the nostalgia of Cavafy" and even the "brush strokes" of Theotokópulos.[15] With the exception of Kostís Palamás, all lived and worked outside Greece. Their peripheral relationship to the geopolitical territory of Hellas is symptomatic of Seferis's spatial atopia. In his neotraditionalist, West-oriented topography of the homeland, it is not the physical occupation of a place but proper lodging in an aesthetic tradition that places one's work among the "discernible landmarks" of Hellenism.[16]

[12] Seferis, Διάλογος πάνω στην ποίηση (Dialogue on poetry), 101.
[13] Ibid., 99.
[14] Ibid., 102.
[15] Ibid., 101.
[16] Yet Seferis was as interested as any of his contemporaries in "rooting" his work in the *topos* of Hellas. In 1941, his good friend Henry Miller observed: "[Seferis] had

By assigning the value of Hellenism to the work of art, Seferis both defended his affiliation with modernist poetics and recuperated the Hellenic as an approachable though difficult standard of value. This paradoxical joining of the modern with the Hellenic, the modernist, international with a neotraditionalist, national sensibility, is the critical foundation of his work. It should be noted that Seferis consistently— and quite successfully, it should be added—posed as both modern and Hellenic: modern in his aim to investigate new forms, Hellenic in his avowal to search for integration, harmony, tradition.[17] By this equivocation, however, Seferis avoided the issue of crisis that had flooded the domain of culture in the interwar period.

Even more deliberately during the next decade, Seferis sublimated the sense of loss. This is not to say that his poetry does not treat the theme of loss. Indeed the loss of significance, foundations, territory, sacred centers, precious paths, and meaningful contexts are major themes in his work. Yet Seferis's work systematically mystifies the theme, making recovery a matter of transcending history, finding the eternal seed to replay an ancient drama rather than facing the inelegant drama of the present.

The 1940s would witness Seferis's more studied repression of present-day crisis. In the diary entry quoted at the beginning of this chapter, dated Tuesday, 4 June 1946, Seferis evokes an emotional moment of cultural return at the close of World War II. Seferis describes what he calls the *topos* 'excavation site' of the Archaeological Museum in Athens, where statues placed in storage at the beginning of World War II for protection from the invading and later occupying German forces are resurrected from their vaults beneath the floors. This is the "second coming" of Hellenic civilization. The "resurrection of bodies," as Seferis refers to the event, becomes a symbol of the

---

begun to ripen into the universal poet—by passionately rooting himself into the soil of his people" (*Colossus of Maroussi*, 50).

[17] In the Tsátsos-Seferis dialogue, Tsátsos's "Hellenicity" attaches itself to a national referent; Seferis's "Hellenic Hellenism" has an aesthetic referent correlating to a national ideal. Insofar as his concerns are national, Seferis betrays the international spirit of many modernist movements, since "the essence of Modernism is its international character. . . . Modernism, in short, is synonymous with internationalism" (Bradbury and McFarlane, *Name and Nature of Modernism*, 26). He remains a modernist, however, insofar as he translates a discussion about national ideals into one about aesthetic form, a discussion about national style into one about individual style that becomes Hellenic by its very consistency and success. It is in this sense that he poses as both modernist and Hellenic.

poet's return to the light of the Greek landscape as well as a figure for the nation's postwar recovery.

But here is something Seferis's journal entry does not record. From December 1944 through October 1949, a cruel civil war set back reconstructive efforts in Greece. Encouraged if not provoked by leaders in England and the United States who wished to counter possible infiltration into the Western bloc by that other rising superpower, the Soviet Union, the Greek civil war marked the beginning of the cold war, of which Greece was the first theater of operations. Seferis does not name the historical moment with any precision—here or anywhere else. Instead, his emphasis on resurrected bodies and intense emotions buries deep in the eschatology of personal rebirth the fact that Greece is in the midst of civil war. Indeed, his powerful juxtaposition of ancient statues, resurrected bodies, and "crazy" feelings deriving from the land bypasses the historical present by crossing an excavation site and entering a life-bearing, emotion-begetting Greek landscape. Seferis's journal entry elides past and present, archeology and nature, politics and theology, civil war and reconstruction. Thus it is not unimportant words but crucial information that Seferis omits.

In all his journal entries that cover this bloody period, Seferis refused to confront the Greek civil war, making only oblique references to the "machine of hatred," "the black and angelic Attic day," the national "shipwreck."[18] This is also the case in his masterful postwar poem, Κίχλη (Thrush) (1946). Seferis's decision to ignore the civil war was typical of artists and intellectuals who did not have leftist leanings. This was the privilege of the ruling class, to claim a distance from the politics of divisiveness, to view civil strife, unlike world war, as irrelevant to the making and unmaking of culture, nonthreatening to the security of museums. Yet the Greek civil war was precisely a contest to control interpretations of Hellenism, and a violent effort to collapse variant versions of Hellenicity into one. Thus to my mind Seferis's "resurrected bodies" take on a political significance despite themselves. They serve as reminders of a forged Panhellenic union. They become an allegory for efforts to orchestrate harmony in a time of internecine war. Hellenism's second coming appears in this passage in the collage of ancient and modern figures, marble and living torsos freely floating in an ahistorical Greek landscape. These are the distinguishing features both of Seferis's postwar corpus and of the Hellenic world that Greece delivered to the West.

[18] George Seferis, *A Poet's Journal: Days of 1945–1951* (1974), 26, 28.

The Road to *Roma aeterna*?

To recover a deeper place of origin for postwar Hellenism, Seferis related his work explicitly to Greek antiquity, in particular to "the literary tradition whose origin is universally attributed to Homer."[19] Before describing Seferis's technique of reactivating the *topos* of Hellenic tradition, however, it may be useful briefly to refer to a parallel case from postwar German letters that suggests that other Europeans, too, made similar efforts to retrace their present-day origins to an ancestral homeland removed from the contingencies of inter- and intranational strife. The work of E. R. Curtius, a critic of modern literature, provides an analogous example. Like Seferis, Curtius responded to cultural transformations by turning his attention away from the broad synchronic plane of contemporary European literatures to a historical line of classical and medieval texts. If Seferis was excavating a tunnel into Hellenism's older layers, Curtius was "seeking, without being precisely aware of it, the road to Rome." He explains: "Ever since my first visit the city had become for me . . . an ancestral homeland and a goal of pilgrimage. Every fresh sojourn in Rome strengthened this relation to my life. I knew myself bound to the *Roma aeterna*. In the course of years and decades I realized that this bond contained a secret with many layers of symbolic meaning."[20]

In *European Literature and the Latin Middle Ages* (1948), his major philological work from this period of exploration, Curtius studied the "transmigration" of structures, allusions, topics, metaphors, modes of inspiration, and curricula of education in the "great intellectual and spiritual tradition of Western culture" from the classical era through the Latin Middle Ages and into the modern period.[21] He mined the literary past. He traced the development of literature "from Homer to Goethe."[22] As he did this, he found himself "gradually penetrating deeper and deeper into my chosen field of study; new connections and

---

[19] Alexander Argyros, "The Hollow King: A Heideggerian Approach to George Seferis's 'The King of Asine'" (1986–87), 315. Andréas Karandónis felt "that Seferis grows out of the deepest layers of our linguistic existence, that he never for a moment lost the conscience of a witness and the sense of a Hellenic literary responsibility. . . . Seferis's role is to clear a road to the deepest depth—not to the scattered, superficial literary successes of our linguistic truth" (Εισαγωγή στη νεώτερη ποίηση [Introduction to contemporary poetry] [1958], 164–65).

[20] Ernst Robert Curtius, *Essays on European Literature* (1973), 498.

[21] Ernst Robert Curtius, *European Literature and the Latin Middle Ages* ([1948] 1973), x.

[22] Ibid., 12.

cross-connections . . . constantly opening up; in the end, a new line of continuity in the history of European culture . . . becoming discernible." Curtius felt that he had finally discovered a site that "transcended history," a center of culture from which there radiated "a new line of continuity in the history of European culture."[23] This was for Curtius *Roma aeterna*, the "ancestral homeland" of culture's origins.

In the same nostalgic tone sustained by Curtius, Seferis, too, would narrate his literary descent through older layers down to Homer. But Seferis's expressive mode was one of quotation, ellipsis, and elision, not of exploration and analysis. Instead of tracing the connections between things, as Curtius tried to do, Seferis's work would elide differences and omit connections. Thus, even as his poetry excavated origins, even as it dug deeper and deeper into the literary past, it subsumed that past in its present without necessarily making crucial links discernible.

The formal correlative to Seferis's decentered homeland is the familiar literary quotation divested of its material and historical context and identified with the fragmented spirit, body, and reality of Neohellenism. Seferis developed the modernist technique of settling disestablished quotations from classical sources into the newly acclaimed autotelic center of culture, the literary text. With unassimilated quotations connected by meaningful ellipses, he would signal the hidden circumstances of a distant cultural homeland, or, by another metaphor, the deep structure of Hellenism that framed everyday existence.[24]

Seferis's techniques of quotation and ellipsis line up perfectly with his poetry's message. Succinctly stated, there is a persistent theme running through his work, namely, that the present age of exhaustion has made Hellenism's ancestral home indistinguishable from the profane surroundings. Home, having lost its holy congealing powers, has disintegrated and merged into a nondescript setting. Through a vague, undifferentiated space, his poetic persona is condemned to pass like a wandering exile in search of some formula that might ultimately bring into focus the nourishing center of civilization. In the setting of ruined landscapes, dilapidated buildings, and abandoned homes, an aging

---

[23] Ibid., 502.

[24] Robert O. Evans offers this explanation of modernists' affinity for ellipsis: "In their eagerness not to be diffuse, 20th-century poets (especially Pound, Eliot, Auden, William Carlos Williams, etc.) are particularly attracted to the device" (*Princeton Encyclopedia of Poetry and Poetics*, s.v. "ellipse"). On poetic ellipsis, see also J. A. Cuddon, *A Dictionary of Literary Terms* (1979), 216–17.

human body clings desperately to the last vestiges of its eternal core. Its commandment is to hold onto some center even as it deserts familiar places, even as it leans toward its disembodiment.

The scene of loss is set in endless variations in Seferis's work. Seferis's *Roma aeterna* is the home once inhabited or the state of being once occupied. It is difficult to locate precisely home, the significance of separation, or the formula for communal integration. His Δελφοί (Delphi) (1961), for example, is an essay about a *topos* that, from an ancient point of view, was the navel of the earth, where two eagles meet. This is the topography of the center. Seferis describes his search for a common mythology in fallen times, when "Phoebus no longer has a shelter."[25] Under present conditions "the temple becomes a *topos* of tourism, with organized guides showing the sights to the masses. . . . Today the common faith is lost and the people who come each have their own different personal mythology. They read or listen to a guide and, based on this information, add up their own story."[26] The people who make their pilgrimage to Delphi have lost access to the "*topos* set apart from the rest of the world" because they have ceased to share a common mythology.[27] Under these conditions, Delphi is commodified, Seferis complains. To this effect, he ostensibly quotes a ντόπιο 'native, man from inside the *topos*', whose lament that "Delphi has become an endless hotel" bears the authenticity of autochthonous experience.[28]

[25] Δελφοί (Delphi) ([1961] 1981), 150. Apparently, Seferis thought a great deal about how to create a Neohellenic mythology. Dimítris Dimirúlis speculates that Seferis's interest in "collective mythology" stems from his desire to create a broad audience. "Personal mythology was not enough to establish for oneself a national Hellenic audience. Collective mythology, on the other hand, offered the symbols that connect present and past and future, making poetry a matter for a collective body and, finally, for the nation" (Το "Άξιον" της ιστορίας και το "Εστί" της ρητορικής· Κριτική φαντασία σε τοπίο ελληνικό [The "Worthy" of history and the "It is" of rhetoric: Critical imagination in a Greek landscape] [1986], 326).

[26] Δελφοί (Delphi), 145.

[27] Ibid., 140.

[28] For George Seferis, the *laós* 'people' sustain the collective soul, which reveals in turn the truth of ancient Hellenism: "The ancients—if we really want to understand them, we must investigate the soul of our *laós*" ('Ένας Έλληνας—ο Μακρυγιάννης [A Hellene—Makriyánnis], 257). Poets and artists must examine the soul of the people for the transhistorical knowledge it reveals about Hellenism. They must investigate the indigenous expression of the people so as to discover the real Hellenic Hellenism within. Seferis himself discussed folk culture in some of his essays. His method was to isolate and define certain qualities in which one discovered both the real ancients and the true values of Hellenism. For a discussion of related populist trends, see Chapter 6.

Δελφοί (Delphi) suggests one grounding point for the scene of loss in Seferis's work. Perhaps the lost center is Delphi, that sacred *topos* in Hellenism's topography where Hellenism's original integrity might have been maintained had Greeks countered the forces of commodification with a viable collective mythology. Yet Seferis's quotation actually refers the reader to a line in the opening section of *Thrush*. Here the poet describes the conditions under which homes age:

> they wither or smile or even become stubborn
> with those who remain with those who leave
> with others who would return if they could
> or who are lost now that the *cosmos*
> has become an endless hotel.
>
> I.17–21

Here it is the entire *cosmos*, not just a cult center of antiquity, which, emptied today of its life force, merges into an "endless hotel." Through cross-referencing of a remarkable consistency, Seferis's work resonates here and elsewhere with a set of related themes: the commodified body that has lost its soul, the house that is emptied of its occupants, the refugee bereft of home, the landscape of ruins sundered from history and meaning, the literary quotation lacking context.

Although it is impossible to settle finally on a single referent as the ultimate scene of loss in Seferis's work, one may identify literary strategies that mark a fragile center as the origin of deferred signification and link the elusive homeland with a Hellenic ideal. To this end it is useful to study *Thrush*, Seferis's masterful postwar poem, in which the form of the literary quotation and the theme of *nostos* are integrally connected. Here Seferis transposed characters and fragments from ancient sources to a modern setting. Here he used the modernizing force of appropriation to translate "poetry's source" into the confused literary horizon of an elliptical modernist work.[29] Here he adapted the

[29] Long ago, Dionysius of Halicarnassus described Homer as poetry's source. Like Homer's Zeus, he wrote, "we must say that Homer is the one 'from whom all rivers and every sea flows, every spring and great well.' The others who have practiced the same mean are very much his inferiors, though well worth study in their own right" (*On the Arrangement of Words* 23). More recently, Harold Bloom has reaffirmed this belief: "It remains not arbitrary nor even accidental to say that everyone who now reads and writes in the West, of whatever racial background, sex, or ideological camp, is still a son or daughter of Homer" (*The Anxiety of Influence* [1975], 33). Charles Segal uses Bloom's theory about anxious influences to analyze intertexts in Seferis in "Orpheus,

narrative voice of the Homeric epic to new purposes and gave it a new position in the contemporary cultural order.

Although critics have discussed Seferis's incorporation of ancient sources, Homer in particular, they have left the matter of appropriation in Seferis's work largely unexplored.[30] Critical attention has remained fixed on how his poetry is "rooted . . . in a universalizing of deeply felt personal experience or insight."[31] Little effort has been made to discuss how a poem like *Thrush* uses fragments of the past as building blocks to reconstruct the *topos* of "Hellenic Hellenism," ostensibly over and above the war-torn landscape of Hellas.[32] Beyond attempts to trace the author's inspired borrowings, there has been little analysis and certainly no topological mapping of Seferis's foray into older texts.[33]

Here I examine in detail important points of convergence and divergence between the modern text and its sources on the subject of

Agamemnon, and the Anxiety of Influence: Mythic Intertexts in Seferis, *Mythistorema* 3" (1989).

[30] For Seferis's incorporation of ancient sources, particularly Homer, in *Thrush*, see Mark Davis, "Seferis' *Thrush*" (1975); Dimítris N. Maronítis, Η νέκυια της "Κίχλης" (The *nekuia* of *Thrush*) (1984); Nikolareízis, Η παρουσια του Ομήρου (The presence of Homer); George Thaniel, "George Seferis' *Thrush* and the Poetry of Ezra Pound" (1974), id., "George Seferis' *Thrush* and T. S. Eliot's *Four Quartets*" (1976); id., "George Seferis' *Thrush*: A Modern 'Descent'" (1977); id., "The Moon, the Heron, and *The Thrush*: George Seferis, Douglas Lepan, and Greek Myth" (1989); Násos Vayenás, Η γενεαλογία της Κίχλης (Genealogy of *Thrush*) (1974); Anthony N. Zahareas, "George Seferis: Myth and History" (1968). For an insightful discussion of Seferis as a reader of Homer for whom Ithaca "summed up . . . the disorder" of present circumstances, see Ruth Padel, "Homer's Reader: A Reading of George Seferis" (1985), 107–21.

[31] Edmund Keeley, "Seferis and 'Mythical Method'" (1983), 78.

[32] During the 1980s, Seferis's critical strategies came under increasing scrutiny. See Vangelis Calotychos, "The Art of Making Claques: Politics of Tradition in the Critical Essays of T. S. Eliot and George Seferis" (1990); Dimirúlis, "The 'Humble Art' and the Exquisite Rhetoric"; Dionísis Kapsális, Κριτική του ελληνικού μοντερνισμού, Μέρος Α'· Στο φως της απομυθοποίησης (Critique of Hellenic modernism, part A: In the light of demythologization) (1984); id., Κριτική του ελληνικού μοντερνισμού, Μέρος Β'· Στη σκιά του μύθου (Critique of Hellenic modernism, part B: In the shadow of myth) (1984); and Lambropoulos, *Literature as National Institution*, chap. 2.

[33] Davis's closing comments are typical of a certain kind of study that features poetic inspiration drawn from antiquity: "'Thrush' . . . signals the consummation of Seferis's search for a transcendent vision in the apparent absurdity and transience of life. He knows well the loneliness, outrage, bitterness and anguish of the search and of our times, but in the end 'Thrush' comes as an affirmative utterance, an utterance which is also a declaration of faith in contemporary man's ability and desire to divine and welcome the light native to the poem called 'Thrush'" ("Seferis' *Thrush*," 298).

homecoming. I offer a parallel reading of *Thrush* and its most obvious literary reference points, books 10 and 11 of Homer's *Odyssey*, Plato's *Apology*, Sophocles' *Oedipus at Colonus*, and Ezra Pound's *Canto 1*. To explore further Seferis's strategies of appropriation, I also take into account his published commentary on the poem, his diaries from the period of its composition, and other essays. I hold these not as proof of intent but as further evidence of tactics. In particular, I am interested in how and why *Thrush* draws its characters and themes from the locus classicus of descent and return: the Homeric *nekuia*, the *katávasis* 'descent' in modern Greek, the episode in which a living hero descends to the underworld and subsequently returns to the light of home. How does the poem navigate the hero's return home? How does *Thrush* repatriate Odysseus into a contemporary scene of uprootedness and longing? Who provides the key to his *nostos*, and what is that key? What is the significance and effect of certain important ellipses, such as the removal of Teiresias from the scene of descent? More generally stated, how does *Thrush* use the techniques of quotation and ellipsis to salvage a shipwrecked Hellenism? In the final analysis, what is gained or lost in Seferis's postwar reconstruction of Hellenism?

Literary Horizons: *Thrush* and the *Odyssey*

From its opening lines, *Thrush* faces the problem of blocked access to a sacred center of culture. The poetic persona, a modern Odysseus, charts the inhospitable forces of modernity in the first section of the poem, "The House by the Sea"; here he contemplates the fragile qualities of home under the conditions of "war, destruction, migration" (1.2) that break down more permanent walls of refuge. In the poem's second section, "Sensual Elpenor," Odysseus overhears the monologue of a mediocre man, which records the difficulties of living in the undifferentiated spatial continuum of modernity. As he closes in on "The Shipwreck of 'Thrush,'" the third section of the poem, Odysseus draws a circle around a calming and stabilizing center assaulted from the outside by a throng of chaotic voices. The question looming on the poem's horizon is a common one in Seferis's work: what might home be, and how might one reach it when "the world has become an endless hotel"?

The horizon of the poem is drawn on two levels, the one representational and the other intertextual.[34] Both reveal the elusive outline of a *spíti* 'house, home'.[35] First there is the "House by the Sea," which offers a window onto Neohellenic reality: its "empty rooms with an iron-framed bed and nothing of my own" (1.25–27) give the vantage point of displacement. From its window, Odysseus contemplates the shipwreck "Thrush" that went down sometime in World War II and remained unsalvaged throughout the Greek civil war. From here, with no stable, responsive center of refuge to escape the surrounding chaos, the transient literary persona reflects on the qualities of lost homes: "The houses which I had they took away" (1.1). He endows the houses with the properties of *filí* 'race, nation' and age and with feelings that reflect the character of their occupants or the circumstances of their abandonment. Under modern conditions, "houses easily become obstinate" and insensitive to habitation "when you empty them" (1.40). The trait of unresponsiveness is typical of the modern human condition. As people give up ground in war, they begin the endless process of exile and migration. They lose both their distinct place and their ability to respond to others. Conversations become common property. One "Elpenor" in the poem is a typical human shipwreck. He is obsessed by voices and images from the past, haunted by "the fragrance of the absence of a youthful form" (2.46).

Because the horizon of the poem connects it to other texts as well as to other worlds, *Thrush* also underscores the theme of lost homecoming through the citation of older works. By way of indirect references to Circe and Odysseus, direct allusions to Elpenor, and the anticipated appearance of Teiresias, whose presence Socrates and Oedipus eclipse, the poem recalls two familiar episodes from Odysseus's adventures: the encounter with Circe and the journey to "the house of Hades," the best-known *nekuia* in Western literature. *Thrush* identifies the "house by the sea," a sign of the relentless inhospitality of the modern hotel,

[34] "Intertextuality" is a critical term that acquired prominence in the United States after structuralism invaded literary criticism in the late 1960s. The term designates a network of texts that absorb and transform one another, and assumes that "every text is absorption and transformation of a multiplicity of other texts" (Oswald Ducrot and Tzvetan Todorov, *Encyclopedic Dictionary of the Sciences of Languages* [1972], 359).

[35] Demotic Greek does not distinguish between house and home; *spíti* designates both. *Oikos*, a Homeric word for 'dwelling place', also remains in use. Its sense is closer to 'house' (specifically the building structure), since it is marked with the greater formality of a word kept in circulation by the purist idiom that sought to replace vernacular words with ancient ones.

with the houses of both Circe and Hades—both of which are by the
sea, as Homer informs us. The poem then links itself to events that
take place between these two boundary points of Odysseus's adventures and adopts the theme of Odysseus's suspended *nostos* 'homecoming, return to light and life.'

The poem draws its literary connection with the *Odyssey* in the first
section through the person of the narrator, who leans subtly on the
character of Odysseus, the literary figure of instability and *wanderlust*:

> Let us *imagine* then that the one who says "I" in *Thrush* is a certain
> Odysseus. Perhaps this even has the advantage of allowing us to con-
> template that people of some instability, of adventures and war, . . .
> always move between the same monsters and the same desires. In this
> way we hold onto the symbols and names which the myth handed over
> to us—so long as we recognize that the typical characters have been
> transformed in accordance with the passage of time and the changing
> conditions of our world.[36]

Now a nameless resident of modernity's endless hotel, the modern
Odysseus peers out of his temporary shelter while the contemporary
world leaks in. Rather than travel to exotic ports, he waits for others to
visit him, hoping that someone might provide the key for return to the
lost homeland. To put it another way, Odysseus is the modern topographer who, studying the present disarray, attempts to recover the
order of another world.

References to the *Odyssey* become more obvious with the appearance of the "sensual Elpenor" in the second section. A brief narration
of Elpenor's fate in the *Odyssey* might help to establish the connections
between the two poems. Elpenor appears in Odysseus's Phaeacian
tales in the *Odyssey* (books 7–12), which include the hero's journey to
the underworld and his conversations with the dead. As Odysseus
describes preparations for the journey from Circe's halls to Hades, he
recalls the circumstances of Elpenor's accidental death. "There was
one Elpenor, the youngest of all, not exceedingly valiant in war or
well-balanced in his mental powers" (*Odyssey* 10.552–53). Elpenor got
drunk at Circe's, climbed onto her roof for fresh air, and fell asleep. In
the morning rush to prepare for Odysseus's journey to Hades, Elpenor
awoke, forgot where he was, sprang up suddenly, and "tumbled
headlong from the roof; so he broke his neck and his spirit went down

---

[36] Seferis, Μιά σκηνοθεσία (Stage directions), 31–32.

to Hades" (559–60), Odysseus took no notice until he encountered a bitter Elpenor at the gate of Hades. Elpenor told him his story and demanded a proper burial.

The first section of *Thrush* anticipates the visit of the dead man dressed

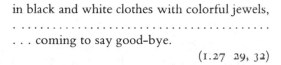

> in black and white clothes with colorful jewels,
> . . . .
> . . . coming to say good-bye.
>
> (1.27 29, 32)

The poem devotes much of the next section to recording Odysseus's recollection of that man's one-sided conversation, overheard on the eve of his death. Here it openly identifies the unfortunate victim with the Homeric Elpenor: "He had the bearing of Elpenor just before his fall and demolition, though he wasn't drunk" (2.4–5). 'A deep-girded, quick-glancing woman' (1.33), a mortal Circe figure, is Elpenor's unsympathetic interlocutor.

> Returning from southerly ports
> Smyrna, Rhodes, Syracuse, Alexandria
> cities closed like hot shutters,
>
> (34–36)

she has become versed in the intoxicating possibilities of "fragrances of golden fruit and herbs" (37) and immune to common suffering (38–39). *Thrush*'s unnamed temptress arouses in Elpenor inexpressible desire.[37]

Elpenor's monologue is an oblique formulation of what he cannot name. The message rides on the metaphor of fragmented statues becoming lifelike and bending in the light. Reverting to the nether world of myth, Elpenor seems to lose himself in the thought that fragments of the past might possess a haunting life of their own, more real than the fleeting present. He privileges broken stones with a permanence the aging body cannot possess. His desire for Circe draws him into the world of the nonrational. He succumbs to his own disintegration of body and will. If the Homeric Elpenor cannot enter

---

[37] Seferis explains that Elpenor metonymically represents all the "mindless and satiated" companions of Odysseus (Μιά σκηνοθεσία [Stage directions], 38); a foil to true heroes, he is typical of the worst "bearers of destruction" (40).

the house of Hades because his corpse remains unburied, the modern Elpenor dwells on the threshold between dead and living because he refuses to come to terms with a modernity that codifies the past as ruin.[38] His way of thinking makes no clear distinction between past and present. For this reason, he can only turn a deaf ear to Circe's persistent, hardheaded reminder: "The statues are in the museum" (2.26 and 54).

Elpenor's intertextual status reflects this temporal and spatial atopia. The transposed quotation evokes Elpenor's homesickness. When Elpenor makes his final appearance in the poem's third section, *Thrush* refers directly to the Homeric passage where the ghost of Elpenor offers to Odysseus his lifeblood, the oar. Here Seferis's appropriation of Homer becomes explicit. We recall Odysseus's encounter with Elpenor at the entrance to the underworld (*Odyssey* 11.51–54). Elpenor approached his leader and requested that his corpse be burned with his armor, a burial mound heaped on the gray sea's shore, and the oar with which he rowed alongside his companions planted in the mound of sand (77–78). The oar is to be a σῆμα *sēma* 'gravestone, sign' marking his fortune ἐσσομένοισι πύθεσθαι 'so that future generations may learn of me' (76). This passage resonates in *Thrush* when Elpenor offers the narrator "the wood that cooled my forehead" as a sign of his toil in "the hours when midday burned my veins." Like Elpenor's oar, the ξύλο *xílo* 'wood' must find its proper end in the hands of others: σε ξένα χέρια θέλει ανθίσει. Πάρ' το, σού το χαρίζω 'it will blossom in someone else's hands. Take it, it's my gift to you' (*Thrush* 3.1–3). Its destiny, however, is altered, since the *xílo* 'wood' must now blossom in living hands rather than mark a resting place for the dead.[39]

The extensive allusion to Elpenor prepares the scene for new literary encounters, which first reach into the heart of the *Odyssey*, then

[38] For the Homeric Elpenor to pass into Hades, he must receive a proper burial, something he motivates by threats: "Do not leave me behind unwept and unburied when you go back there, / lest I bring upon you the wrath of some god" (*Odyssey* 11.72–73).

[39] Seferis's image of "the wood" blossoming into another's hands also counteracts Achilles' absolute claim in his oath sworn on Agamemnon's scepter than cut wood οὔ ποτε φύλλα καὶ ὄζους φύσει . . . οὐδ' ἀναθηλήσει 'will never again grow leaves and branches . . . nor will it ever blossom' (*Iliad* 1.234–36). Seferis radically revises the archaic view of an absolute distinction between the living and the dead. For the modern poet, a living spirit never completely runs its course; instead it passes into new things, for example, the modern poem, and gives them life.

suddenly swerve toward other texts. Elpenor receives no recognition or thanks for his gift of "the wood" because the narrator's attention is already drawn elsewhere along the horizon of the *Odyssey*:

> Κι άλλες φωνές σιγά σιγά με τη σειρά τους
> ακολούθησαν· ψίθυροι φτενοί και διψασμένοι
> που βγαίνουν από του ήλιου τ' άλλο μέρος το σκοτεινό.
> Θά 'λεγες γύρευαν να πιούν αίμα μια στάλα·
> ήτανε γνώριμες μα δέν μπορούσα να τις ξεχωρίσω.
> (*Thrush* 3.12–16)

> Other voices slowly followed
> one by one; whispers thin and thirsty
> coming out of the sun's dark side;
> you would say they were looking to drink a drop of blood;
> familiar voices, but I couldn't distinguish them.

This passage clearly alludes to the description of the ghastly throng that encircled Odysseus at the house of Hades:

> αἱ δ' ἀγέροντο
> ψυχαὶ ὑπὲξ Ἐρέβευς νεκύων κατατεθνηώτων. . . .
> . . . .
> οἳ πυλλοὶ περὶ βόθρον ἐφοίτων ἄλλοθεν ἄλλος
> θεσπεσίῃ ἰαχῇ· ἐμὲ δὲ χλωρὸν δέος ᾕρει.
> (*Odyssey* 11.36–37, 42–43)

> There gathered
> spirits of the dead out of Erebus. . . .
> . . . .
> The throng moved toward the bloody pit from every side
> with a deafening shout; and pale fear seized me.

As *Thrush* reaches this moment of near convergence with the *Odyssey*, it becomes possible to assess the relationship of the modern to the ancient poem. Poetic recollection has effaced the distinctive outlines of epic figures and whatever narrative detail might be incongruous with the modern setting. At the same time, it highlights features especially suited to the tenor of times. The once insignificant Elpenor takes center stage. Recognizable Homeric elements, the dark scenery of Erebus (το σκοτεινό *to skotinó* 'that which is dark' in *Thrush*), the throng thirsting for blood, all these things are transported into the modern poem, but the narrator's reaction remains muted, appropriately so, perhaps, for the poem's unheroic setting.

With the approach of the thirsty throng, *Thrush* takes a step toward what is arguably the center of the *Odyssey*, the exchange between the hero and Teiresias, which is the goal of Odysseus's underworld journey "to the halls of Hades and dreaded Persephone" (*Odyssey* 10.491). As Circe explains:

> you will consult the spirit of the Theban Teiresias
> the blind seer whose mental powers are still intact;
> for Persephone provided him with a mind even after death
> so that he alone has *noos* [understanding], while others flit about like
>   shadows.
>
> (10.492–95)

In the underworld, Odysseus discovers that none of the spirits—not even his mother—is capable of recognizing him before drinking his offering of dark blood. The exception is Teiresias, who "recognized me and addressed me: 'Son of Laertes, sprung from Zeus, Odysseus of many devices!'" (11.91–92). Teiresias drinks from the blood and forthwith pronounces the crucial word, *nostos* (100), which he alone can dispatch. Teiresias thus becomes the guide for Odysseus's safe return to the light of home.

Teiresias's oracular procedure is to place *epi phresi* 'in the mind' of Odysseus the proper *sēma* 'sign', which should not escape the hero's notice (11.126). He identifies Poseidon as the god who is detaining Odysseus (101–3). He entreats Odysseus to curb the appetite of his companions when he arrives at Thrinacia and finds Helios's fatted flocks grazing there (104–14). He describes a woeful state of affairs in Ithaca. He predicts Odysseus's violent revenge against Penelope's voracious suitors. Finally, he describes the subsequent inland journey that Odysseus is to make and the unmistakable *sēma*, the misnamed oar, that will indicate his wanderings are over.

The latter is a strange and haunting story, recounted by Odysseus after his return to Ithaca but never fulfilled in the epic:

> Then you will take up a well-shaped oar and go
> until you come to a place where men do not know the sea
> or eat food mixed with salt;
> they do not know purple-prowed ships
> or well-shaped oars, like wings to ships.
> A clear and inescapable sign I give you:

when another traveler encountering you
says that you are holding a winnowing shovel over your famed
   shoulder,
then you shall plant the well-shaped oar in the earth
and make sacrifices to lord Poseidon
a sheep and a bull and a mounting boar
and depart for home and offer sacred hecatombs
to the immortal gods who hold broad heaven
each in order. Death will then come to you from the sea, a gentle
   death,
when you are quietly overcome with old age, and your people
will be prosperous. These things I have spoken truthfully to you.
                              (*Odyssey* 11.121–37)

Since the journey is not made in the epic, the prediction appears
without closure. This seems to contradict the seer's word: for he
stresses that he has spoken νημερτέα 'truthfully' (137) and given a
σῆμα . . . ἀριφραδές, οὐδέ σε λήσει 'clear and inescapable sign'
(126). Perhaps the story is taken up in another epic, or deliberately
unrealized in the Homeric poem so as to tease the audience and suggest
that the greatest of journeys are never really complete. Perhaps there
are just too many inconsistencies in the *Odyssey*.

These are plausible suggestions, though not altogether satisfying.
The appeal to aesthetic interpretations of closure or compositional
theories about the epic poem's multiple layering does not do away
with the sense that the epic tradition has a functional self-sufficiency,
developed "within the *social* framework of performer-audience interaction."[40] Both the *Iliad* and the *Odyssey* serve social purposes that
somehow make themselves manifest in the poems: "Between the two
of them, the *Iliad* and the *Odyssey* manage to incorporate and orchestrate something of practically everything that was once thought worth
preserving from the Heroic Age."[41]

Given the orchestration of a complex of social signs within the
Odyssey, we might consider carefully how the poem indicates the
fulfillment of Teiresias's prophecy in its narration of Odysseus's wanderings and *nostos*. To this end, one should not overlook the significance of the ἐρετμός *eretmos* 'oar' as a sign of the journey's closure. We
saw that Elpenor also commands his leader to plant an oar in the shore

[40] Gregory Nagy, *Comparative Studies in Greek and Indic Meter* (1974), 11.
[41] Gregory Nagy, *The Best of the Achaeans: Concepts of the Hero in Archaic Greek Poetry* (1979), 18.

by the sea as a *sēma* 'sign' (11.75) of his toil and, in his case, a *sēma* 'gravestone' to mark his death. After returning from Hades, Odysseus puts his companion to rest:

> τύμβον χεύαντες καί ἐπὶ στήλην ἐρύσαντες
> πήξαμεν ἀκροτάτῳ τύμβῳ εὐῆρες ἐρετμόν.
>
> (12.14–15)

> piling up a mound and drawing up a pillar,
> we stuck a well-shaped oar at the top of the mound.

The oar that Odysseus plants may not be the *sēma* 'sign' of which Teiresias has spoken. After all, Odysseus fixes this oar in a mound *near* the sea rather than "where men do not know the sea" (11.124), in the middle rather than at the end of his adventures. Yet Elpenor's unusual burial may suggest something of the significance of Teiresias's story. If the oar planted in Elpenor's mound signifies the end of the oarsman's toil and offers a lesson for others, the oar planted away from the sea may also indicate both the completion and the meaning of the hero's contest with the elements. In each case, the oar is a sign that closes a period of restless wandering and institutes learning for others.

The knowledge that Odysseus bears to the uninformed is not confined to the lessons of the oar, however, as may be the case with Elpenor. A much-quoted line from the *Odyssey*'s opening informs us of the outcome of the hero's wanderings: πολλῶν δ' ἀνθρώπων ἴδεν ἄστεα καὶ νόον ἔγνω 'he saw many cities of men and learned their *noos*' (1.3). Odysseus's special power is his ability to recognize the *noos* 'mind, way of thinking' of others by the power of his own *noos*, and to act accordingly. It is this that distinguishes him from his *nēpioi* 'childish, senseless' companions.

This possession of *noos* also bears upon Odysseus's relationship with Teiresias. We have already seen that Teiresias retains the power of *noos* even after his passage into Hades. The gift of interpreting *terata*, another word for 'signs', more specifically, 'signs or wonders through which people might read the future', is encoded into his identity as *teres-ias* 'one having to do with signs'.[42] This makes Teiresias the appropriate guide for Odysseus, whose special power is his ability to recognize the *noos* of others. Teiresias is ideally suited to offering

[42] Pierre Chantraine (*Dictionnaire étymologique de la langue grecque* [1977]) and Hjalmar Frisk (*Griechisches etymologisches Wörterbuch* [1961]) agree that Teres-ias (Teiresias in epic poetry, with the first syllable augmented for metrical reasons) is derived from the noun *teras* 'a significant sign or token'.

Odysseus insight into significant matters such as his elusive *nostos*, the goal of his wanderings.[43]

Furthermore, *nostos* shares an etymological root with *noos*.[44] As Teiresias delivers the *sēma* 'sign' of *nostos* 'return, homecoming', Odysseus applies his *noos* 'mind' to decode this *sēma* and thus bring about his *nostos*. Gregory Nagy describes the process of encoding and decoding *nostos* thus:

> The seer Teiresias is giving a *sēma* to Odysseus, and the follow up expression "and it will not escape your mind" raises the expectation that getting the sign is linked with its recognition. The word *nóos* is indeed overtly linked with the concept of *sēma* here, but the attention is as much on the *encoding* and on the *decoding* of the sign. The narrative stresses that Teiresias, who is giving the *sēma* to Odysseus, is exceptional among the *psūkhaí* in Hades in that his cognitive faculties—or *phrénes*—are intact (x 493): it is because Persephone had given him *nóos* (x 494). This *sēma*, then, is implicitly encoded by the *nóos* of Teiresias—and presumably must be decoded by the *nóos* of Odysseus.[45]

Although the *Odyssey* does not give special status to any one event above others as the sign of homecoming, nevertheless there are several important junctures in the epic where Odysseus is seen to apply his skill of *noos* with the effect of moving one step closer to returning home, securing his rule, and teaching others the lessons of the sea. Those are the three signs of his successful rehabilitation. In each case the hero appears to fulfill Teiresias's odd prophecy by instituting learning from his own example. One crux appears late in book 11, when the Phaeacian king Alkinoos 'the one of powerful mind', whose mental powers are encoded in his name, interrupts Odysseus's story to observe that the teller has the unusual gift of speech coupled with a powerful mind:

> On you is the grace of *epos* and in you are noble *phrenes*.
> You tell your *mūthos* with skill like a minstrel—
> the one about all the Argives' and your own grievous sufferings.
> (11.367–69)

[43] See *Odyssey* 11.100, quoted above.

[44] On the etymology of *noos* see D. Frame, *The Myth of Return in Early Greek Epic* (1978), 1–5. Frame offers formal evidence that *noos* and *nostos* derive from the same Indo-European root-verb, *nes-*, 'return to light and life'. See also his "Origins of Greek ΝΟΥΣ" (1971).

[45] Gregory Nagy, "*Sēma and Nóēsis*: The Hero's Tomb and the 'Reading' of Symbols in Homer and Hesiod" (1990), 212. This article, with the title "*Sēma and Nóēsis*: Some Illustrations," initially appeared in *Arethusa* 16 (spring-summer 1983): 35–55.

Odysseus then resumes his narration, showing precisely how he uses his twin gifts to graft his own ten-year plight to the epic of the ten-year Trojan War, and so to confirm his special greatness among the illustrious Argives. It is the signature of Odysseus alone that he applies his *noos* to gain a safe *nostos*, and that he applies the power of *epos* 'speech' to transform his suspended homecoming into *mūthos* 'myth'. Even with this first-person narration of descent into Hades, Odysseus is shown eternalizing the values of mind and speech in myth, thus securing authority over each new audience through the ages. One might argue, then, that the epic depicts its *telos* in this scene: what Odysseus is doing here in book 11 of the *Odyssey*, artfully telling his story to the Phaeacians, is proof that Teiresias's sign—the mark of authority in the epic tradition—has not escaped him; the *nostos* of eternal *mūthos* belongs to the hero of the *Odyssey*.

Another important modernist poem bears witness to the irretrievable social and cultural context of the epic exchange of signs. I refer to Ezra Pound's first *Canto*, which Seferis translated into Greek in 1939.[46] This poem offers an archaizing English rendition of a Latin version of *Odyssey* 11, translated by the obscure Andreas Divus in 1538.[47] It faithfully recounts Odysseus's descent "to the place / Aforesaid by Circe" (17–18), his meeting with Elpenor, "pitiful spirit" (26), and his initial neglect of Anticlea "whom I beat off" (58). When the poem reaches the interview between the peregrinating hero and "Tiresias Theban," however, it takes a significant turn away from its textual source, though not from Teiresias. The soothsayer appears, gives his sign of recognition, then asks: "A second time? why? man of ill star, / facing the sunless dead and this joyless region?" (60–61). Here he addresses not the hero who reportedly traveled to Hades in mythic times but the twentieth-century literary persona who intends to retell this event.

After drinking the blood, "Tiresias Theban" divines a familiar answer, but in the third person: "Odysseus / Shalt return through spiteful Neptune, over dark seas, / Lose all companions" (65–67).

---

[46] Seferis's translations of *Cantos* 1, 13, and 30 appeared as Ezra Pound, Τρία "Canto" (Ezra Pound, Three "Cantos") in the journal *Ta néa grámmata* (April–June 1939) and are reprinted in his volume of translations, Αντιγραφές (Copyings) (1965). See Thaniel, "George Seferis' *Thrush* and the Poetry of Ezra Pound." For a discussion of Ezra Pound's poetic uses of Hellenism, see Martha E. Klironomos, "Formation of the Nation/State: Hellenism in the Poetry of Ezra Pound, William Butler Yeats, and Odysseas Elytis" (1993).

[47] George Kearns, *Guide to Ezra Pound's Selected Cantos* (1980), 18.

With the shift in address, the context of the prophecy also shifts. No longer does Teiresias address the hero of the *Odyssey*; instead he reports his prediction of Odysseus's pitiful homecoming to the suddenly anonymous narrator, who is himself given no such reassurance. There follows a series of interruptions, so that the message of a prospective homecoming reaches the reader only through a mass of "cultural layering"—that is to say, through numerous voices that have edited, revised, translated, interpreted, or in some way appropriated Homer's *Odyssey*.[48] Pound's homesick modern persona has such great difficulty hearing Teiresias's response that he registers a complaint to the noisy translator: "Lie quiet Divus. I mean, that is Andreas Divus / In officina Wecheli, 1538, out of Homer" (68–69). Other voices interject from the Babel-like configuration.[49] These, too, relay the message that numerous literary voyagers stand between moderns and ancients—so many, in fact, that the scene of pure origins remains hopelessly out of reach. Through the din of literary interjections, the modern poet makes his own voice heard by this seemingly nonsensical addendum: "So that" (76). This is his introduction to the 116 cantos that follow. In an age when poets' too great consciousness of secondariness has blocked passage to the original centers of culture,[50] Pound attempts to project the fresh voice of a modern medley.[51] He offers songs with

[48] Kearns documents these sources and adds: "Once we are aware of all the voices in the *Canto*—Homer, Virgil, Divus, the Cretan, the Anglo Saxon bard, Pound—we see more clearly in the structure of the *Canto* one of Pound's essential methods, 'cultural overlaying'" (*Guide to Cantos*, 21). Seferis calls this technique a "mosaic" of words (Αντιγραφές [Copyings], 151).

[49] Lines 71–76 are rich in cultural layering. They refer first to "the Cretan," Georgius Dartone, who called himself Cretensis and translated *Homeric Hymns* into Latin. Aphrodite is then described in both Latin and Greek as *veneranda* 'worthy of worship' in her "orichalchi" 'bronze' form. The "golden bough" plucked by Aeneas before his descent into Avernus—a descent that echoes the *nekuia* of Odysseus—is that bough made familiar to an English-speaking audience by James George Frazer.

[50] This inconclusive finale may be supplemented by Pound's programmatic statement: "Quite simply: I want a new civilization. It must be *as good* as the best that has been. It can't possibly be the same, so why worry, novelty is enforced" [1928] (quoted in Kearns, *Guide to Cantos*, 23; Kearns supplies the date 1928 but no precise reference).

[51] James Longenbach argues that the full effect of literary quotation in Pound's work is something more than pastiche: it is an "imaginative reconstruction" of the literary past: "Just as Odysseus gives life to ghosts, Pound gives his own life to a dead poet, translating Divus's translation of Homer into English and filtering the result through the ancient rhythms of 'The Seafarer'. . . . Pound's poem including history begins with an invocation of the dead, a seance that reveals how historical knowledge is acquired by infusing the ghosts of the past with the life of the present" (*Modernist Poetics of History: Pound, Eliot, and the Sense of the Past* [1987], 17 18).

deliberate anachronisms and simultaneous readings from Homer to
Ovid, troubadour tales to Renaissance history, Chinese calligraphy to
ideograms.

Declarations of Ignorance, Modernist Ellipses, and the Return to Light

Seferis takes a very different approach from Pound in his appropriation of Homer.[52] He omits Teiresias's divinations entirely and dangles
in their place a literary quotation from another canonical classical text,
Plato's *Apology*:

> Κι ά με δικάσετε να πιώ φαρμάκι, ευχαριστώ·
> δίκιο σας θα 'ναι το δίκιο μου· πού να πηγαίνω
> γυρίζοντας σε ξένους τόπους, ένα στρογγυλό λιθάρι.
> Το θάνατο τον προτιμώ·
> ποιός πάει για το καλύτερο ο θεός το ξέρει.
>
> (*Thrush* 3.20–25)

> And if you condemn me to drink poison, I thank you;
> your justice will be my justice; why should I go
> wandering through foreign *topoi* like a rolling stone.
> I prefer death; god knows who goes to the better lot.

These words recall the conclusion of the *Apology*: ὁπότεροι δὲ ἡμῶν
ἔρχονται ἐπὶ ἄμεινον πρᾶγμα, ἄδηλον, παντὶ πλὴν τῷ θεῷ 'which
of the two of us goes to a better lot is not evident to anyone except the
god' (42a). *Thrush*'s turn from Homer to Plato comes at a crucial
point, indicating an adjustment of textual strategies. Until this moment, Homeric figures and episodes appeared as foils for a modern
quest for home. They added literary depth by marking major continuities and ruptures between the archaic order—with its hierarchy
of gods and heroes—and the contemporary world—with its over-

---

[52] One might also consider another poem where Teiresias is the presiding consciousness, Eliot's *Waste Land*, which Seferis also translated into Greek. See especially
part 3, with Eliot's invaluable commentary on the persona of the poem. Longenbach
observes that Tiresias (like Pound, Eliot employs a non-Homeric spelling) "was to
function not only as the 'most important personage in the poem' but as an observing
consciousness who can penetrate the everyday world of Sunday outings and closed
carriages to 'trace the cryptogram' of a higher reality—transforming that everyday
reality into a visionary world of myth" (*Modernist Poetics of History*, 214). The voice of
Tiresias "*seems* to be the voice of history itself, an expression of the 'entire past' woven
into the texture of the present" (208).

whelming chaos. The unexpected quotation from another major text, however, complicates the intertextual horizon, deters the Homeric *sēma* 'sign' of *nostos*, and relocates the cultural center of the poem.

One may recall that the virtues attached to the figure of Socrates are *sophia* 'wisdom' and *dikē* 'justice'. Contrary to the Homeric value of *noos* 'mind', Socratic wisdom is acquired through an ironic profession of ignorance and fearless submission to the unknown. In the *Apology*, Socrates defends his reputation as *sophōtatos* 'the wisest' ironically by admitting his ignorance, specifically on the subject of death: "To fear death, gentlemen, is nothing else than to think one is wise when one is not; for it is thinking one knows what one does not. No one knows whether death is not the greatest of all blessings to man, yet they fear it as if they know that it is the greatest form of evil" (*Apology* 29a).

When Socrates chooses death as his punishment, he offers τοῦ θείου σημείου 'the divine *sēmeion* [sign]' (40b) as proof that he may meet with a better fate than his accusers: 'for the customary *sēmeion* would surely have opposed me, if I had not been going to meet with something good" (40c). As he submits to Athenian law, Socrates pronounces his final words, through which he derives the ultimate argumentative advantage by claiming that his accusers are no less ignorant than he is about the quality of their future: ἐμοὶ μὲν ἀποθανουμένῳ, ὑμῖν δὲ βιωσομένοις· ὁπότεροι δὲ ἡμῶν ἔρχονται ἐπὶ ἄμεινον πρᾶγμα, ἄδηλον, παντὶ πλὴν τῷ θεῷ 'I am about to die, while you will continue to live; which of the two of us goes to a better lot is not evident to anyone except the god' (42a). These are the passages that *Thrush* incorporates into its scene of descent. The modern poem gives prominence to Socrates' calm submission to fate ("And if you condemn me to drink poison, I thank you"), his compliance with the ruling system of justice ("your justice will be my justice"), and his loyalty to place ("why should I go wandering through foreign *topoi* like a rolling stone"), but also to his plea of ignorance and his deferral to "god" on the subject of unknown destinations: "I prefer death; god knows who goes to the better lot."

One should not overlook the fact, either, that Socrates' modern declaration of agnosticism is heard from *to skotinó* 'that which is dark' (*Thrush* 3.14). In Seferis's poetic corpus, this word becomes a figure for the meaningful "void behind the mask" of perceptible existence.[53]

---

[53] The phrase "void behind the mask" occurs in "The King of Asine," which names the generative void ἕνα σημείο σκοτεινό 'a dark point or sign' (line 29). In his deconstructive reading of the poem, Kapsális takes this "dark sign" as evidence both of

Set in plain analogy to the *Apology*'s ἄδηλον *adēlon* 'that which is not evident, invisible, obscure, inscrutable', *to skotinó* represents that site where human language and perception reach a productive stopping point. Even more resonant is the allusion to the *Republic*'s dark cave (book 7). There an elect group from the multitude imprisoned with backs facing the sunlit exit frees itself from the bonds of illusion when it perceives the bondage of the human senses, and passes from reliance on ephemeral physical sensations to the use of reason and finally to insight into the absolute. The image of a *skotinó* 'dark' or blind side of human existence in *Thrush* signifies a deeper understanding of things hidden from plain view. This understanding can be claimed only by a Socratic turn, that is to say, through a declaration of ignorance about origins and destinations. Indeed, it is a Socratic declaration of ignorance that provides the key for a return to light. In *Thrush*, Socratic ignorance takes the place of the Teiresian *sēma* of *noos* and *epos*, by which the Homeric Odysseus transformed his suffering into *mūthos* 'story', brought closure to his journey, and instituted learning for others.

Seferis offers this explanation of "why there was this replacement of Teiresias by Socrates in *Thrush*": "My first answer is this: because I sensed that the *tónos* [tone] of the whole which I was trying to create was elsewhere; I didn't even consider the Theban. Then—autobiographically speaking—because the *Apology* is a text that greatly influenced me in my life; perhaps because my generation grew up and lived in a period of injustice. Third, because I have a very organic intuition that identifies humanity with the Hellenic *physis*."[54] The first point that Seferis makes is predictable enough. Aesthetic criteria concerning the "*tónos* of the whole" bear final weight in the poet's decision to incorporate certain sources and discard others. Seferis imagines the poetic work harmoniously reorganizing literary particles drawn from a synchronically available tradition. This calls to mind T. S. Eliot's idea of the poetic whole as the harmonization of historical layers, in which older layers resonate with the more recent "particles" and together form a new whole.[55] Eliot's influential essay "Tradition and the

---

"mythopoeia which demythologizes itself" and of "the process of demythologizing which in turn becomes blind" (Κριτική του ελληνικού μοντερνισμού [Critique of Hellenic modernism], B, 45).

[54] Seferis, Μιά σκηνοθεσία (Stage directions), 54.

[55] Seferis systematically discussed and translated Eliot's work into Greek. His translation of *The Waste Land* in 1936 included a lengthy introduction; this truly introduced the American poet to the Greek cultural scene. Seferis's essay, Κ. Π. Καβάφης, Θ. Σ.

Individual Talent" (1920) describes tradition as the cumulative pool of literary material surviving from all ages.[56] All texts have a "simultaneous existence."[57] That is to say, they exist contemporaneously and are synchronically available to the poet both in principle—in that they can be read and understood with a properly receptive attitude—and in fact—since they are housed together in vast libraries. Writing involves selecting from this cumulative "living whole."[58] The conscious or unconscious borrowing of existing images and phrases then unites with the poet's experience "to form a new compound."[59] Older layers must resonate with the more recent "particles" to form a new whole. Such a resonance is what Seferis calls the *tónos* of the poem. He therefore argues that the choice of Socrates over Teiresias makes for the organic coherence of the whole, so that it meets with the standard of "the harmonious word." And Seferis gives special emphasis to the word "*harmonious*, in the sense of the attention paid to the connection, flow, correspondence, and contrast of one idea or feeling with another."[60]

Seferis's second point about the substitution of Socrates for Teiresias derives from personal experience. Here he offers the *Apology* as the appropriate antidote to contemporary injustices—perhaps having to do with the civil war? One can only guess, since Seferis avoids mentioning specifics, as it is his custom to avoid making clear references to the sordid details of present-day Greek politics.

With his third statement of justification, however, Seferis seems to move in another direction altogether: "I have a very organic intuition that identifies humanity with the Hellenic *physis*." This sentence involves several crucial ellipses, which, only when elaborated, connect it with the matter at hand: Socrates' particular mediation of homecoming in *Thrush*.[61] Seferis neglects to elucidate the connection between

---

Ἐλιοτ· Παράλληλοι (C. P. Cavafy, T. S. Eliot: Parallel cases) ([1947] 1981) became another standard work on Eliot. On Seferis's and Eliot's parallel strategies of self-promotion, see Calotychos, "The Art of Making Claques."

[56] For an interesting discussion of Eliot's uses of tradition, see Gregory S. Jay, *T. S. Eliot and the Poetics of Literary History* (1983); and Sean Lucy, *T. S. Eliot and the Idea of Tradition* (1960). Jay relates important contemporary theories of the poetics of tradition to the influential views of Eliot.

[57] T. S. Eliot, "Tradition and the Individual Talent" (1920), 49.

[58] Ibid., 50.

[59] Ibid., 55.

[60] Seferis, Μιά σκηνοθεσία (Stage directions), 53.

[61] As always, ellipsis is at work in Seferis's rhetoric. Critics have mistakenly interpreted Seferis's brevity as a sign of simplicity, humility, and directness. See, for

"humanity" and Socrates, though one may infer this from his earlier claim: "In *Thrush*, the interpreter of homecoming is not Teiresias, but someone whom I feel to be more human than Teiresias: the one who is just."[62] Perhaps he associates Socrates with "humanity" because of his interest in justice. Without warning, however, Seferis introduces the subject of "the Hellenic *physis*," with its geographical and racial connotations. How can one justify Seferis's appeal to "the Hellenic *physis*" as a final factor deciding which trait (humanity, say, as opposed to the gift of divining the future) his poem should admit at its crux? Even references to harmony and *tónos*—aesthetic criteria that subject the "particle" to the demands of the "whole"—do not adequately anticipate the movement to *physis*, or to the specification that this is Hellenic.

The poem exhibits similar ellipses. Leaping from Socratic agnosticism to the narrator's prophetic complaint about place, *Thrush* laments a modern condition in which *ílios* 'sun' and *ánthropos* 'human being', two important attributes of the land, are not adequately appreciated:

Χώρες του ήλιου και δεν μπορείτε ν' αντικρίσετε τον ήλιο.
Χώρες του ανθρώπου και δεν μπορείτε ν' αντικρίσετε τον άνθρωπο.

(3.25–26)

Lands of the *ílios*, and yet you cannot face the *ílios*.
Lands of *ánthropos*, and yet you cannot face *ánthropos*.

These two terms, *sun* and *man*, are bound together under the rubric To φως *To fos* 'The Light', the subtitle of the poem's closing section. Light is something one experiences properly only when one has lived long enough, the narrator asserts:

As the years pass
the critics who condemn you multiply;
as the years pass and you converse with fewer voices
you observe the sun with different eyes.

(3.27–30)

example, Yánnis Dállas, Μιά αίσθηση πέρα από τον Καβάφη· Με το κλειδή της Κίχλης (A feeling beyond Cavafy: With *Thrush* as key) (1981), 303. For a critical analysis of Seferis's rhetoric of simplicity, see Dimirúlis, "The 'Humble Art' and the Exquisite Rhetoric."
[62] Seferis, Μιά σκηνοθεσία (Stage directions), 52.

Passage beyond a devalued modern existence to a real *nostos* 'home-coming, return to light and life,' is, as I have suggested, the *telos* of the poem. The poem traces the path of return through eminent literary sources that lead, as it suggests, back to the physical landscape of Hellas radiating with light. Culture emanates from "the light" of the Hellenic *topío* 'landscape' in this literary topography of Hellenism. Neohellenic poetry as well as the Homeric epics, the tragedies of Aeschylus, and the philosophy of Anaximander and Heraclitus all constitute sophisticated but "natural" reactions to the element of light.

Here Seferis's critical thinking reveals its ultimate debt to aesthetic nationalism, in particular, to Yannópulos's ideas examined in the previous two chapters. Indeed, the fact that Seferis so deftly elides humanity with the Hellenic *physis* suggests that postwar Neohellenism had come to presuppose a natural link between a particular physical landscape and certain ways of behaving, feeling, seeing, and appreciating things. If Seferis unequivocally claims to experience "the condition of nonexistence, the abolition of the self . . . when facing the grandeur of certain foreign *topía* [landscapes]," on the one hand, and senses a "humanizing function" in "the principally Hellenic natural *topía*" filled with *fos* 'light', on the other hand, this has become a *koinos topos* of postwar Neohellenic thought.[63] The light of the Hellenic *topío* 'landscape' is seen ultimately to merge with a living force that runs through not only "the blood of man" but also the cultural tradition of Hellenism, from Homer to the present: "It's so simple: Imagine that the light of day and the blood of Man are the same thing? *How* deeply can one actually experience this? . . . If the humanizing function which I referred to gave birth to the *Odyssey*, *how* far can we actually *see* the *Odyssey*?"[64]

I would argue that the conflation of culture and nature is a fundamental feature of *Thrush*. The poem renders the literary *topos* of cultural return identical with return to the physical *topos* of Hellas, with its dominant characteristic of *fos* 'light'. We might briefly summarize how the poem conflates culture and nature, tradition and geography, in the *topos* of return. First, literary quotation from ancient sources lays the foundation for return. Then, not only do the modernist techniques of quotation and ellipsis render the distant past more hospitable to

[63] Ibid., 54–55.
[64] Ibid., 55–56.

latecomers who suffer under the burden of their ancestors' priority;[65] they also mark the boundaries of home for a fragmented and scattered tradition. Finally, if the poem defines the condition of modernity as a loss of home, the literary sign of Socratic agnosticism provides the means for homecoming. The modern reader is called upon to recognize the limits of knowledge as a precondition for reaching Hellenism's natural home, the *fos* 'light' of the Greek landscape.[66]

As the last section of the poem develops, references to ancient sources increasingly enter into conjunction with one another. *Thrush* incorporates fragments from other venerated texts, including loose translations from Aeschylus's *Prometheus Bound* (3.57), the *Iliad* (58), Sophocles' *Oedipus at Colonus* (59ff.), Vintzéntzos Kornáros's *Erotokritos* (65), Hesiod's *Theogony* (72), *Pervigilium veneris* (74), and, once again, the *Odyssey* (80). The reference to Oedipus is extensive and worth examining, particularly for the way it integrates Oedipus's reported benefit to Athens in its Socratic sign of a return to light. Here literary quotation takes the form of an apostrophe to the ambivalent "light" of religious revelation:

> Αγγελικό και μαύρο φως
> γέλιο των κυμάτων στις δημοσιές του πόντου,
> δακρυσμένο γέλιο
> σε βλέπει ο γέροντας ικέτης
> πηγαίνοντας να δρασκελίσει τις αόρατες πλάκες
> καθρεφτισμένο στο αίμα του
> που γέννησε τον Ετεοκλή και τον Πολυνείκη.
> (*Thrush* 3.56–62)

> Angelic and black light
> laughter of the waves on the crossroads of the sea,
> tearful laughter,
> it's you the old suppliant sees

[65] I refer to Bate (*Burden of the Past*), who argues that tradition became a burden only when specific cultural conditions occurred. An increase in the means of distributing and preserving literature, which resulted in the expansion of archives available at a given time to a poet, a deepening self-consciousness about the wealth of this legacy, and an imperative that (new) poetry be original combined to create a sense that the possibilities of language were being exhausted and that the poet had to work against very difficult odds.

[66] Seferis identifies the *fos* 'light' as the new home of Odysseus, "*his own* home, the home to which Odysseus wishes to return" (Μιά σκηνοθεσία [Stage directions], 50).

going to cross the invisible fields
light mirrored in his blood
which bore Eteocles and Polyneices.

Clearly αγγελικό και μαύρο φως *angelikó ke mávro fos* 'angelic and black light' refers the reader to the Sophoclean text's φῶς ἀφεγγὲς *phōs aphenges* 'blind light' (*Oedipus at Colonus* 1549), just as "the old suppliant . . . going to cross the invisible fields" brings to view Oedipus passing the ultimate threshold at Colonus, today one of Athens's working-class neighborhoods.

In *Oedipus at Colonus*, the wandering Oedipus, blinded by his own hands and exiled by his own decree, finds refuge in Colonus, though not without facing hostility from a chorus of Athenian elders. A suppliant to Athens, Oedipus offers *onēsis* 'benefit' to Athens in return for kindness. Though interpretations of the tragedy have traditionally identified Oedipus's boon with his dead body, the centerpiece of hero worship, at least one recent study focuses on the political and moral benefit of the living Oedipus:

> If the Athenians are capable of accepting Oedipus, of sharing in a perspective that sees his nature as ultimately viable, even beneficent, they will be able, and will deserve, to inherit his spiritual, his hard-won sense of "love" (*to philein*; 1617). It is not, finally, what happens to his corpse that matters. . . . If they cannot accept Oedipus alive, they do not participate, as Athens does, in that extension of spirit, and they cannot possess him dead.[67]

When the Athenians finally do receive Oedipus and reintegrate him into society, they exhibit both political unity—something Oedipus's native war-torn Thebes completely lacks—and the integrity of their essence and reputation as hospitable and just. They prove themselves enlightened.

It is at this point that *sēmata* 'signs' from the gods indicate Oedipus's approaching death. Oedipus prepares to pass through the gates of Hades. He addresses for the last time the *phōs aphenges* 'light that is no light', which belonged to him. He refers here to the contradiction of

---

[67] Laura Slatkin, "*Oedipus at Colonus*: Exile and Integration" (1986), 218. Nagy explains that "the Greek hero is a product of the polis, in that the cult of heroes is historically speaking a transformation of the worship of ancestors on the level of the polis" (*Pindar's Homer*, 143).

human insight. Out of the sight he extinguished when he recognized his flawed understanding comes his moral and political insight, though admittedly the insight of a blind man. It is only as a blind man that he acquires insight into people's contradictory behavior. Perhaps death will bring passage beyond the oxymoron of life's light that does not illuminate:

> ὦ φῶς ἀφεγγές, πρόσθε πού ποτ' ἦσθ' ἐμόν,
> νῦν δ' ἐσχατόν σου τοὐμὸν ἅπτεται δέμας.
> ἤδη γὰρ ἔρπω τὸν τελευταῖον βίον
> κρύψων παρ' Ἅιδην.
>
> (Oedipus at Colonus 1549–51)

> O light that is no light, once in the past you belonged to me,
> now for the last time my body touches you.
> Presently I creep ahead to the end of life
> which hides beyond Hades.

One is correct to anticipate that *Thrush* sublimates the political message of *Oedipus at Colonus*. Its appropriation of the Sophoclean oxymoron *phōs aphenges* 'light that is no light' in the phrase *angelikó ke mávro fos* 'angelic and black light' assigns an apocalyptic meaning to the Sophoclean contradiction of a light that is no light.[68] It identifies *fos* 'light' not with the chasm between sight and insight but with an unspecified "apocalypse" that takes place in the poetic persona's "continuous exchange with the sea, mountains, light, and air" of the Attic landscape.[69] Quite typically, both in *Thrush* and in his diary entries on the poem's composition, Seferis stops short of describing the process by which the identity of the poem's persona becomes submerged "elsewhere, in other places": "Impossible for me to express this apocalypse better. From here on, it makes no difference whether or not you exist as a single person. Better, the person is no longer *you*, it is *there*. If you can, you complete it. If you can, you perform a holy act. . . . This is an agon that takes place elsewhere, in other *topoi* [places]. . . . How can one pass this abyss? . . . The black and angelic Attic day."[70] The ellipsis

[68] Seferis was not indifferent to religious apocalypse. He translated the New Testament Book of Revelations into modern Greek (Η Αποκάλυψη του Ιωάννη [The apocalypse of John] [1975]). Sofía Skopetéa briefly discusses this translation, claiming that "Seferis's purpose was to make the *Apocalypse* accessible to the uninitiated" (Μυστήρια και αποκαλύψεις [Mysteries and apocalypses] [1987], 29).

[69] George Seferis, Μέρες (Days), 5:37.

[70] Ibid., 38.

of apocalypse intimates a point of crossing from the murky darkness of modernity's cultural indistinction to some sacred *topos* "elsewhere." Suddenly, the modern Odysseus finds himself lifted up from his descent. "There" under the light of "the black and angelic Attic day," his personality becomes immaterial, while Hellenism, broadly Christianized through direct reference to apocalypse and narrowly localized in the Attic *topío*, achieves its resurrection.[71] Apocalypse, with no specified vision except an admission of the inexpressible and an image of light, opens the gateway to Hellenism's home above.

Salvaging the Postwar Shipwreck

The textual strategy of omitting crucial links and deferring to revelation initially led to difficulties in the reception of *Thrush*. During the first years after its publication, readers complained that it was too fragmentary.[72] They cited allusions that broke off before coming clearly into focus. They felt it even more inexcusable, however, that this Neohellenic poem displayed an ambivalence toward tradition that was typical of European modernism. The poem's obscurity quickly became a point of concern for the postwar audience, just as the indeterminacy of modernist poetics had become an issue before World War II for the defenders of a Hellenicity.

Seferis took the opportunity to mediate differences between unappreciative readers and modernist innovators. His supplementary essay Μιά σκηνοθεσία για την Κίχλη (Stage directions for *Thrush*) took the form of a personal letter addressed to the journal's editor, Seferis's

---

[71] "Seferis's relationship with ancient Greek authors is deeper than any one borrowing, recollection, use of mythical material that offers itself for anachronistic games; it is a structural relationship. The structure of Greek tragedy is the path from passion to human dignity: the transformation of the Furies into the Eumenides . . . from the fall into darkness of the instincts to the arrival into the light of balance and justice. This is precisely the structure which *Thrush* follows. The voice of the wise old man . . . is the voice of justice, which will speak of a death that is full of dignity. From inside the deeper symbolism of the instincts, the soul serves one of the highest moments of human conscience: the mystical experience of apocalypse which resolves the agon" (Lína Lihnará, Το μεσογειακό τοπίο στην ποίηση του Γιώργου Σεφέρη και του Οδυσσέα Ελύτη [The Mediterranean landscape in the poetry of George Seferis and Odysseus Elytis] [1986], 87).

[72] *Aprospélasto* 'unapproachable' is the word Seferis used to describe readers' experience of the poem (Μιά σκηνοθεσία [Stage directions], 30). Karandónis describes his frustration in Ο ποιητής Γιώργος Σεφέρης (The poet George Seferis).

close friend Yórgos Katsímbalis.[73] Here Seferis blocked the positions of the ancient figures in *Thrush*. His declared purpose was to ease the difficult descent to the shipwreck of "Thrush" through Odysseus's renowned *nekuia* 'descent', and back up into the haunting "angelic and black light" of Socratic humanism. By pointing out convergences and explaining divergences between the ancient sources and the modern poem, he appeared to answer the difficult question of consistency: what held together the heterogeneous fragments of tradition in his contemporary vision.

While insisting that his interpretation was inspired by merely personal motive and bore no greater weight than the reading of "any more or less competent common reader," Seferis nonetheless offered his "private letter" for public scrutiny.[74] Its publication met with success, if mediation (and publicity) was indeed its purpose. For an increasingly broader audience, it revealed the poet's ultimate respect for tradition—and antiquity's personal effect on him. Thus the essay set the stage, as it were, for a discussion of Homer's, Plato's, and other ancient authors' direct influence on Seferis's poetic psyche, making the question of individual inspiration the crux of the poem. Even as the author attached further disclaimers with each successive reprint, rejecting both the essay's status as a "prose supplement" to the poem and his own status as a privileged interpreter,[75] critics began publishing articles explaining how the "Hellenic spirit" of George Seferis had succeeded in resurrecting antiquity and sacralizing the landscape of Hellas.[76]

Because his personal "tragic experience" of loss became regarded as perfectly analogous to Neohellenism's, Seferis gained a reputation for offering, both in his person and in his work, a profound if uneasy link

[73] The essay first appeared in print in 1950 in the journal *Angloellinikí epitheórisis*. The full text of the letter has been translated by James Stone, "A Letter on *Thrush*" (1980).

[74] Μιά σκηνοθεσία (Stage directions), 30.

[75] In the 1962 edition of Δοκιμές (Essays, Attempts), Seferis added this quotation from his earlier essay on Calvos: "No artist has given an authentic interpretation of his work" (Μιά σκηνοθεσία [Stage directions], 353 n. 1).

[76] By its own ellipses, noted above, the essay reinforces the idea that a complex composition such as *Thrush* is nested within not an intertext of images, icons, and ideas but "the non-text, the experience of Hellenism" (Kapsális, Κριτική του ελληνικού μοντερνισμού (Critique of Hellenic modernism), B, 45). Seferis offers aesthetic "reinforcement" so as to create an illusion of an apparently natural site nested in the contemporary landscape where "the nostalgia emanating from the weight of the past" can disappear.

between ancient and modern Greek sensibilities: "No Greek poet is more intensely aware of the abyss between a great past and dismal present than George Seferis."[77] The tug-of-war between the mediocrity of the modern world and the greatness of the classical appeared to be played out in the poet's soul. Seferis himself was said to advance from "present breakdowns" to "heroic memories."[78] He experienced a "lively sense of his *topos* paralyzed under the double burden of present misfortune and ancestral glory."[79] He composed his "personal mythology" from "memory and sensation."[80] "Symbolism of the instincts" rendered deep and meaningful a collective sense of a Neohellenic trauma.[81] "Private and general catastrophes" experienced by Neohellenes through years of "war, destruction, and migration" became harmoniously integrated in Seferis's stately, diplomatic, public persona.[82]

Readers will recall the passage from Seferis's published diaries where the poet refers to a "second coming" of Hellenism on the site of the Archaeological Museum. There we saw the unexplained contiguity of ancient statues, resurrected bodies, and "crazy" feelings for the Hellenic *topos*. At the same time, Seferis repressed in this passage reference to the contemporary reality of an ongoing civil war and limited it elsewhere to oblique phrases such as "the black and angelic Attic day." That expression, slightly modified in *Thrush* to read "angelic and black light," functions both to designate the darkness of present understanding and to reveal the healing power of the Attic landscape—the "humanizing function in the Hellenic light."[83] That is to say, it obfuscates contemporary details while it sublimates the contours of the physical and cultural horizon.

Indeed, these two functions, obfuscation and sublimation, should not be viewed as contradictory. They constitute the double movement found in all of Seferis's work. While representing the complex contemporary *topío* 'landscape' in such a way as to hinder analysis of the various forces that made it dark, crowded, and indistinct, Seferis also offered to his readers "faith in ancient signs within the landscape . . . ,

[77] Zahareas, "George Seferis," 190.

[78] Ibid., 191.

[79] Nikolareízis, Η παρουσία του Ομήρου (The presence of Homer), 231.

[80] Eléni Ladiá, Ποιητές και αρχαία Ελλάδα· Σικελιανός, Σεφέρης, Παπαδίτσας (Poets and ancient Greece: Sikelianós, Seferis, Papadítsas) (1983), 83.

[81] Lihnará, Το μεσογειακό τοπίο (The Mediterranean landscape), 37.

[82] Zahareas, "George Seferis," 197.

[83] Seferis, Μιά σκηνοθεσία (Stage directions), 55.

faith that they have their own soul."[84] This double movement allowed Seferis forever to equivocate on the matter of Greece's growing post-war dependence—in particular, on its loss of control over the development and uses of its land. Seferis promised that Neohellenism could regain access to its Hellenic origins by bypassing the problems of a belated modernity. The point of crisis might well become the stepping-stone to revelation.

What is lost in this reterritorialization of Hellenism's sacred homeland is analysis of how commodification transformed a *cosmos*—especially the sunny, underdeveloped Mediterranean exposure of the Western world—into an "endless hotel." Anxiety concerning commodification appears only in the margins of Seferis's work, for example, in his essay on the interpretation of dreams, entitled "Γλώσσες" στον Αρτεμιδώρο τον Δαλδιανό ("Commentary" on Artemidoros Daldianos) (1970). Here Seferis narrates the nightmare of his ascent to the Acropolis on the day it is auctioned.[85] Typically he refuses to interpret the dream he narrates. Is this refusal his way of coordinating "a dialogue between the poet's senses and Hellenic space and Hellenic time"?[86] Or is it a way of generating mass relief? The subject of this narration, too, is representative of what Seferis refuses to treat. What Seferis "hasn't the power to analyze," as he claims, is one of the most important concerns of postwar Neohellenism: the ill effects of Hellas's postwar reconstruction; the social, cultural, and environmental bankruptcy that evolved as Greece opened its doors to foreign investors and tourists and commodified its ancient monuments.[87]

In Seferis's nightmare, a state auction is taking place on the Acropolis. The purpose of the auction is to bring in revenue to the state by selling ancient monuments to the highest bidder. Suddenly the crowds cry out in triumph: "The Americans have won!"[88] An American toothpaste company has purchased the Parthenon: "Then I saw the Parthenon frightfully bare, without its pediment and peak, its col-

---

[84] George Seferis, Πάντα πλήρη θεών (All is full of gods) ([1971] 1981), 346.

[85] George Seferis, "Γλώσσες" στον Αρτεμιδώρο τον Δαλδιανό ("Commentary" on Artemidoros Daldianos) ([1970] 1981), 326ff.

[86] Maronítis, Η νέκυια της "Κίχλης" (The *nekuia* of *Thrush*), 16.

[87] More analytical was the condemnation of a 1991 advertisement by Coca-Cola, which rendered the Parthenon's Doric columns in the shape of Coca-Cola bottles. This time, Greeks became more self-critical of their own promotional uses of ancient monuments.

[88] Seferis, "Γλώσσες" ("Commentary"), 327.

umns chiseled and buffed in the shape of colossal tubes. It is not within
my power to analyze this dream. . . . But for me it is didactic. . . .
The relief I felt [when I awoke], which has accompanied me all my
life, could not be intensified or shaken by any interpretation of the
dream—this I know. Thus I believe that my dream of the Acropolis
was a didactic warning. Such is our life, an island within sleep."[89] Like
a character in his own poems, Seferis focuses on the light of the
landscape while he remains blind to its pitfalls. Surely Seferis's failure
to spell out his contemporary reference point is typical of the modernist literary approach that chose not to be "diagnostic" about the effects
suppressed dissent and too rapid modernization would have on the
social, political, and geographical horizon.[90] In his topography, Seferis
colors "the light" of Hellenism's physical scenery with a spiritual hue.
His reinvention of the sacred facilitates a relatively painless homecoming for Hellenism, which bypasses major obstacles on the national and
international front. This is his way of salvaging the postwar shipwreck
of Neohellenism.

[89] Ibid., 327–28.
[90] In "Beyond the Cave: Demystifying the Ideology of Modernism" ([1975] 1988),
Fredric Jameson criticizes the modernist literary nonreckoning with the "bondage" of
contemporary ideology. He countersuggests a "diagnostic" approach: "Our task—
specialists that we are in the reflections of things—is a more patient and modest, more
diagnostic one. Yet even such a task as the analysis of literature and culture will come to
nothing unless we keep the knowledge of our own historical situation vividly present
to us: for we are least of all, in our position, entitled to the claim that we did not
understand, that we thought all those things were real, that we had no way of knowing
we were living in a cave" (132).

CHAPTER 6

Cosmos: Modernist
Poetics in a National Universe

> Probably the great revolution of difference . . . is precisely people's
> last attempt to grapple, to attach themselves to their earth, before
> they abandon it, before it abandons them like leftover trash. Small is
> beautiful. And there's a good chance these three words, the contests
> of nations, will slowly erode the empire of Europe that is trying to
> take shape.
> —Mimíka Kranáki, Φιλέλληνες (Philhellenes)

> Defining a regional identity was a response to Modernism.
> —Steven S. High, "The Significance of Place"

Some forty years before Europeans—Eastern and Western—were
to find themselves again in "the contests of nations," grappling in the
1990s to dig in their roots, "to attach themselves to their earth,"
Odysseus Elytis's poetry precociously anticipated the passion of reas-
serting one's regional, ethnic identity. Initially a *protoporiakós* 'avant-
garde' surrealist more interested in literary developments in Paris than
in Greece,[1] Elytis emerged as a national poet after World War II. In
what was becoming an ever more Europeanized Greek world, he
campaigned for indigenous art and condemned Greece's subservience
to Western Hellenism. Contradictory as this may seem, it was as a
national poet that he consolidated his reputation worldwide.[2]

---

[1] Elytis's circle included the poets who introduced surrealism to Greece: Andréas
Embiríkos (1901–75), Níkos Engonópulos (b. 1910), Yórgos Sarandáris (1908–41), and
Nános Valaorítis (b. 1921). In France, Elytis knew André Breton (1896–1966), Tristan
Tzara (1896–1963), Giuseppe Ungaretti (b. 1888), Pablo Picasso (1881–1973), Alberto
Giacometti (1901–66), Henri Matisse (1869–1954), and others.

[2] Elytis first published poems in the journal *Ta néa grámmata* in 1935. *Prosanatolismí*
(Orientations), his first collection of poetry, appeared in 1940. Two other collections

Elytis's postwar vision redirected the course of a borrowed, Third World modernity from the dissolution of the small nation to its miraculous reassertion. Like other Neohellenic modernists, Elytis attached certain powers of determination to the Greek landscape. His particular claim was that the elements of the Aegean—the sun, sea, water, air, and rocky crags—could actually link eras of civilization divided by time, provided a poet existed who could discover their *orthografía* 'correct spelling'. The Aegean shorelines, "the wise digestive track of Hellenism," possessed a certain eloquence that might "correctly spell" civilization.[3] The visionary poet who accurately traced the landscape's *orthografía* might actually recover that *cosmos* 'world order, universe'. This was Elytis's calling, anyway: to render Hellenism's topography "orthographically."

The Self-Sufficient Universe: Two Versions of Autonomy

To the degree that Elytis's literary revolution involved the dismantling of conventional boundaries, it remained accountable to a high modernist project. Through experimental language, it promised to surmount contradictory realities, recover lost freshness, and overcome ideological crisis. Unusual, however, at least by a high modernist standard, was Elytis's effort to reconstruct the nation, specifically the geopolitical entity of Hellas, through his poetic universe. The *cosmos* of his poetry is self-contained but not self-enclosed. It connects itself by analogy to the landscape and the people, constituent elements of the nation, the story of which it tells. Furthermore, it attempts to synthesize a self-sufficient national tradition, one integrating nature and culture, geography and discourse, dream and reality.[4]

---

followed in the early 1940s. After a long hiatus, during which he was reported to be working feverishly on a longer work, he published the *Axion Esti* in 1959. Since the early 1960s new poetry and essays by Elytis have appeared almost every year. Elytis achieved international recognition in 1980 with the conferral of the Nobel Prize in literature.

[3] Elytis, Η σύγχρονη ελληνική τέχνη (Contemporary Greek art), 414. In Henry Miller's romantic vision of Greece, too, the landscape opens up like a book: "I see the geometric pattern of nature expounded by the earth itself in a silence which is deafening. The Greek earth opens before me like the Book of Revelation" (*Colossus of Maroussi*, 244).

[4] Karandónis, describing "Elytis's primary historical contribution to the renewal of poetic feeling and writing," saw "an entirely new *cosmos* of visual miracles at once real and dreamlike. For the first time in our poetry, the boundaries are abolished between reality and its dreamlike reconstruction. From their abolition emerges the assumption

Cosmos (Greek κόσμος) is Elytis's transcendental *topos* of Hellas. In its normative Neohellenic usage, this word has a fairly straightforward meaning, although its literary and philosophical resonances are certainly as rich as those of *topos* and *nostos*. *Cosmos* refers to people or the world. Of people, it indicates any group ranging in size from at least one person (the expression έχω κόσμο *ého kósmo* 'I have visitors' might suggest the presence of as few as one visitor) to a complete group (όλος ο κόσμος *ólos o kósmos* 'everybody') or even the entire world (ο κόσμος ολόκληρος *o kósmos olókliros* 'the entire world'). In a more philosophical sense, *cosmos* is a worldview or order, whether an individual's eccentric outlook (ζει στο δικό του κόσμο *zi sto dikó tu kósmo* 'he lives in his own world'), a poetic universe (ο κόσμος του Ελύτη *o kósmos tu Elíti* 'the universe projected in Elytis's poetry'), a sphere of being (ο κοινωνικός κόσμος, ο φυσικός κόσμος *o kinonikós kósmos, o fisikós kósmos* 'the social world', 'the natural world'), or the universe of heavenly bodies.

The literary resonances of *cosmos* include its philosophical uses. In ancient Greek, it "originally signified 'right order' in a state or other community" under the governance of *dikē* 'justice'.[5] More broadly, *cosmos* referred to the natural order of things. Of people it suggested good order, behavior, discipline, form, fashion, or government. Of art it indicated ornament, decoration, or ornaments of speech. Of the physical world it came to signify the universe in the works of Pythagoras, Parmenides, Heraclitus, Aristotle, and the Stoics; the firmament, the earth as opposed to heaven or the underworld, or the sphere whose center is the earth's center and whose radius is the straight line joining earth and sun for Archimedes.

Elytis builds on the normative Greek usage of *cosmos* and its ancient philosophical resonances, as well as the word's romantic appropriation by Greece's poet laureate Dionísios Solomós.[6] He creates his own seemingly transparent, though certainly not unprecedented, use of the

---

of a new and unrestricted freedom for poetic creativity" (Η ελληνική αίσθηση [Hellenic feeling], 160).

[5] J. B. Wilber and H. J. Allen, *The Worlds of the Early Greek Philosophers* (1979), 39.

[6] Dionísios Solomós developed a romantic sense of the organic unity of *cosmos*, revealed in sublime moments when matter underwent disintegration, as when a British subject was torn to pieces by a shark off the coast of Corfu:

Πριν παψ' η μεγαλόψυχη πνοή χαρά γεμίζει·
Άστραψε φως κι' εγνώρισεν ο νιός τον εαυτό του·

term.[7] *Cosmos* in Το 'Αξιον Εστί (Worthy it is) (1959), Elytis's most amibitious postwar poem, means, quite simply, 'world'; but it implies a certain kind of world order, a particular set of relationships between voice and being, part and whole.[8] The Neohellenic *cosmos* is a living organism, a national body whose connected and interdependent parts share a complex evolution and a common voice.

Elytis's brief essay of 1947, written during the Greek civil war, Η σύγχρονη ελληνική τέχνη και ο ζωγράφος Ν. Χατζηκυριάκος Γκίκας (Contemporary Greek art and the painter N. Hadzikiriákos Gíkas), reflects on the relationship between Hellenism's vital parts — nature, earth, landscape, people, language, artistic expression — its voice, and the organism, the living whole.[9] The essay assumes that artistic expression shapes matter; artistic form may synthesize discrete parts into a unified whole, provided it obeys inherent rules for its organization. The essay narrates Neohellenism's difficult evolution from the first years of the newly established Greek state to the mid-twentieth century, then seeks to justify Neohellenism's belated development and to point out avenues for future growth. This is typical

---

Οι κόσμοι γύρου ν' ανοίγαν κορόνες να του ρίξουν.
(*Pórfiras* 8.2–3)

Before ceasing, the great-hearted spirit fills with joy;
Light flashed and the young man came to know himself;
Cosmoi around him opened to throw crowns upon him.

[7] Cf. Periklís Yannópulos, who wanted to lay "the foundations for the creation of a New Hellenic *Cosmos*," including "first the physiology of the Hellene and second the physiology of the Hellenic race" (Νέον πνεύμα [New spirit] [1906], 5).

[8] In their notes to the English translation of the poem, Edmund Keeley and George Savídis give this explanation for the title *Axion Esti*: "In the Greek Orthodox ecclesiastical tradition, these two words . . . have a double Mariolatric connotation: first, the title of a Byzantine hymn glorifying the Virgin Mother of God; and, second, the name of a famous holy icon of the Virgin still extant on Mount Athos" (Odysseus Elytis, *Axion Esti* [1974], 79). Although the *Axion Esti* won the National Prize in Poetry in 1959, nevertheless Savídis, an eminent Greek critic, complained that the nation lacked "spiritual health" because it effectively ignored so great a national poem (Yórgos P. Savídis, 'Αξιον Εστί το ποίημα του Ελύτη [Worthy is the poem by Elytis] [1974], 142). He set about rectifying this situation by proving "why the poet of the *Axion Esti* is worthy of the nation" (143).

[9] Elytis's essay first appeared in *Angloelliniki epitheórisis* 2, no. 11 (January 1947), the same year Nikolareízis published his important essay discussed in Chapter 3 and Seferis published *Thrush*, and one year after Pikiónis's study of form, discussed in this chapter, and Kiriakídis's "Language and Folk Culture of Modern Greece."

of Neohellenic essays on art; we have already discussed critical works by Yannópulos, Nikolareízis, and Seferis that also seek to ground their assumptions about art in the story of Neohellenism—a story they never tire of retelling.

Typical, too, is the narrative pattern of stubborn impasse and remarkable breakthrough. The essay recounts recent Greek history thus. In the beginning was the independent state of Hellas, a "recently born organism that remains culturally alive if searching even after four hundred years of apparent death."[10] In vain it sought to find a voice to express its spirit, one of its crucial parts. In vain it tried to give a self-sufficient expression to the entire organism. Under the oppressive influence of Western institutions, in this case European secular art, the Neohellenic "organism" found little room to develop its authentically "Hellenic voice" and so remained effectively mute.[11] It was unable to synchronize its vocal parts to express the organic essence of Hellenism in a style wholly its own; the *plastikí axía* 'plastic value' of the specifically Hellenic landscape eluded art and sculpture.

The essay largely blames the Greek educated elite for the impasse confronting Neohellenism: *they* freely accepted foreign influences; *they* grafted Western forms; *they* interrupted the natural course of development. Foils to this unapologetically Westernizing project, a few iconographers and folk artists sought to preserve a native strain. The colossal difference in orientation between educated and uneducated artists left its mark of silence, or perhaps inarticulate expression, on Neohellenism. "Two parallel *cosmoi* follow their own respective paths, the one far from nature and the youthful exuberance of life, the other far from cultivation and the possibility of any change."[12] Whereas the combined forces of native authenticity and education might have given a cultivated indigenous form to the national landscape, instead the lack of common ground between autochthonous and heterochthonous products created an immense *hásma* 'chasm', and "the Hellenic *topío*, as a plastic value, remains without expression. Until the third decade of the twentieth century, the Attic *earth*, the *Aegean*, do not find a single person to render their essence with one unmediated gesture."[13]

[10] Elytis, Η σύγχρονη ελληνική τέχνη (Contemporary Greek art), 408.
[11] Ibid. According to Elytis, Greek cultural history continues to be shaped by European techniques, even though these fail miserably, each in succession, to give "voice" to the Greek soil.
[12] Elytis, Η σύγχρονη ελληνική τέχνη (Contemporary Greek art), 408–9.
[13] Ibid., 409 (my emphasis).

In the broader context of Western artistic movements, Elytis found Neohellenic artists moving from classical allegory to representations of everyday life when, with "pseudo-classicism's" demise, the center of European culture moved from Munich to Paris. French impressionism, which called for the complete "dissolution of forms in an orgy of impressions," revived hopes in Greece "that the time had arrived for this *topos* to discover its authentic expression."[14] Yet this artistic revolution, too, would ultimately run against the grain of Hellenism. European technique would again prove "incurably 'antiplastic' for our *topos*," incapable of grounding artistic form in the Hellenic earth.[15]

Elytis's essay on contemporary Greek art marked a turning point in the 1930s, like so many other essays written by liberal supporters of the modernist revolution during the mid- to late 1940s. It finds in the previous decade a window of opportunity, a horizon of change. The road to discovery was taken by an entire *yeniá* 'generation' of artists, critics, novelists, and poets, Elytis concluded. They focused their attention on the native arts of the Greek world. They learned "the deeper meaning of Byzantine art, . . . the graceful works of the people, handmade objects, Karagiózis, . . . the unschooled, itinerant artist of Lésvos, Theófilos, . . . the older vernacular texts of *Erotókritos* and Makriyánnis."[16] The same group also followed the developments in

[14] Ibid., 409.

[15] Ibid.

[16] Ibid., 409–10. Karagiózis refers to the genre of shadow puppet theater that takes its name from its trickster-hero. On the shadow puppet tradition in Greece, see Linda Myrsiades, "Aristophanic Comedy and the Modern Greek Karaghiozis Performance" (1987); id., "The Karaghiozis Performance in Nineteenth-Century Greece" (1976); id., "The Karaghiozis Tradition and Greek Shadow Puppet Theatre: History and Analysis" (1973); and Linda Myrsiades and Kostas Myrsiades, *Karagiozis: Culture and Comedy in Greek Puppet Theater* (1992). On the ideological uses of Karagiózis by Neohellenism, see Stathis Gourgouris, Η μυθοπλασία του Καραγκιόζη και το εθνικό ασυνείδητο (The mythification of Karagiózis and the national unconscious) (1988). Theófilos Hadzimihaíl (d. 1934), or Theófilos, as he became known, was a self-trained mural artist who painted on Lésvos in the early 1900s. E. Teriade discovered his work and began collecting Theófilos's more portable paintings. He organized a Theófilos exhibit in Paris in 1936 and in Greece in 1947. Teriade donated his collection to the Museum of Variá on Lésvos, where it remains today. Surrealist poet Andréas Embiríkos also collected his paintings. Modernists found in Theófilos's work an indigenous aesthetic of Hellenicity. See Elytis's and Seferis's essays on Theófilos for representative evaluations of his work (Odysseus Elytis, Ο ζωγράφος Θεόφιλος [The painter Theófilos] [(1973) 1986]; George Seferis, Θεόφιλος [Theófilos] [(1947) 1981]). The contemporary painter Daniíl, who retells the story of Theófilos's discovery in Το φαινόμενο Θεόφιλος 40 χρόνια μετά την "ανακάλυψη του" (The phenomenon Theófilos 40 years after "his discovery") (1975), is especially critical of tenuous links that Elytis produced

the West, especially the cubist revaluation of "plastic values." But their ambivalent orientation, specifically their will to conflate the native and the Western, allowed them to suppose that they had discovered self-sufficient values in a Hellenic universe. As Elytis puts it, they saw that the whole story about a chasm between the Hellenic tradition and modern art was nothing but a myth. His generation found the "*rízes* [roots]" of modern perceptions buried deep in "ancient *hómata* [soils] watered by . . . unchanging rules."[17]

The metaphorical language in the reference to "ancient soils" stands out, calling attention to Elytis's conception of both the determinant powers and the self-sufficient values of the Hellenic *topío*. Here the image of a culture rooted in the generative "soils" of Hellas allows Elytis to derive the rules of modern art from Hellenism's natural *orthografía*, as he imagines it. As in the beginning of the essay, where he describes the "chasm" between the European-educated Greek elite and the uneducated traditional Greek artists, so throughout the essay Elytis represents a break between present and past, European high art and Hellenic folk art. The medium of the message is the spatial metaphor, the great abyss. When he proceeds to describe how his comrades managed to bridge the chasm between two discrete worlds, however, Elytis deftly shifts to the metaphor of the plant deeply rooted in primordial soils. To these soils Elytis attributes the powers not only of enrichment but also of metabolism. The earth of Ionia, the southeastern Asiatic hinterland and its Aegean shoreline, becomes "a field of a miraculous assimilative energy, the laboratory of nuclei of art which constituted always some of the greatest mysteries of Hellenism's success," "the wise digestive track of Hellenism," or, by another metaphor, "the depths of the collective unconscious":

> From the time of the pre-Socratic philosophers through the Hellenistic, early Christian, and Byzantine eras, and even during the Ottoman occupation the exchange of influences and mixture of cultures never ceased to mark the deepest spot in the collective racial unconscious. . . .
> In the wise digestive track of Hellenism, Egyptian, Arabic, Syrian, and Persian lose their local plastic idiom . . . and take on a new, exemplary essence that is also purely personal in accordance with the rules of light and the commands of this earth where they will now stand.[18]

between Theófilos's paintings and cubist art. *Erotókritos* is a seventeenth-century epic poem by the Cretan Vintzéntzos Kornáros. On Yánnis Makriyánnis see Chapter 2. It is noteworthy that Greek modernists canonized his semiliterate memoirs.

[17] Elytis, Η σύγχρονη ελληνική τέχνη (Contemporary Greek art), 411.
[18] Ibid., 414–15.

In Elytis's narrative, Neohellenism recovers its authentic voice when artists of his own generation enter into "communion with the essential content of Neohellenic reality," not through slavish philology or chauvinistic nationalism but "with a simple biopsychological movement toward the sources."[19] At the "deepest" level, his generation of Neohellenes reached antiquity itself. At an intermediate level, it delved "into the memory of the race from Byzantium to the Turkish occupation."[20] In the living present, on this end of a vertical time line that took a nose dive into the depths of the past, Elytis found his contemporaries becoming "more and more familiar with popular sensibilities" as they discovered "themselves naturally in harmony with the feeling and movements dictated by the soil of Neohellenic life."[21]

Because Elytis's essay links the landscape so inextricably to the fate of the Neohellenic people, it can argue that harmony with nature follows directly from an artist's understanding of the people. Elytis consistently places "the needs of the people" alongside the forces of nature—"the bare rocks, the light, the winds" in an unspecified contiguity. These are the two constituent parts of his Neohellenic *cosmos*. By a grammatical closeness to the soil of the Aegean, he suggests that people "continue directly the traditions of the ancients" as naturally as the sun shines in the Aegean.[22] Elytis further suggests that contemporary artists can link their work to the vernacular traditions of archaic, classical, postclassical, Byzantine, and Ottoman Hellenism by drawing on the natural resources of the landscape.

We might now explore the form Elytis gives to his perplexing formula for Neohellenic modernism, a paradoxical synthesis that subjects the autonomy of artistic activity, admittedly a European idea, to the determinations of soil and people, a core doctrine of aesthetic nationalism. Elytis argues that contemporary art should emerge as a product of soil, land, and blood. But how can the modernist work be authentically national, the product of an artist's "reading" the landscape, perusing the contemporary scenery, studying the national traditions, cultivating indigenous forms, and so excavating and discovering the Hellenic *cosmos* that preexists within?

Let us consider one specific line of poetry. The expression Αυτός ο κόσμος ο μικρός ο μέγας *aftós o kósmos o mikrós o mégas* 'This *cosmos* the

[19] Ibid., 415–16.
[20] Ibid., 416.
[21] Ibid.
[22] Ibid., 412–13.

small the great' appears repeatedly in the *Axion Esti*.[23] The line is well known to a broad Greek audience, though the familiarity of the verse does not make the referent of αυτός ο κόσμος 'this *cosmos*' any more stable. What are the possible referents of this verse? There are at least three interpretations in currency. First, a nationalist reading claims a real referent: Hellas, the small geographical entity that has generated cultural greatness throughout the ages. Second, a, modernist, New Critical reading suggests that 'this *cosmos*' can refer no farther "outside" itself than to the universe of poetic language.[24] The poem offers also a third reading, no less nationalist or modernist, I would argue, in which there are *two* referents. The *mikrós* 'small' *cosmos* is the universe of the poem, while the *mégas* 'great' is the geographical, social, historical, political, and cultural entity identifiable as "Hellas." Through analogy the poem gives order to Hellas in accordance with its internal coherence. "This" becomes both self- and extrareferential. The poem is the small *cosmos*, a universe unto itself, self-instituting, autonomous, capable of naming itself and thus creating itself without heteronomous intrusion. It is more perfect than any other *cosmos* because it resists invasion, closes itself off; it controls itself. In its self-creation, the poem finds a proper place for each irreducible element of language. It composes a universe of language. It then subsumes a greater *cosmos* by the analogy of its own perfection. Through the achievement of perfection, it undergoes transubstantiation. Language becomes matter. The poetic map subsumes the place. "This" self-referential *cosmos* of language cocoons "this" terrestrial nation of sun, sea, and Hellenic people. Αυτός ο κόσμος ο μικρός ο μέγας 'This *cosmos* the small the great' becomes a *topos* both in the rhetorical and in the geographical sense: it is a common-place—a place shared by the deeply rooted universe of language and the wide expanse of the Hellenic nation.

This third reading of the verse suggests that there is something unusual about modernist works from currents tangential to the Euro-

---

[23] Elytis's cultural ideal is reflected almost explicitly in Andréas Karandónis, Γύρω από το Άξιον Εστί (Surrounding the "Axion Esti") (1980), first recited on national radio in 1958, in anticipation of the poem's publication. Karandónis discovered in the poem "a Hellenic *cosmos*, a tangible *cosmos*, born alongside that other *cosmos* when it was decreed, 'Let there be light'. The magical mystery of this *cosmos* is that each individual, even the most humble, the most unwitting, creates this *cosmos* from the beginning, from the moment, that is, when it is not yet a *cosmos* but only matter and images, things and objects thrown under the light and unrelated to one another" (170).

[24] On the connection between modernist and New Critical assumptions about the status of the text, see Leontis, "Modernist Criticism."

pean mainstream. Contrast Elytis's world-encompassing poetic word with the aspirations of modernist poets following the lead of Stéphane Mallarmé (1842–98), who tried to create a self-sufficient, self-enclosed universe of language. Assuming that an ailing modern world needed purification, they sometimes chose to treat it linguistically, though they were pessimistic that they could make the world a more integrated and harmonious place by perfecting any system of language. Literary modernists therefore distrusted the common word as a bearer of meaning, norms, and values. Instead of perfecting the referential powers of language, they sought to restore to language itself a lost purity or integrity. As evidence of a broader trend within modernity, one can point to the many attempts to invent new codes of expression, from twelve-tone music to cubism and surrealism, from Esperanto to Ludwig Wittgenstein's *Tractatus*. In the language arts, individual authors sustained efforts to create what Roland Barthes has referred to as "a self-sufficient language" rooted in the depths of one's "personal and secret mythology."[25]

While Elytis frequently expressed the wish to discover the *orthografía* 'correct spelling' of a self-sufficient *cosmos*, his aim was not only to produce an autonomous semiotic system but also to reproduce an integrated, transhistorical Hellenic world. His project involved a peculiar kind of introspection: Elytis recently declared his intent to "excavate and discover the Hellas that preexists within me," *without* the guilt of belatedness.[26] His has been no historical or biographical search for lost origins; instead his poetry becomes a topographical register of that small, intimate space in the heart of the Hellenic *cosmos* where language remains luminous, where signs are natural. Unlike other European modernists, including his contemporary George Seferis, Elytis viewed past layers of civilization not from the individual perspective of a secret personal mythology but from the absolute perspective of the self-fulfilled nation, a point above, from which the *cosmos* of Hellenism appears clear, unproblematic, and eminently readable.

Elytis's project may seem to contradict a standard modernist assumption that pure art and the sullied world, especially the propaganda machine of the nation-state, are at odds. Yet Elytis's idealization

---

[25] Roland Barthes, *Writing Degree Zero* ([1953] 1968), 10.

[26] Odysseus Elytis, Τα δημόσια και τα ιδιωτικά (The public and the private) (1990), 29.

of both poetry and landscape as a topographical holdout resisting the cannibalism of capitalist markets conforms to a certain vision of aesthetic modernity.[27] What is unusual in modernist circles is not his valorization of poetry but his view of the rule of autonomy.

We can trace aesthetic autonomy to German idealism, from which there evolved an idea that art should be *auto-nomos* 'self-governing' in order to be free. Without the intervention of heteronomous, external laws (moral norms, political demands, religious commandments), the processes of artistic creation can correctly apportion their materials and means. As the institutions of art evolved, art created an autonomous space for itself; it became the medium for its own (re)production.[28] Alongside this view of artistic autonomy, though not necessarily in contradistinction to it, there also evolved an important notion of political—specifically national—autonomy in modern society: the autonomy of the nation, the social "organism" defined by the unique particularity of its language, history, and culture. The rule of national autonomy is that a group may declare itself distinct based on shared culture, history, and blood and, given this distinction, aspire to self-rule. The argument for self-rule is the claim of distinction. There usually follows an instituting act of affixing nation to geography and grounding identity on a map. As we saw in Chapter 3, the nation may designate a *topos* or territory for itself. Furthermore, it may infuse that territory with identity by way of culture. Ideally, a national group seeks to gain full control over its cultural, social, and political (re)production within the territory to which it sutures its identity.

It is to this second view of national autonomy that Elytis's aesthetic *cosmos* is tied. This is not to say that Elytis's poetry radicalizes a modernist aesthetic by rendering it political. Instead, it presupposes one element of aesthetic nationalist ideology found repeatedly in Yan-

---

[27] Matei Calinescu's careful differentiation of aesthetic from scientific conceptualizations of modernity finds the aesthetic ideal of autonomy and purity opposed to "modernity as a stage in the history of Western civilization—a product of scientific and technological progress, of the industrial revolution, of the sweeping economic and social changes brought about by capitalism" (*Five Faces of Modernity: Modernism, Avant-Garde, Decadence, Kitsch* [1987], 41).

[28] For Peter Bürger "autonomy" refers to the institutional status of art after aestheticism, when artistic production became a distinct institutional subsystem: "The evolution of art as a distinct subsystem . . . began with l'art pour l'art and was carried to its conclusion with Aestheticism" (*Theory of the Avant-Garde* [(1974) 1984], 32), when art finally lost its social function. Art became autonomous, with its own system of production, canonization, promotion, and reproduction, when the artistic avant-garde thematized its radical disjunction from the social world.

nópulos's philosophy of art: that artistic expression is an important act of political self-institution, in particular, of nation building.[29] Furthermore, it gives form to the idea that the work of art is the highest expression of the national-popular spirit. As I have mentioned, *cosmos* is Elytis's *topos* of Hellenism. More specifically, *cosmos* is the space where the Hellenic nation projects its spirit onto the soil and water of the Aegean, where it becomes readable. Since, in Elytis's view, the *cosmos* of Hellenism has its own *orthografía* 'correct spelling', its irreducible elements—the sun, the sea, the land, the earth, the tolling winds, the mountains, the trees, and the people—require only a luminary poet who can "read" them from the outside in. It is the everyday details of the landscape that reveal the autonomous spirit of Hellenes. The *cosmos* of poetry presents a reading of the Hellenic *cosmos*. It registers on the surface of the poetic text the *orthografía* of the landscape, including vignettes from the people's everyday life. Thus it reproduces the *cosmos* of Hellenism—nature and people—so perfectly that the poetic *cosmos* itself becomes the *cosmos* of Hellenism by absolute analogy.

It is no accident that critics have promoted Elytis as the authentic spokesman for the Hellenic *laós* 'people' (the preferred socialist term) or *éthnos* 'nation' (the preferred conservative term).[30] Especially in the *Axion Esti*, Elytis offers both an autotelic poem and a national work. He "reads" the "small but great *cosmos*" of Hellenism in a way that identifies his first-person voice with the constituent body of Hellenes. He projects his poetic voice as the living memory of his people. Each subsequent reading of the *Axion Esti* promises the people/nation the glory of eternity, as one Greek critic's evaluation attests: "The first person (speaker) is the poet and the people in an indivisible identification. . . . The fate of the poet (individual) is identified with the fate of his nation (general) in a specific place and . . . time. . . . So let this small world reveal the glory of the eternal. For the world the small is potentially the great."[31] But how exactly does a modernist artist make himself an organ of the people? Any assumption that there is an

---

[29] Klironomos, "Formation of the Nation/State," chap. 4, "The Nation as Aesthetic and Ethical State in Elytis' Poetry," makes an important contribution to this subject.

[30] Tzióvas says that the term *laïkós politismós* 'popular culture' was not used until after 1920, i.e., after urbanization had progressed in Greece and the Russian Revolution had stimulated Greeks in the labor movement to think about socialism (*Nationalism of the Demoticists*, 324). Although Elytis was not a socialist, he borrowed from socialist rhetoric.

[31] Tásos Lignádis, Το ᾽Αξιον Εστί του Ελύτη (Elytis's "Axion Esti") (1970), 26–27.

"indivisible identification" between "poet," "people," and the "fate of the nation" in a self-declared modernist work raises interesting questions about the problematic link between late modernism and populism on the margins of the West. Is such a link possible, without divesting the term "modernism" of any meaning? And to what end does Elytis make his poetry the rallying point for the people/nation? How can he give dramatic form to the fate of the people through his own personalitty, without denying the superiority of free, original, autonomous artistic expression? How does he subject his personal voice to the collective mythology of a nation without making every modernist illusion painlessly peripheral or eccentrically decorative?

To answer these questions, I shall examine the rise of Greek intellectuals' interest in the *laós* 'people' at the beginning of the twentieth century. My approach is again genealogical: I collect scattered references to the *laós* 'people', which I consider to reflect relevant moments in the formation of a discourse of populism in Neohellenic letters. As I analyze specific passages, I advance the argument that populism permeates Neohellenic vernacular culture from its early demoticist to its late modernist phase, approximately from 1880 to 1960, before taking hold of the state apparatus in the postmodernist 1980s. For nearly a century, critics and poets promoted works they viewed as speaking directly to the people of Hellas through their usage of a more "natural" language. The rule of populism certainly defines demoticism, but it also gives shape to Greek modernism. In Elytis's difficult modernist epic, the *Axion Esti*, populism lends simple sense to a complex pattern of literary citations from the Hellenic tradition, including the classical canon. Populism incorporates familiar and obscure literary *topoi* in an engaging national narrative, the story of the small nation's quest to cling to its *topos* against the rule of hostile, invading forces.

Demoticism and the Discourse of Populism

The discourse of populism has thrived in Greek intellectual circles from the turn of the twentieth century to the present. I call populism a discourse because it comprises a complex of signs, techniques, strategies, and truth claims that compete against other signs, techniques, strategies, and truth claims for the power to organize Greek social practices and political and cultural life.[32] Foremost is the sign of the

[32] Populism has also been discussed under the rubrics of ideology, rhetoric, syndrome, and movement. Torcuato S. di Tella ("Populism and Reform in Latin America"

laós 'people', with a range of signifiers, including the *palikári* 'young man', *fandáros* 'infantryman', *kléftis* 'klepht, guerrilla fighter', Romiosíni, Karagiózis, Makriyánnis, Theófilos, Kazantzídis and Marinélla, Vuyukláki, and, more recently, Andréas and Mimí.[33] Through these signifiers, the discourse of populism conveys the message that "virtue" (or purity of heart, at the very least) "resides in the simple people, who are the overwhelming majority, and in their collective traditions."[34] Furthermore, it promises self-governance through self-assertion.

Neohellenic populism, like populism everywhere, incorporates the people as hero in its very powerful account of history, that is to say, it

---

[1965]) and Peter Wiles ("A Syndrome, Not a Doctrine. Some Elementary Theses on Populism" [1969]) discuss the last two categories. Regarding the ideology of populism, Kitching (*Development and Underdevelopment*) makes a significant contribution, as do Donald MacRae ("Populism as an Ideology" [1969]), Angus Stewart ("The Social Roots" [1969]), and Peter Worsley (*The Third World* [1967] and "The Concept of Populism" [1969]). To call populism an ideology is, however, to become entangled in the vexed issue of whether populism inherently serves conservative or progessive causes. Doris Sommer manages to escape this issue in her very interesting study of populism in Dominican novels (*One Master for Another: Populism as Patriarchal Rhetoric in Dominican Novels* [1983]). She refers to populism as a rhetoric, following Kenneth Minogue ("Populism as a Political Movement" [1969]). The value of this term is that "instead of distinguishing one cause from another, rhetoric often constitutes the common (battle) ground for competing ideologies that vie for the authority to establish the referents of a shared rhetoric" (Sommer, xii). It is certainly true that the rhetoric of populism may index an ideology that differs in significant and substantial ways from what its users appear to be trying to say. Yet I would argue that both the rhetorical and the ideological uses of "the people" depend on the signs, techniques, strategies, and truth claims that set into motion ways of talking about "the people." A discourse in fact combines ideology and rhetoric, in that it manages ways of talking about an object of knowledge. See Margaret Canovan, *Populism* (1981), for a good discussion of scholarly trends. Primary sources include A. J. Herzen, *From the Other Shore* and *The Russian People and Socialism* (1956); F. List, *The National System of Political Economy* ([1841] 1904); P. J. Proudhon, *What Is Property? An Inquiry into the Principle of Right and Government* ([1840] 1898).

33 The struggle over the value and content of Romiosíni has a very interesting history in the early twentieth century, which I discuss below. Stélios Kazantzídis and Marinélla are two popular singers who paired up in song and life during the 1950s and 1960s; they won Neohellenes' hearts with their music and romance. Alíki Vuyukláki, a perennially youthful actress, for decades has displayed childhood innocence and sexual charm in film and on stage. Andréas and Mimí are the names by which most Greeks refer to Andréas Papandreou, prime minister of Greece from 1981 to 1989 and again beginning in October 1993, and to his wife, Dímitra Liáni. In the mid-1980s during Papandreou's second term, Greeks intensely followed the drama of Andréas and Mimí's less-than-secret affair. The Andréas and Mimí soap opera culminated in a large marriage ceremony, with local publicity rivaling that of Charles and Diana's ill-fated royal wedding.

34 Wiles, "Theses on Populism," 166.

claims to assert the truth about the people by unfolding the people's meaning in narrative time. The story goes something like this. While the people unconsciously promoted the causes of harmony and continuity in their *topos*, some unwanted conspirator—the educated pedant, the elitist Westernizer, rationalism, the amoral capitalist, the foreign invader, or, more abstractly, *to sístima* 'the system'—tried to disrupt the integrity of their lives so as to break their ties to the land.[35] The project of the conspirator was to erect alien structures—an artificial language, Western clothing, non-Greek metrical patterns, a Bavarian king, foreign institutions—on native foundations. When carried out, this plan inevitably led to catastrophe. Only the *laós* 'people' could combat its ill effects, by relying on the existential necessity of their identity.

Populism's conspiratorial narrative produces a set of dichotomies (native-foreign, majority-minority, direct-mediated, nature-culture, people-scholars), which create, in turn, an internal sense of belonging and outward sense of otherness. Thus the discourse of populism not only expresses a struggle against domination; it also contests the right to represent the people on whose behalf it claims to speak—a serious contradiction, to be sure. It warns against the intrusion of an elite minority, whose aim is "to check the majority opinion of this people."[36] It counterproposes, finally, a "theology of roots arrayed against the 'impasse of Western thought.'"[37]

As a discourse, populism may permeate a variety of relatively autonomous fields, institutions, or movements: history, anthropology, folklore; culture, education, politics; the Megáli Idéa, demoticism, PASOK.[38] In politics, the appeal to a single, undifferentiated community is a gesture of coalition building, directed ultimately to-

[35] A figure of ill repute in the eyes of supporters of the Greek vernacular, the educated pedant was associated with Adamantios Koraes by Dionísios Solomós in his *Diálogos* (Dialogue) of 1824 and with Koraïsmós by Psiháris and by Psiharismós 'Psiharism' (the linguistic, cultural, and social idiom created by Psiháris's more literal-minded followers). Fílipos Ilíu (Ιδεολογικές χρήσεις του κοραϊσμού [Ideological uses of Koraïsmós] [1989]) argues that the derogatory image given to Greek Enlightenment figures by Psihárism and more recently by certain Marxist and Neo-Orthodox leaders reveals how populism sought to undermine the Enlightenment educational tradition in Greece.

[36] Harry Lazer, "British Populism: The Labour Party and the Common Market Parliamentary Debate" (1976), 259.

[37] Gerásimos Likiardópulos, Ρωμιοσύνη· Ιδεολογία και αθλιότητα του νέου εθνικισμού (Romiosíni: Ideology and paltriness in the new nationalism) (1983), 9.

[38] For an introduction to the political party known as PASOK, see Richard Clogg, *A Concise History of Greece* (1992), chap. 6.

ward (re)constituting the middle class.[39] Assuming the common cultural background and aspirations of that group, the discourse of populism offers to a national audience a coherent mythology. It addresses issues of national crisis in terms of territorial determinism, native authenticity, and national identity. Its implicit goal is to escape from the burden of history and politics by defending the beauty, simplicity, integrity, and purity of an alleged national community.[40]

The usage of *laós* 'people' to signify the carriers of the eternal Greek spirit and authentic Greek culture is quite recent. It seems that the populist image of a *laós* began to regulate Greek culture in the late nineteenth century. Margaret Alexiou gives this history and definition of the usage:

> Throughout the Tourkokratia, and even during the War of Independence, the words *genos*, *ethnos* and *patrida* predominate in appeals to Greek consciousness. Only after the establishment of the Greek state, was the word *laos* used increasingly to mean 'people' in the Herderian sense of *Volk*, as carriers of the eternal spirit (*pneuma*) of the Greek nation (*ethnos*), whose values are transmitted "in the blood." The nationistic and religious overtones of the word continue to this day. . . . Yet *laos* is rarely, if ever, used by ordinary people *of themselves*: it denotes not "real" people, but a concept of the collective consciousness for popular will and power, so generalised as to exclude direct reference to the speaker or addressees.[41]

---

[39] In his polemical book Ανάλυση της νεοελληνικής αστικής ιδεολογίας (Analysis of the ideology of the Neohellenic middle class) (1989), Gerásimos Kaklamánis argues that populism emerged concurrently with the Greek middle class. This is no historical accident. Populism assumes the common cultural background and aspirations of a middle class, while it also aims to consolidate a national audience by offering the middle class a coherent mythology of its "spirit." Populism appeals to the dream of native authenticity repelling the invasion of Western rationalism.

[40] MacRae ("Populism as an Ideology") suggests that populism seeks to escape from the burden of history and is therefore apolitical. Populism is especially effective where a national culture aims to express the spirit of a people and territory. For this reason it is extremely pervasive in Greece, where we find even the libertarian defender of internationalism Yórgos Theotokás appealing to a kind of territorial determinism in this airy description: "Hellas is entirely spirit, a land of pure and clear ideas. Its view is the deliverance of thought, the catharsis of the soul. There is no place here for heavy, dark intellectual edifices, for nebulous systems, for pompous and grandiloquent declarations, for defiant and brutal colors. You would think that our *topos* dismisses far away whatever is superfluous and graceless . . . and retains only its supreme essence. Here everything is simple, so beautiful, so deeply simple, that simplicity was named a miracle" (Η διαύγεια [Clarity] [1931], 30).

[41] Margaret Alexiou, "Folkore: An Obituary?" (1984), 14–15.

An obvious example of the more crass regulatory efforts of the late nineteenth century is bureaucratic *folkorismós* 'folklorism', which glorified an authentic national body and celebrated its spirit and traditions through officially sanctioned festivals and shows. These festivals, in fact, managed the activities of the *laós* while appearing paradoxically to "serve images of spontaneity and *naïveté*."[42]

More subtle was the case of demoticism itself. A bold and coordinated attempt to make vernacular the language of high culture, demoticism also played a formative role in producing knowledge about the rural *laós*: its beliefs, customs, and forms of expression. Representatives of literary and artistic movements that swelled in the 1930s again revived arguments for native authenticity in the arts. In their imaginative works, they sought to strike a balance between Hellenicity and modernity by aesthetically upgrading folk forms.

Even a cursory glance at these important trends indicates that populism has an important discursive history in Greek culture. Here I sharpen my focus to study a particular category of populist statements that depict the *ancient* Hellenes living in a contemporary agrarian or urban working-class setting. My intent is to understand how the Greek *laós* became viewed as the authentic carrier of ancient Greek civilization, and how ancient Greek texts came to be read as expressions of the Greek *laós*. How, when, and why did it become a sound option to claim, as Elytis does, that the virtues found in Hellenism's deepest historical layers continue to reside in the *laós* and in its collective traditions?[43] And how does ancient Greek become a carrier of the

---

[42] Michael Herzfeld, *Anthropology through the Looking Glass: Critical Ethnography in the Margins of Europe* (1987), 13.

[43] A contemporary example may serve the purpose of clarification. In a remark made during an interview about his record album Το κούρεμα (The haircut) (1988), composer-musician Dionísis Savvópulos complained that "Greece as a state is continuously distancing itself all the more from the values of Hellenism." Savvópulos identified the Greek *stratónas* 'army barracks' as one place where traditional values prevail. He advanced his argument by equating the modern *fandáros* 'infantryman' with the Homeric hero: "Fortunately the ancient code of honor first taught by Homer—according to which we live not for ourselves, but in order to achieve something exceptional—continues to exist somehow in the army barracks today" (Χρειάζονται συντηρητικές λύσεις [Conservative solutions are necessary] [1989], 29). Homeric scholarship might have a hard time comprehending why Savvópulos found it rhetorically effective to invoke Homer as the original teacher and guarantor of Hellenism's pure presence in the company of modern Greek infantrymen. But Savvópulos was relying on well-tested tactics: by reference to the venerated name of "Homer"—which represents not only the primal scene of instruction but also, in a Greek context, the immediacy, intimacy, and

message that Hellenism persists in everyday life? What complex of signs and truths makes it comprehensible to equate ancient figures and texts with the ethos of the contemporary rural or urban Greek? What rhetorical tropes, poetic techniques, and tactical arguments erase the differences between past and present, rendering the ancient an enduring expression of nature preserved in popular culture? How and why do ancient Greek authors, once venerated by the purist tradition in Greece, long prototypes for high art in Europe, become emblems of a popular, demotic tradition—hence available for appropriation by the proponents of a vernacular culture?

There are two important phases in the development of the national-popular *míthos tis Ellinikótitas* 'myth of Hellenicity' that extends from the ancients to the homespun philosophy of the *kafenío* 'coffee-house'.[44] The first phase began when demoticists appropriated ancient authors as demotic writers—writers, that is to say, of the Greek vernacular. The second phase may be linked to the modernist quotation of ancient *topoi* as textual signposts of Neohellenism. I shall discuss the emergence of a demoticist ideology of the *laós* before studying modernist transpositions.

The differences between purist and demoticist attitudes toward the Greek people and their past are evident in a debate that took place just after 1900 concerning the name and nature of a Greek national identity. The appearance of Aryíris Eftaliótis's book, Ιστορία της Ρωμιοσύνης (History of Romiosíni) (1901), precipitated this debate, with its promotion of Romiosíni as a signifier of the national-popular body.[45] In

authenticity of everyday life—Savvópulos transplanted the cultural capital of the ancient past from literary history to the everyday present. His appeal to Homer's "teachings" somehow offered Greeks assurance that the most valuable tradition lived on in the hearts of the people who really mattered.

[44] Vakaló links the phrase *míthos tis ellinikótitas* 'myth of Hellenicity' to a "neopopulist" trend in art. An example is artist Yórgos Sikeliótis, who takes "popular themes and forms, raises them to an archetypal expression, and develops them into a personal mythology" (Ο μύθος της ελληνικότητας [The myth of Hellenicity], 52; see also Vakaló's chapter on "neopopulism"). Vakaló's source for the "myth of Hellenicity" may well be Níkos Nikoláu's Η περιπέτεια της γραμμής στην τέχνη (The adventure of line in art) (1986); see especially p. 49.

[45] For a definition of Romiosíni, see Chapter 3. Entering the fray of battle on the side of Romiosíni were Kostís Palamás, Yánnis Psiháris, Karl Krumbacher, and Gregórios Xenópulos, whereas Geórgios Sotiriádis, Geórgios Mistriótis, Geórgios N. Hadzidákis, and Nikólaos G. Polítis stood up in defense of Hellenism. Relevant works are G. Hadzidákis, Νεωτάτη φάσις του γλωσσικού ζητήματος (The newest phase of the language question) (1902); Krumbacher, Το πρόβλημα της νεωτέρας γραφο-

the aftermath of the book's publication, intellectuals lined up either in support of Romiosíni or in opposition to its usage and in defense of Ellinismós 'Hellenism'. At issue were not only the national epithet but also the cultural affiliation and historical self-representation of contemporary Greeks. Although both sides appealed to the principle of continuity, they disagreed on its medium and message.

Exponents of Ellinismós stressed the "unbroken continuity of the *víos* 'life' of the Greek *éthnos* 'nation' from antiquity through the painful era of *sklaviá* 'slavery' under the Turks until the restoration of a free *patrís* 'fatherland, homeland'."[46] What remained undisturbed from the age of Pericles to the Greek Revolution was the value given to national unity and the pursuit of military glory. This value "the name Hellene" symbolized best, whereas the name Romiós, the origins of which lay in the Roman conquest of Hellas, made it subject to ridicule.[47]

Advocates of Romiosíni claimed, to the contrary, that evidence of Greek continuity resided in the nation's single unbroken tradition: oral, folk culture.[48] They extolled the Byzantine and Ottoman-Christian

μένης Ελληνικής (The problem of modern written Greek) (1905); Polítis, Έλληνες ή Ρωμιοί (Hellenes or Romií); Psiháris's and Palamás's essays, both entitled Ρωμιός και Ρωμιοσύνη (Romiós and Romiosíni) (1903 and 1907); and Xenópulos, Ιστορία της Ρωμιοσύνης υπό Αργύρη Εφταλιώτη (History of Romiosíni by Aryíris Eftaliótis) (1902). G. Sotiriádis, professor of classical archeology at the University of Athens, kindled the hot debate with his review of Eftaliótis's book, Ιστορία της Ρωμιοσύνης (History of Romiosíni) (1901), in which he argued that it would be an inconceivable insult for Greeks to use this name, since Romiós had the derogatory meaning of a base and vulgar man. It took public intellectuals of the stature of Palamás and Psiháris to counteract this devastating blow to the cause of Romiosíni. The entire debate is well documented. For a brief summary, see Alki Kiriakídu-Néstoros, Λαογραφικά μελετήματα (Folklore studies) (1975), 221–38; and Tzióvas, Οι μεταμορφώσεις του εθνισμού (The transformations of nationism), 35. Tzióvas's discussion in *The Nationism of the Demoticists* (77–85) is even more extensive. For a critical bibliography on Romiosíni, see María Mantuvála, Ρωμαίος, Ρωμιός και Ρωμιοσύνη (Roman, Romiós, and Romiosíni) (1983).

46 Polítis, Έλληνες ή Ρωμιοί (Hellenes or Romií), 132. A supporter of Ellinismós, Greek folklorist Nikólaos G. Polítis worked with his own conception of the Greek *laós* as a retainer of survivals from the past. His pioneering effort to record demotic songs aided in the emergence of the discipline of *laografía* 'folklore' in Greece. See Alexiou, "Folklore: An Obituary?" 14–15, on his early contribution.

47 Politis, Έλληνες ή Ρωμιοί (Hellenes or Romií), 132.

48 In his novel Όσοι ζωντανοί (As many as survive) (1926), Íon Dragúmis contrasted the competing oral with the written Greek tradition: "Two traditions live in Hellenism from the time when Atticist civilization declined, the one inherited by an oligarchy, the educated elite, among whom teachers ruled supreme, supported by the

vernacular heritage, with its demotic language and folk songs, along-side an ancient genealogy. They argued, furthermore, that Romiosíni represented this heritage best, since it possessed "something poetically and musically colored, something winged, manly, and light—something that Ellinismós does not possess, with its heavy, immobile grandeur."[49] In celebrating the survival of a continuous religious and folk tradition rather than the revival of a glorified classical past, the champions of Romiosíni highlighted the people's everyday contributions to the continuation of an unbroken heritage, especially the part they played during the Byzantine and Ottoman periods.

Yet demoticist authors did not denounce outright the values of Hellenism or the ancient origins of Greek culture. Demoticists never finally selected Romiós over Éllinas as the chosen epithet for Neo-hellenes; nor did they renounce the terms Éllinas or Ellinismós.[50] Instead, they made the two equivalent titles of honor. And they kept both in circulation. Their reasoning was that both names had eminent origins; they each bore witness to the twin glory of being Greek. As Psiháris argued, "N. G. Polítis proved . . . that the name Éllinas also has its legitimate credentials in the Middle Ages and in Byzantium. . . . Palamás showed that Romiós was a sacred and honorable name even during the years of the Revolution; so much the better for us to have two glories rather than one. . . . No one said that we must rebaptize Hellas and make it a Roméic Kingdom."[51] Although referred to as a "solution of compromise,"[52] this seems instead a formula for profit; it is the ultimate expression of a Panhellenic ideology, the impulse of which has been to repossess *all* layers of Greek history (even those identified with conquerors) and *all* signifiers of Hellenic identity in the name of a common spirit. Psiharis's "compromise" allowed demoticists to appropriate all aspects of the national past, including its most

---

church and state. The other was inherited by the *laós*, illiterate, but always alive. By speaking and writing the language which the *laós* speaks and sings and enjoys and cries, demoticists come closer to the life of the nation than the teachers and educated elite. Between the demoticists and the nation there is no intervening wall dividing them; they communicate directly" (21–22).

[49] Palamás, Ρωμιός και Ρωμιοσύνη (Romiós and Romiosíni), 279.

[50] Today both Ellinismós and Romiosíni remain in usage, each representing a different symbolic order, as Herzfeld argues in *Anthropology through the Looking Glass*. In brief, *Romiosíni* refers to self-knowledge, while *Ellinismós* involves self-presentation for external consumption.

[51] Psiháris, Ρωμιός και Ρωμιοσύνη (Romiós and Romiosíni), 51.

[52] Kiriakídu-Néstoros, Λαογραφικά μελετήματα (Folklore studies), 224.

valued cultural possession, ancient texts—a contested *topos* that no one could afford to relinquish. Thus, while demoticists included post-classical periods in their narrations of Greek history, while they made Byzantium an indispensable component of Neohellenic literary history,[53] they also began to translate the *ancients* into the demotic idiom, to "put their seal on them by using demotic language, folk diminutives . . . and *dekapentasyllavos* [15-syllable verse], which was considered by them to be the national verse form."[54]

The demoticist struggle to interpret Greek history and to define the parameters of Greek culture focused on language and folklore. Demoticists' goal was to overpower the language of historical origin and purity with their own glorification of an authentic folk culture. Demoticists employed the discourse of populism to counter purist appropriations of the ancient past, to caricature the apologists of *katharévusa* 'purist Greek' as conspiring, elitist fools, and to present themselves as legitimate representatives of the people, with direct access to their folk language and oral culture.

In the effort to reclaim the classical past for a vernacular tradition, Psiháris's Το ταξίδι μου (My journey) is certainly a tour de force. It even advances a controversial position on the *Homerische Frage*, the question of the composition and language of the *Iliad* and *Odyssey* and the existence of a historical Homer. In one scene from this fictionalized journey, Psiháris's first-person narrator records his disagreement with

[53] A pioneering effort to view Greek history as a continuum with emphasis on the Byzantine period was the pre-demoticist Ιστορία του ελληνικού έθνους (History of the Hellenic nation) (1970) by Konstandínos Paparrigópulos (1815–91), first published by installment from 1853 to 1857. The enhancement of Byzantium's reputation in Neohellenic culture continued with Spirídon Zambélios (1815–81), who inquired, "Whence the common word, to sing?" in his 1859 work of the same name. Zambélios recognized the importance of medieval Greek history in the development of an indigenous poetic tradition. Among demoticists, Dragúmis, Eftaliótis, Psiháris, and Palamás gave Byzantium a central position in Greek history. The enhanced reputation of Byzantium in Greek circles is not unrelated to the rise of Byzantine studies in Germany in the late nineteenth century. For a comprehensive survey of the history of Byzantine scholarship excluding the Greek scholarship, see A. A. Vasiliev, *History of the Byzantine Empire* (1928).

[54] Tzióvas, *Nationism of the Demoticists*, 78. The most remarkable demotic rendering of ancient Greek is Aléxandros Pállis, Η Ιλιάδα μεταφρασμένη από τον Αλέξανδρο Πάλλη (The *Iliad* translated by Alexandros Pállis) ([1904] 1932). Pállis translated the *Iliad* in the manner of a δημοτικό τραγούδι *dimotikó tragúdi* 'folk song'. He adapted the *Iliad* to the prosody of the fifteen-syllable stressed verse and demoticized its heroes' names: Ἑλένη *Helenē,* the *causa belli,* for example, becomes the folk diminutive Λενιό *Lenió.*

a Chian native, who points to the place on the coast where Homer might have written the opening of the *Iliad*. The narrator responds categorically: "Homer didn't write, because he didn't know how to write. . . . A single Homer did not exist. Homer was many people. Hellas thus proved itself to be a very rich *topos*—one poet was not enough; it produced many poets at once, all of whom wandered here and there throughout Greece, each telling his own tale. . . . Poetry and imagination were not the possession of a single person, but of the entire *laós*."[55] The narrator argues that the Homeric epics derive from neither a written source nor a single historical poet. Instead, these poems represent the composite oral creation of a plurality of anonymous authors who, like contemporary illiterate villagers, stitched together the poems they created in the spirit of folk songs. In other words, the ancient epic poems appear to be no different from *dimotiká tragúdia* 'folk songs'. Homer, finally, is none other than the *laós* of antiquity who spoke the Greek vernacular and produced folk poetry.

The German philologist F. A. Wolf first advanced the theory Psiháris adopted in this passage. Wolf's *Prolegomena ad Homerum* (1795) aroused great controversy in European philological circles. Furthermore, it instigated a debate that has yet to be resolved.[56] It described a four hundred-year oral tradition begun by a certain Homer in approximately 950 B.C., gradually written down by a series of authors, and deliberately revised even after the epic poems' redaction. It argued that one could not attribute the Homeric poems to a single creator. Cer-

---

[55] Psiháris, Το ταξίδι μου (My journey), 116–17.

[56] Wolf's theory about the poems' oral composition, if not multiple authorship, made its way into diverse discussions and contexts. J. Davidson and Albin Lesky's surveys of the development of the "Homeric question" in English and German scholarship are comprehensive, but somewhat dated (see Davidson, "The Homeric Question" [1969]; Lesky, *Die Homerforschung in der Gegenwart* [1952]). More recently Nagy rebaptized the topic "Homeric questions" (1992). Jenkyns describes the reaction of Victorian authors to Wolf's challenge (*Victorians and Ancient Greece*, 192–226). In Greece, Zambélios adopted the view that Homer composed orally, though he never questioned Homer's historical existence. Zambélios began his controversial critique of *metafisikomanía* 'mania for metaphysics' in modern poetry by tracing the roots of Hellenic *tragudó* 'to sing' to Homeric *áïdō* 'to sing'. Homer in Zambélios's work appears as the inspired oral poet who documented extraordinary historical developments in the Greek world: "Behold the blind creator of Epic, divine Homer! The teller of many tales, goaded by the novel sight of the Panhellenic army marching against the barbarian under the one and only king, sings, glorifies, trumpets—sings as poet, sings as historian—the nation's first step toward consciousness of its own totality and wholeness" (Πόθεν η κοινή λέξις τραγουδώ; [Whence the common word, to sing?], 5).

tainly from our own perspective it makes sense that an age that saw German romantic poets turning to the *Volk* as a source of inspiration and scholars collecting popular tales also produced a philological argument that the *Iliad* and *Odyssey* were orally composed and enjoyed a plurality of authors.

Psiháris, too, adapted Homer to the spirit of *his* times and the purposes of *his own* cultural project. What is remarkable about his theory is its conflation of Wolf's arguments and linguistic demoticism. If the Homeric poems could be conceived as multiply layered, anonymously conceived, and orally composed, might one not also argue that they were a string of folk songs composed by and for the people in their own language?[57] In his effort to align the linguistic and cultural borders of the nation with the Greek vernacular, Psiháris made room for Homer by transporting him from an antiquated past into the everyday present. He thus extended the *topos* of the Greek vernacular to include not only the *dimotiká tragúdia* 'folk songs' of Romiosíni but also the Homeric epics—the entire span of the Roméic-Hellenic world.

By this gesture, Psiháris claimed the right to interpret all layers of Hellenism's past as well as to define its present and to invent its future. Since Homer remains, as Psiháris rightly conceded, a weighty precursor for a modern nation that feels nothing if not the *város* 'burden' of its past, he is an important cultural *topos*—one that must find its place in the front line of the forward-moving contemporary vernacular. Psiháris made Homer fit this culture by transforming him from the unique genius of a chosen individual to the exceptionally vibrant *pnévma* 'spirit' belonging to no one in particular and everyone in general: to the village, to speech, to purity, to simplicity, to the everyday, to the present. A sign of what the Grekí (another vernacular appellation for 'Greeks') are rather than of where they come from, Homer becomes the national communal organism diligently at work spinning its copious though ultimately unified cultural traditions.

---

[57] For a comparable view, consider Karl K. F. W. Lachmann's "lay" theory, developed through comparative study of Homeric and Finnish national epic. In *Betrachtungen über Homers Ilias* (1974) Lachmann argued that the epics were composed from separate "lays" that treated similar themes and a single myth. These "lays" were then "stitched" together. Again, it should be stressed that Psiháris's contribution to this and other arguments by the German analyst school was his insistence that common villagers composed the epic poems in the vernacular language of the age.

Modernist Form: An Internal Sense of Belonging

In the struggle to define national identity, demoticists prevailed in the cultural sphere but not in the state apparatus. Indeed, the state did not adopt the Greek vernacular as its official language until the late 1970s. Yet intellectuals and poets who appeared in the 1930s provided the aesthetic foundations for the later state recuperation.[58] This group of writers, critics, and scholars made the boldest move in appropriating all layers of Greek history, including the ancient Greek, for a national, popular, *high* vernacular culture.[59] They managed to redefine high culture as a continuation of Neohellenism's communal self-formation.

As heirs to the cultural project of demoticism, Neohellenic modernists adopted many demoticist views about the past. One will recall Elytis's narrative of Greece's anonymous artists quietly perpetuating Hellenism's living traditions, even while a self-serving, prejudiced elite minority of narrow-minded Westernizers sought to intervene in its affairs and dispossess it of its past. Modernists like Elytis shared demoticists' goal of integrating traditional material into an elevated, modernized vision of Hellenism. The key to their broader success was that they framed their project as a "continuous renewal" of the Hellenic tradition through the recovery of forgotten links with the past.[60] They claimed to have rediscovered previously overlooked manifestations of

---

[58] From the preceding discussion, one should not infer that populism served only hegemony. It also offered ammunition for the causes of resistance to dominant party politics. Consider the leftist poetry of Yánnis Rítsos or the early music of Míkis Theodorákis. Certainly it has been a staple of the rhetoric of the Greek Left that the *laós* is the authentic carrier of civilization. Appeals to the *laós* have motivated resistance to foreign invaders. A poignant example is found in Kiriakídis's essay "The Language and Folk Culture of Modern Greece" (1946), self-described as a "rebuttal to what the German occupation forces wrote during World War II in order to indoctrinate their soldiers. They said that the modern Greeks had no connection whatsoever with the ancient Greeks but that, for the most part, they were descendants of the barbaric Slavic tribes which flooded Greece during the Middle Ages" (47). The populism of resistance movements in Greece is an area that deserves broad exploration.

[59] In the view of Kaklamánis, Neohellenic populism emerged full force after 1930. Kaklamánis discusses the work of Theotokás and Spíros Melás in detail (Ανάλυση της νεοελληνικής αστικής ιδεολογίας [Analysis of the ideology of the Neohellenic middle class], 128–51).

[60] For the phrase *adiákopi ananéosi* 'continuous renewal', see Dimarás, Ιστορία της νεοελληνικής λογοτεχνίας (History of Neohellenic literature), xiii.

Hellenism. Although they effected their renewal of tradition through the eclectic assimilation of *foreign* influences into a demoticist framework, their rhetoric identified the act of modernizing Hellenic *morfí* 'form' with giving Neohellenism its authentic, *ntópia* 'native' expression.[61] This was their contradictory strategy: to reconcile the demoticist ideal of an unrestrained, unlearned orality with the literary modernist requisite for a self-referential textuality—a tall order indeed, since the process of a spontaneous orality and a well-wrought writerliness appear fundamentally at odds from a certain perspective.

Yet the formula of their project has remained unchallenged in Greece. Furthermore, it is a formula that artists everywhere are adopting more and more frequently when they wish to present the distinctiveness of an oppressed group they claim to represent. Today writers and artists in Greece continue to pay close attention to the rule of Hellenism's internal *morfí* 'form' in all its phases of development as they try to capture contemporary manifestations. Indeed, the systematic reconsideration of *morfí* 'form' is the neoteric, properly aesthetic contribution of Elytis and his contemporaries, I would argue.[62] Perhaps we should specify what they meant by *morfí*, however, so that we do not automatically assume that Greek notions completely coincide with other contemporary theories of form from which they may have borrowed ideas.

When Elytis refers to the successful "plastic" rendering of the Hellenic landscape, he assumes that *morfí* is a shaping principle that derives from nature. Although apparently mutable with the passage of time, it is nevertheless a transcendental essence, the ideal organization of a living organism. It consists of whatever in the object's construction welds all the parts into a whole and, in addition, gives a comprehensible *foní* 'voice' to the *pnévma* 'spirit' of the whole. Since outward manifestation may change with time and place, the artist must discover shaping principles that give an object life under a specific set of historical, geographical, climatic, and cultural conditions. What re-

---

[61] For Elytis, all forms of speech—artistic, political, educational, religious—must have "the necessary and fundamentally appropriate structure. . . . Nothing . . . becomes a passport to the soul, if it has not previously had the beneficial 'visa' of expressive means. The rules of the arts are the rules of life. The politician should not differ from the artist in his views. And in the artist's view the struggle for the salvation of human beings is the struggle for appropriate expression and nothing else" (Τα δημόσια και τα ιδιωτικά [The public and the private], 33–34).

[62] In *Belated Modernity and Aesthetic Culture*, Jusdanis argues that Greek letters did not entertain properly aesthetic considerations before the 1920s.

mains immutable, however, is the rule of immanence: principles of structure must derive from nature. Furthermore, artistic expression must recover the spiritual dimension of the *topío* 'landscape'. This process involves a communion of language and soil.

The most extensive consideration of *morfí* 'form' in the postwar era appears in an essay appropriately entitled Το πρόβλημα της μορφής (The problem of form) (1946). Its author, architect and theorist Dimítris Pikiónis, designed and executed landscaping on the hills of the Acropolis and Philopappos in Athens, which has been described as "the best known work of a sensitive and populist eclecticism, which particularly appealed to modern Greek intellectuals."[63] His essay defines *morfí* as "the spiritual dimension of this earth."[64] Like Elytis, Pikiónis presupposes that there must be an absolute "identity between principles of structure and principles of nature" in any work that achieves its ideal form.[65] To determine what relationship binds Neohellenes to the Hellenic *cosmos*, Pikiónis studies fragments from centuries of civilization on Rhodes. He very eloquently argues that the spiritual radiation of antiquity, the true value of ancient aesthetics, lies in its discovery that the beauty of the human body as manifested in sculpture, the essence of the physical world as captured in architecture, and the power of soul and mind as explored by philosophy—all these things—reveal the beauty of the divine. The Byzantine world supplements this discovery with the belief that the grace of the *iperúsios* 'superbeing' sheds mystical light on every form of expression. Everything depends on incarnation, which, in turn, relies on the identity of principles of structure and nature.

In a standard narrative turn, Pikiónis argues that the importation of Western aesthetics into the Hellenic world breaks this absolute identity. Again and again one finds Greek artists and theorists very much under the influence of French, German, and English ideas bemoaning the Hellenic turn to the West and working hard to mark the Neohellenic difference. Pikiónis discovers false, foreign shapes grafted onto Hellenism where first the Frankish, then the Italian, occupying forces "add the seal of their presence everywhere in this Hellenic *topos*. This imposition of their own measure, their own ideal values onto

---

[63] Helen Fessas-Emmanouil, *Public Architecture in Modern Greece, 1827–1992* (1993), 63. Pikiónis also first imagined the center of Athens as a pedestrian archeological park, an idea that may be consummated by the year 2000.
[64] Pikiónis, Το πρόβλημα της μορφής (The problem of form), 206.
[65] Ibid., 212.

those of others . . . takes the form of a high-handed intrusion on the
'karma' of a people, an unbearable rape of the Hellenic consciousness."[66] Although the Ottomans came nearer to realizing a Hellenic
ideal, according to Pikiónis, the spirit of Hellenism remained wholly
intact only in Hellenic *hómata* 'soils', on the one hand, and in the heart
of the *laós* 'people', on the other.[67] It was finally the common *laós* who
kept alive the essence of antiquity for Pikiónis: "Yes, in him live the
divine seed, ancient speech, and the rhythms and musical modes, the
shapes and essences from ancient times. Here it was destined that they
be conceived. If they were to die here, not even God himself would be
able to resurrect them. . . . For this reason it was His will that they be
preserved here—hidden away, far from the peaks and declines of
history, in the *pnévma* 'spirit' of the simple man and the unspoiled
surprise of his soul—so that the poet could take them over from
here."[68]

Pikiónis was certainly not alone in concluding that educated Greeks
must investigate the *pnévma* 'spirit' of the *laós* 'people' together with
the *hómata* 'soils' of Hellas to uncover the eternal *morfí* 'form' of
Hellenism. Elytis arrived at the same conclusion in his essay on contemporary Greek art, as we have seen, while Seferis also anticipated
that the soul of the people could reveal something transhistorical to the
poet or intellectual: "If we really want to understand the ancients, we
must always investigate the *psyche* [soul] of our *laós*."[69] In the years
immediately following World War II, Greek authors and artists sought
to cultivate in their own work an inherent popular understanding of
Hellenism in all its manifestations, including the ancient.

Certainly Elytis was preeminent among those who placed *laós* 'people' alongside the Hellenic *topío* as constituent, even determinant,
elements structuring a poetic *cosmos*. He envisioned a natural community, an element of the landscape itself sprung from the *hómata* 'soils',
ordering itself within the poetic word according to the rules of immanence. For Elytis the poet's task is to give a contemporary order to
Hellenism's eternal spirit. And, contradictory as this combination of
elements may appear, he argued that it was modernist, specifically
surrealist techniques that could ground Neohellenic artistic expression
in the determinant powers of the *laós* 'people' and *topío* 'landscape'.

[66] Ibid., 208.
[67] Ibid., 207.
[68] Ibid., 220.
[69] Seferis, Ένας Έλληνας—ο Μακρυγιάννης (A Hellene—Makriyánnis), 257.

In sum, Elytis's aim was to overcome linguistic aridity by making poetic language so luminous that it could somehow spell the Hellenic *cosmos*. To put it another way, his poetry gives form to an idea he recently expressed thus: "places here and there in the soils of the Aegean," bearing signs of the "many-century presence of Hellenism," furnish their own "*orthografía*, where each omega, each ipsilon, each accent mark or iota subscript is nothing but a small bay, a slope, the vertical line of a rock over the curved line of a boat's stern, winding grapevines, a decoration over a church door, red and white dotted here and there from pigeon houses and potted geraniums."[70] Not only does Elytis's poetry seek to abolish the duality between world and word; it tries to recover a *cosmos* where nature spells itself. Language becomes purified not because it cleanses its universe of worldly referents; rather it finds for each physical element its natural location in culture.

Elytis's elision of the move from language to landscape, orthography to nature, is not incidental to the passage quoted above; instead it is eminently programmatic. Everywhere we find his work slipping back and forth between literary and natural referents, each co-determining the other. Important to observe, Elytis's recent essay draws its natural monuments — the "small bay," the "curved line of a boat's stern," the "pigeon houses and potted geraniums"—from the vast storehouse of *topoí* that appear in *his own* literary corpus. These are the distinctive, irreducible phonemes of Elytis's poetic *cosmos*. They do not correspond to actual physical elements and objects but to the proper ordering of words and images in his poetic topography. Thus *orthografía* represents the latent movement of his poetry from language to entopia,[71] it suggests his poetry's internal belonging to the Hellenic landscape and its native peoples. Elytis's poetry tends to cultivate the aesthetic potentialities of words and images in ways that makes them fit naturally, as it

---

[70] Elytis, Τα δημόσια και τα ιδιωτικά (The public and the private), 8–9.

[71] Clearly Elytis's aesthetic ideas about the relationship between poetry and the Hellenic *topío* 'landscape' reflect a vogue from the late 1930s and early 1940s. Not only can this be traced to Greek modernism; it shares something with the official cultural doctrine of Ioánnis Metaxás's Fascist regime and with the "national aestheticism" of Nazism. Martin Heidegger is the German thinker who sought to establish a subtle philosophical "tie between art and the grounding of the 'world' of the people" (Jean-Joseph Goux, "Politics and Modern Art—Heidegger's Dilemma" [1989], 14). See especially his essay "The Origin of the Work of Art" ([1935–36] 1971). For an interesting discussion of Heidegger's "dilemma" concerning modern art, see Goux. It should be noted that unlike Greek Fascists or German Nazis, both Elytis and Heidegger took language rather than blood to be the element that grounded a poetic world in the nation's soils. Both also acknowledged their debt to Hölderlin.

were, into a particular *cosmos*, which is, finally, none other than his literary corpus. The assumption is that when words find their "natural" location, they can spell perfectly Elytis's own "*cosmos* the small the great."

In that *cosmos*, as I have mentioned, the *laós* 'people' appear to project their own image onto the *hómata* 'soils' of the Aegean. In fact, a fundamental presupposition of Elytis's work is that Neohellenic poetry is, in its purest form, an extension of the natural world, with which it may find itself in perfect communion. In the same essay, Elytis expressed the wish that the objects of everyday life, the "phonemes" of literary expression, be "in continuous communication with the sun," the element his poetry nearly worships: "Let there exist a kind of phototropism like that which allows plants to obtain the necessary chlorophyll for their eternal revival . . . , which enables all those [cultural artifacts] to leap from one century to another and to stitch through the hide of time. . . . For no other reason than that we dwell on the same *hóma* [soil]."[72]

Surely Elytis's desire for a cultural "phototropism" can be placed alongside his idea that a culture that follows its natural inclination can "leap" through time so as to attach itself to eras temporarily distant but physically grounded in the same *hóma* 'soil'. What unites these two ideas is their incompatibility with the premise of autonomy shared by an internationalist, modernist standard. By the novelty of the form they introduced, most modernist movements both announced a clear break with history and refused to subject art to external contingencies such as the demands of national politics. Yet—as critics are now asking of Martin Heidegger's philosophical and critical project after 1935—is the effort to establish a "tie between art and the grounding of the 'world' of the people" necessarily contrary to the assumptions of modernist art?[73] Does it contradict a modernist aesthetic at its metaphysical foundations? Elytis, like Heidegger, proclaimed his own modernity by dislodging the ego from the sovereign place of the center, while also resettling in the place of the ego a landscape and its people. Was this a repercussion of the disturbance of the modern—a conservative reaction to the formal decomposition of culture, particularly after the traumas of the 1930s and 1940s? Or was it a modernist expression of rupture?

---

[72] Elytis, Τα δημόσια και τα ιδιωτικά (The public and the private), 18–19.
[73] Goux, "Politics and Modern Art," 14.

Although Elytis's idea of recovering a physical ground for literary creation conflicts with the irreducible premise of aesthetic autonomy, it is not entirely irreconcilable with the metaphysics of modernism. Here I refer to the idea that the subject achieves perfection within the self-enclosed realm of literature or art. Within this purified space, artistic creation enacts a fragmentary self-formation. Elytis's work, however, employs modernist techniques to express not the disembodied voice of a solitary individual who quietly suffers social decomposition but the body of a national community proudly marching forth to reclaim its *cosmos* from foreign usurpers. Form expresses the content not of a battered individual consciousness but of Neohellenism's communal self-awareness, which achieves perfection precisely when it faces the threat of foreign invasion.

Elytis felt he could adopt European techniques to assert Neohellenism's distinctiveness, particularly against foreign appropriations of its past. Paradoxical as this may seem, we should recognize it as a common strategy. Certainly the move to assert a premodern, non-Western identity through arguments and techniques borrowed from Western European texts is a salient feature of Eastern European populism. And we should understand that Elytis acquired artistic authority and ideological power by using the surrealist revolution to mediate not only between tradition and modernity but also between an authentic Hellenism and its appropriations. Elytis assumed a very powerful role when he promised to reclaim for the Neohellenic people the classical past appropriated by Western rationalism. To a Neohellenic audience, the goal of transforming Hellas from a historical ideal into an eternal, luminous expression of the Neohellenic *laós* 'people' and their *topío* 'landscape' seemed truly revolutionary.

The National Body as Literary Palimpsest

In the effort to reclaim the classical alongside the Byzantine and Ottoman Greek traditions as constituent elements of the national-popular body, the *Axion Esti* is a culminating achievement. It transposes Hellenism from a venerated historical conceptualization (the purist mode) and a glorified folk setting (the protodemotic mode) to an important new *topos*: the literary text. Although itself an assemblage of styles, symbols, fragments, heroes, and commonplaces from a select Greek corpus, the *Axion Esti* gives the impression of creating

its own Neohellenic mythology, from the *topío* 'landscape' and customs, from the historical consciousness of freedom, from the mysteries
of the Greek language, from Byzantine hymns and the liturgy of the
Greek Orthodox Church, with its survivals of Dionysian and Eleusi-
nian elements, and above all, from the sea, the sky, the rocks, and the
whitewash of the contemporary Aegean *topío* 'landscape'.[74]

The overall strategy of the poem is to translate Hellenism from the
remoteness of history to the immanence of form, to incorporate Hellenism in the autonomous *cosmos* of the well-structured modernist
poem. The poem inscribes within itself allusions to ancient authors,
mythical heroes, and canonical texts, which appear as if sutured to the
"entrails" of the "newly created" poet, the poem's incarnated ego. The
poet's body is written through with mythical and Christian figures,
classical, biblical, and modern texts, then conflated with the autochthonous body of the people as represented by a community of Hellenes "made up of all generations and ages, some from now and some
from ancient times, turned white by too much beard," marching
toward a communal destiny on the Albanian front in World War II.[75]

But what exactly might it mean to read the *Axion Esti* as if it were "a
palimpsest where the text and the words that cover it have accrued,
mingled, digested one another, and crossed"?[76] Perhaps we should
first consider the nature of the palimpsest, in order to describe more
accurately the composite effect of the poem. A palimpsest is the
product of erasing and reinscribing a writing surface. The final product is a surface where several layers may become visible, so that the
discernible text becomes a complex mosaic of various other texts that
happen to show through in different places.

The three parts of Elytis's *Axion Esti*, entitled "The Genesis," "The
Passion," and "The Gloria," reflect the life of a palimpsest conceived as
a self-sufficient *cosmos* with a meaningful *archē* and *telos*. "The Genesis"
presents the dialectic of creation: the activities of erasing and rewriting
that produce the palimpsest. In "The Passion," we find the populist
narrative of a conspiracy to crucify the defiant national–popular body-
as-hero superimposed over older stories about passion, including the
stories of the ancient Greek and romantic Prometheus and the biblical

---

[74] Kimon Friar, Άξιον Εστί το τίμημα (Worthy is the honor) (1979), 49.

[75] *The Axion Esti*, trans. Keeley and Savidis, 21.

[76] Dimirúlis, Το "Άξιον" της ιστορίας και το "Εστί" της ρητορικής (The "Worthy" of history and the "It is" of rhetoric), 315.

and liturgical Christ. Here hidden layers, reemergent surfaces, and final inscriptions all tell a story of near-fatal conflict, though they confuse the identity of the invading forces. "The Gloria" offers a medley of native expressions. These become visible in the landscape of the modern text through a process of self-reconstruction. The surface recovers some layers from its ageless tradition, while it also digests other layers in the most recent incarnation of Hellenicity.

Although Elytis reflects pejoratively on the meditated usage of the written tradition, he does not reject outright the literary appropriation of older texts.[77] To put it another way, whereas he describes his own work as a "primal inscription of reality" the goal of which is to express the soul clearly,[78] in the Axion Esti Elytis identifies creation with the activity of reading. On the first day of the "Genesis," the creator unequivocally introduces the poet's first commandment for the newly created cosmos.

> "Your commandment," he said, "is this cosmos
> and it is written in your entrails
> Read and strive
> and fight," he said.
> (The Axion Esti, trans. Keeley and Savidis, 3)

Here the readable surface is not the literary text but the poet's "entrails." Yet the image itself represents a conflict between the natural body and the cultivated literary space. Nature and culture are then mediated by a personification of "memory become the present," which takes on "the voice of the trees, of the waves" (3) when it introduces the poet to reading.

The image of memory as words written on the hearts of mortals has its own literary history. One conventional ancient Greek metaphor likens the faculty of memory to a writing tablet contained in the heart.

[77] Elytis's essays express a formal opposition to "a certain kind of neointellectualism that tends toward abstract expression, studied silence, . . . overworked citations, and mediated references to older layers of education" (Πρώτα-πρώτα [To begin] [1982], 15).

[78] Elytis, Πρώτα-πρώτα (To begin), 41. On another occasion, Elytis described how he sought long and hard to discover a method capable of "incarnating," or literally "giving body" to, the senses: "It was quite natural that I should seek a poetic method that could be made capable, by my own soul's intervention, of incarnating something analogous to the senses that charm me" (Odysseus Elytis, Το χρονικό μιάς δεκαετίας [Chronicle of a decade] [(1973) 1982], 243).

The phrase μνημόνες δέλτοι φρενῶν 'memory tablets of the heart' is crucial to Io's story in Aeschylus's *Prometheus Bound*. The relevant scene follows Prometheus's famous monologue in which he enumerates his gifts to human beings. These include a marvelous discovery:

γραμμάτων τε συνθέσεις
μνήμην ἁπάντων, μουσωμήτορ' ἐργάνην.
(*Prometheus Bound* 460–61)

the combining of letters,
Memory of all things, industrious Mother of the Muses.

Here "the combining of letters," or writing, becomes the ultimate source of artistic inspiration on which even Memory, Mother of the Muses, depends.[79]

After this speech, Io arrives. She requests that Prometheus reveal to her what sufferings are in store for her. Prometheus commands Io: ἐγγράφου 'engrave' a prophecy of πολύδονον πλάνην 'sorrowful wanderings' μνήμοσιν δέλτοις φρενῶν 'on the memory tablets of the heart' (789). What Io is to engrave on her *phrenes* 'the seat of thoughts and emotions in living persons' is Prometheus's map of her wanderings through the Greek world.[80] Prometheus quite literally maps Io's destiny—that is to say, his speech contains so much geographical detail that it presents a map of the Greek world. Io must engrave this map within. To remember Prometheus's words, she must bring them out of storage, so to speak, so as to recollect the signposts of suffering from her private map.

The *Axion Esti* recalls the literary image of a text engraved within the body. Like the unfortunate Io, the poet's fate rides on his ability to decipher the inscription, which also bears a miniature *cosmos*. Whereas Io was commanded to record and then recall what is marked on her

---

[79] James A. Notopoulos suggests that the invention of writing, like the purloined firebrand, would significantly disturb a preliterate social order. Thus "Prometheus's gift of letters wherewith to hold all things in memory is a radical and rather opposite view to that of conservative members of an oral society. Here we see the clash between the two views of early peoples on letters, the conservative element of the oral society maintaining that it destroys memory, while the progressive element maintained that it would conserve rather than destroy memory" ("Mnemosyne in Oral Literature" [1938], 476).

[80] In pre-Socratic literature, *phrēn* 'mind' is equivalent to the 'living spirit' of humans; it is what endows the living person with the capacity to both feel and think. Human shades are without it.

heart, however, the modern poet must *read* the body already engraved with the creator's words. Indeed, the act of reading is what the poet learns from the creator during the seven days of genesis. The story of his initiation into the processes of reading "this small *cosmos* the great" inscribed within is a prominent theme of "The Genesis." There we are given a step-by-step account of how the poet learns to "read his entrails" and so to understand the world within and around him. The poet first observes the creator:

> the One not made by human hand
> > drew with his finger the distant
> > lines
> sometimes rising sharply to a height
> sometimes lower: the curves gentle
> > one inside the other
> > > (*The Axion Esti*, 4)

Then the poet prepares a blank slate by "erasing History with my heel" (6). In a parallel action, the creator speaks and creates first the sea, then "in its center he sowed little worlds [*cosmoi*] in my image and likeness" (6). Each word brings into creation a new *cosmos*.

After a day of writing, the creator turns the poet's gaze in the direction of the broad sky to "read the infinite on your own" (6). When charged to "see and receive" this *cosmos* (7), the poet finally takes the first hard steps toward reading. He clears a space of silence "to plant the seeds of phonemes and golden shoots of oracles," then pronounces "secret syllables through which" he strives "to utter my identity" (7). The creator congratulates him for learning to read and points him in the direction of το Ασήμαντο to *Asímando* 'the Insignificant' (7). The poet pronounces "words strange and enigmatic / ROES, ESA, ARIMNA / NUS, MIROLTAMITY, YELTIS" (8).[81] When the creator describes these as "Precious names, . . . ancient oaths, / saved by Time and the sure ear of the distant winds" (9), the poet learns that language is his most important weapon. He prepares the seed within his love-stricken entrails for "This world [*cosmos*] the small world the great!" (9).

Another day of *áskisis* 'isolated study' passes, and the poet, "bent over papers and bottomless books" (9), seeks "whiteness to the utmost

---

[81] These are anagrammatic forms of key words in Elytis's poetry: "rose," "sea," "marina," "sun," "immortality," and his signature, "Elytis."

intensity / of blackness" (10). Now he completes his "Genesis." He has fully located the text within and learned to read it productively. As he reads, his identity expands, and the creator god fully occupies him:

> And the One I really was, the One of many centuries ago
> the One still verdant in the midst of fire, the One still bound to heaven
>   entered into me, became
>   the one I am
>
> (*The Axion Esti*, 13)

Finally the poet can identify the body with the *cosmos* written within. Through oral recitation of his internal "orthography," he becomes "This I, then, and the small *cosmos* the great."

"The Passion," the second part of the *Axion Esti*, juxtaposes the poet's reading voice to older layers of texts.[82] The poem's apparently primordial orality hides books from the Old and New Testaments, Byzantine hymns, the liturgy of St. John Chrysostom, Greek folk songs, the poetry of Dionísios Solomós, and the memoirs of Makri-yánnis. As the story of passion progresses, images accumulate; the isolated hero becomes a modern transubstantiation of Prometheus, Christ, the naval leaders of the Greek Revolution, and many others.

It becomes possible to analyze how the *Axion Esti* integrates classical works into its populist narrative by following one ancient thread in the poem: the very subtle references to the figure of Prometheus. Although textual allusions to Aeschylus's *Prometheus Bound* are only occasionally obvious or certain, a comparative reading of the two texts is not only possible but illuminating. One finds a few choice passages from Aeschylus incorporated into Elytis's altogether different narrative of foreign interference and popular defiance—a nontragic myth of Greece's unjust suffering before an evil and barbarous enemy.[83] Close

---

[82] "The Passion" is the largest section of the poem, composed of eighteen psalms (represented by Roman numerals), twelve odes (represented by lowercase letters), and six readings. These are grouped in the following pattern, PPOROPPOROPP, repeated three times. The three parts of "The Passion" have as their respective themes Consciousness Facing Tradition, Consciousness Facing Danger, and Consciousness Surpassing Danger.

[83] In a very early appraisal of the poem, Pános Thasítis referred to it as a "tragedy." Clearly he used this term in an unspecific way when he defined "tragedy" as a "conflict of catholic powers . . . [that] finds an optimistic solution in the victory of good over evil" (Επτά δοκίμια για την ποίηση [Seven essays on poetry] [(1960) 1979], 59). Yet the term has been applied generously to the *Axion Esti* since Thasítis first set the tone of discussion. In the analysis that follows, I would like to suggest that the conception of

comparison enables one to investigate how the ancient references find a new setting in the modern text—how they become visible on the modern poem's legible surface.

The narrator identifies himself with Prometheus through his inventiveness, the discovery of writing, recourse to the creative forces of fire and mind, and through the circumstances of his victimization. In the final hour of passion, the *Axion Esti* recalls Prometheus's repeated torment through several transparent allusions to the *Prometheus Bound*:

> They came
> with their gold braid,
>   the fowl of the North and the beasts of the East!
> After dividing my flesh in two
>   and quarreling finally over my liver,
> they left.
>   "Theirs the smoke of sacrifice," they said,
> "and ours the smoke of fame,"
>   amen."
> And the echo that was sent out of the past
>   all of us heard and knew.
> We knew the echo and once again
>   we sang in a dry voice:
> Ours, ours the bloody iron
>   and the treble-wrought betrayal.
> . . . .
> But you, mouth of the innocent, gate of Paradise,
> with your word you lit the star's lamp
>   in our hand!
> We see in the future the might of smoke,
>   a plaything of your breath,
> its power and its glory!
>
> (*The Axion Esti*, 32)

Like Aeschylus's Prometheus, Elytis's poetic persona finds himself betrayed by a powerful enemy, the beneficiary, like Zeus, of "the smoke of sacrifice"—against whom the modern hero refuses to take up firearms. Indeed, the enemy's "weapons and iron and fire" are made weightier by references to Aeschylus, where Hermes is said to have carried the message of Zeus's threat: "Zeus will send a πτηνὸς

---

power put forth by the *Axion Esti* conflicts with that which moves the action of ancient Greek tragedies.

κύων 'winged dog' (*Prometheus Bound* 1022) to devour the Titan's liver day after day; similarly τα πετεινά 'fowl', 'birds of prey', quarrel over the hero's liver.[84]

Yet the Manichean division in Elytis's populist conception of a war-torn *cosmos* split into parties of good and evil becomes all the more apparent by contrast to Aeschylus's world of power play, blackmail, and fierce negotiation. One discovers the clearest signs of how Elytis renders tradition populist in the contrast between the two texts. The *Axion Esti* bifurcates justice and power. The voice of purity, a force of good brandishing the creative torch of poetic language, remains innocent of the knowledge of power that wields the might of smoke. Forces from the North employ a destructive form of fire to extend their unjust rule, while the sun-filled South defends itself with poetry. The story of the conflict between these two cosmic forces, fire and sun, power and justice, good and evil, North and South, ignores the ancient tragedy's anticipated reconciliation between Zeus and Prometheus, while it also gives moral rather than political or social significance to the element of fire.

It may be useful to reflect more extensively on the *Prometheus Bound*, where fire, in Aeschylus's words παντέχνου πυρὸς σέλας 'the blaze of fire skilled in all the arts' (7), becomes the focus of a power struggle between Prometheus and Zeus. Indeed, Prometheus, who stole fire from Olympus intentionally to provoke the new ruler, has some interesting things to say about the place of fire in the cosmic order. In his opening and closing statements, he makes his counter-allegations against Zeus. He calls upon the element of aether (*aithēr*, commonly translated as 'air' or 'heaven' but also identified with fire) to be the first witness to his oath.[85] Prometheus naturally avoids invoking the supreme god Zeus, from whom he is alienated. Yet it is significant that he names the δῖος αἰθὴρ 'illustrious heaven' (88) in the place of Zeus.[86] In this invocation, Zeus remains powerfully present, since ΔΙΟΣΑΙΘΗΡ, as the words would appear in a fifth-century B.C. text, could be interpreted as either δῖος αἰθὴρ 'illustrious heaven' or Διὸς αἰθὴρ 'heaven of Zeus', since Διός is also the genitive case of Ζεύς.

---

[84] From the same root verb πέτομαι 'to fly'. The words πτηνός and πετεινός (or πετηνός), adjectives meaning 'able to fly' (the nominalized form designates a 'bird' or 'fowl'), are both documented in antiquity.

[85] The formula is Homeric. See *Iliad* 3.276ff.

[86] This, too, is a Homeric formula. See *Iliad* 16.365: αἰθέρος ἐκ δίης 'out of the illustrious aether'.

Prometheus addresses the aether again in the closing lines of the tragedy as he falls into a new abyss of torment:

ὦ πάντων
αἰθὴρ κοινὸν φάος εἱλίσσων,
ἐσορᾷς μ' ὡς ἔκδικα πάσχω.
(*Prometheus Bound* 1091–93)

O aether
who rotate the common light of all
you see how lawlessly I suffer.

The meaning of this passage depends on a pre-Socratic use of *aether* that appears in fragments from Empedocles, Parmenides, possibly Heraclitus,[87] and most certainly Anaxagoras.[88] The image is of a gaseous medium that catalyzes the sun's combustion through its own rotation. This cosmic image of the aether conforms with the etymological root, *aeth-* 'to light up, kindle, or burn'.

More important, the image assumes knowledge of Anaxagoras's cosmology. Anaxagoras was the first Ionian philosopher to take up residence in Athens during the fifth century B.C.[89] At about the time when the *Prometheus Bound* was first being performed in Athens, Anaxagoras was probably stirring up citizens with his scientific theories on the nature and order of the *cosmos*. His cosmology portrayed the sun, moon, and stars as fiery stones carried round by the aether's περιχώρησις 'rotation'. For unlike ἀήρ 'air', a dense, moist, cold, and dark element, the aether was a thin, dry, hot, and light element; indeed it was the equivalent of fire, as Aristotle informs us: Ἀναξαγόρας . . . ὀνομάζει γὰρ αἰθέρα ἀντὶ πυρός 'Anaxagoras refers to aether rather than fire' (*De caelo* A3.270b24).

Aeschylus could not have been ignorant of this cosmic theory, or of Anaxagoras's substitution of aether for fire. In light of this substitution, Prometheus's apostrophe to the ΔΙΟΣΑΙΘΗΡ is deeply suggestive. Whether taken to mean "illustrious fire" or "fire of Zeus," it names the object of contention between Prometheus and Zeus. In his

[87] "The pure cosmic fire was probably identified by Heraclitus with *aither*, the brilliant fiery stuff which fills the shining sky and surrounds the world" (G. S. Kirk and J. E. Raven, *The Presocratic Philosophers: A Critical History with a Selection of Texts* [1957], 200–201).

[88] C. J. Herington, "A Study in the *Prometheus*, Part I: The Elements in the Trilogy" (1963), 180 n. 3, lists these references.

[89] Anaxagoras stayed in Athens from approximately 480 to 450 B.C. John Burnet (*Early Greek Philosophy* [1957], 251) lists sources for Anaxagoras's life.

closing prayer, too, Prometheus recognizes the role fire has played in his struggle with Zeus. He is now at the mercy of the same element that he wielded against Zeus. The sustained rotation and redistribution of the elements has made him, once the aggressive player, a "plaything" of fire. This Prometheus admits to himself in a moment of deep despair, νῦν δ' αἰθέριον κίνυγμ' ὁ τάλας 'now I, the wretch, am moved about by the aether' (158).[90]

Prometheus also describes himself as the chance victim of wandering calamity:

> Πλανωμένη
> πρὸς ἄλλοτ' ἄλλον πημονὴ προσιζάνει.
> (275–76)

> Misery roams
> unpredictably around and settles on different people in turn.

In this case he uses the verb πλανάω 'to wander', which entered medical discourse in Aeschylus's time to denote "fevers that recur at regular intervals."[91] Here Aeschylus's tragedy has extended the metaphor of moving fields of fire to explain the arbitrary suffering that befalls mortals and immortals. This is to give a sociological application to a cosmological and medical model. Within a schema of relentless elemental rotation, there is little room for individual agency or just arbitration. As Prometheus struggles to designate Zeus's crime against him, he suppresses his own role in disturbing the new ruler's *nomos* 'just distribution of things'. He thus renders himself its arbitrary victim.

---

[90] We saw these lines elegantly revised when the poetic persona calls himself τῆς πνοῆς σου παίγνιο 'a plaything of your breath' (*The Axion Esti*, 32). The theory of the powerful motion and the exchange of burning elements appears in other speeches by Prometheus, notably his narration of the battle between Zeus and the sons of Earth and Heaven. The fate of the hundred-headed giant, Typhon, is exemplary. When fighting against Chronus's sons and daughters, Typhon flashed hideous lightning from his eyes. Yet an undaunted Zeus dared to withstand his force and struck him with an "unsleeping dart / descending thunderbolt that breathes out flames" (*Prometheus Bound* 358–59). This burnt him to ashes, leaving his corpse sprawling beneath the roots of the mountain Aetna. Yet "there will burst forth one day / rivers of fire devouring with savage jaws / the level fields of Sicily, rich in fine fruit" (367–69). The root of Typhon's name, τυφ-, 'to raise or consume smoke', derives from the Indo–European root *dhu* (see Frisk, *Griechisches etymologisches Wörterbuch*, 950).

[91] M. Griffith, *Aeschylus, Prometheus Bound* (1983), 138.

Prometheus's rhetoric in the tragedy's opening lines, however—his repeated use, for example, of forms of the word αἰκεία 'outrage' to name Zeus's action against him[92]—betrays his strategy. Through repetition, he persuades the sympathetic chorus of his vague charge against Zeus. The chorus concedes that Zeus indeed ἀτίμως . . . αἰκίζεται 'commits outrage unpunished' (195); hence Prometheus suffers αἰκὲς πῆμ' 'outrageous misery' (472). In the process of explaining his present situation to the chorus, Prometheus provides valuable information about his struggle with Zeus. For his part, Prometheus admits: ἑκών, ἑκὸν ἥμαρτον 'willingly, willingly I missed the mark!' (266).

It is reasonable to ask why he willingly disturbed the cosmic order and set it into furious motion. What did he gain by this disturbance?[93] Certainly Prometheus "the sophist," as Hermes pejoratively refers to him (944), had something else in mind. The issue for him was the survival of his descendants, the mortals whom the Titans created and civilized. Every generation faced the threat of its destruction by future generations. Zeus himself was not exempt from this rule of violent succession. Just as "Zeus vanquished the older generation of giants" (150–51) and planned "to replace mortals with his own creation after destroying their race" (231–33), so his own offspring would "hurl him from his sovereignty and throne into oblivion" (909–10).

Prometheus stole fire for human beings in order to dispense arms to Zeus's only surviving opposition. This was a first step in a long-term struggle for power. Prometheus took up the cause of mortals not as a champion of justice and civilization over tyranny and barbarism but as a power broker arming his allies. Mortals, a remnant of his own generation, needed arms to face Zeus, who intended to destroy them in order to seal his absolute sovereignty. By passing the secret of fire to mortals, Prometheus willfully shifted the scales of power in his favor. This move set the combustible elements of the *cosmos* into a violent, rotating motion. Prometheus would take a temporary beating; but he also held another card. He knew precisely when and how Zeus would be vanquished by the next generation in return for having usurped power. In an act of blackmail, Prometheus made Zeus dependent on

[92] Nominal and verbal forms of αἰκεία appear in lines 93, 97, 168, 176, 227, and 256.

[93] Oceanus is unable to see the payoff when he advises Prometheus to forget his anger, beg for release from suffering, and adjust himself to Zeus's system of justice (310–16).

his own well-being by advertising (without revealing the content of) his valuable foreknowledge.[94]

Throughout the process of tough negotiation, Prometheus stood ἔκδικα ek-dika 'outside justice' (1093) only because he removed himself from the protection of Zeus's rule of justice by ignoring the ruler's regulations. This is in accordance with a rule of justice in which the ruler determines what is just, as Prometheus himself declares: τὸ δίκαιον ἔχων Ζεύς 'Zeus holds justice' (187). Justice is not arbitration by natural law but a system for regulating community life. Due process of law is accorded only to the community member. Whoever takes a fateful step outside community life, whoever removes himself from the community by trespassing its regulations, becomes an "outlaw." He loses the right to seek legal reparations, meaning that he may experience outrage by the standards of community justice without this outrage's being labeled an unjust act. He stands, quite literally, ek-dika.

We should therefore read Prometheus's cry of frustration at the end of the tragedy as a cry of recognition: "You see how I suffer outside justice" (1093). His call for witnesses against Zeus's outrage meets with meaningful silence from the ruling authorities. He has gained the sympathy only of a powerless chorus, who nonetheless has learned "to despise traitors" (1607) because they upset the cosmic order. The tragedy's moral lesson reflects as much on Prometheus in his relationship to Zeus as it does on Zeus in his relationship to the precursors whose power he eclipsed.

The Populist Repossession of the Classics: A Modernist Transposition?

The *Axion Esti* adjusts the story of Prometheus to fit a populist narrative. According to this narrative, a powerful intruder victimizes a native hero. In the poem, the Prometheus recalled stands completely outside the domain of power. No longer the mythical Titan who used

---

[94] "Aeschylus's *Prometheus* seems to be a continuous discussion of a fundamental political problem: what is power? And it is one of the deepest things that have been thought and artistically formulated in antiquity on the essence of power. Hardly anywhere has the problematic and mysterious essence of power been described in such a concrete way as in the progress and construction of this play. Force has only the appearance of power: the threats and punishments of Zeus are illusory; in reality only powerlessness rages in this way. Only seemingly does the chained and tortured Prometheus succumb; despite his lack of force, there is superior strength, real power, in his knowledge and his will" (F. Stoessl, "Aeschylus as a Political Thinker" [1957], 128–29).

blackmail to call a contest of power, the poem's hero puts all his bets on the principle of Right. His goal is to defend an autochthonous people seeking delivery from the intruder who would supplant them. With justice transported from the realm of power to righteousness, the enemy becomes a wholly pernicious force while the hero becomes a saint.

This Manichean reorientation allows the poem to balance an ancient Greek prototype of political defiance with a popular Christian narrative of passion and resurrection. Furthermore, it can ignore the pre-Socratic conception of power that permeates the Aeschylean drama, exemplified in the tragic conflict between Prometheus and Zeus. The *Axion Esti* thus divests Prometheus and Zeus of textual identity. The powerful usurper becomes, in the words of Karandónis, "anything foreign and northern, . . . European barbarism."[95] Natural forces, the Aegean landscape, "the sandy shores of Homer" (To 'Αξιον Εστί [*The Axion Esti*], 28), "the whitewash" where "I now enclose and entrust my true Laws" (70)—all these serve native justice. Prometheus achieves a modern everyday incarnation within the whitewashed landscape of Elytis's *cosmos*. He becomes a luminous image of Hellenism's pure presence in Neohellenic vernacular culture. No longer an emblem of distant pagan origins, he is another natural element in the Hellenic *cosmos*, created in "The Genesis," purified of foreign intervention in "The Passion," and glorified in "The Gloria," the final section of the *Axion Esti*.

This closing hymn of praise presents a collage of diverse elements from Hellenism's literary history. It is a Christian-pagan, saintly-erotic litany to the Hellenic *cosmos*. It joins mermaid with Madonna, common housewife with Penelope, the child's unanswered question with the fragmented *logos* of Heraclitus. By juxtaposing modern, Byzantine, and ancient, vernacular and classical, small and great, in unlikely linguistic combinations, "The Gloria" suggests that the Greek language is able to invoke the sky and sea by their real, undiluted names, *uranós* 'sky' and *thálassa* 'sea', "exactly as Sappho did, exactly as Romanós did, for thousands of years, *and only thus* to view in truth the blue of the aether or to hear in truth the roaring of the sea."[96]

Elytis's entire poem reenacts a mystical union of the poetic word

[95] Karandónis, Γύρω από το " 'Αξιον Εστί" (Surrounding the "Axion Esti"), 171.
[96] Elytis, Το χρονικό μιάς δεκαετίας (Chronicle of a decade), 321–22. Romanós the Melode, a Byzantine hymnographer of the first half of the sixth century, is credited with over a thousand Orthodox hymns, including the *Akathistos Hymnos*, perhaps the best known of all Byzantine hymns.

with *topos*, glorifying its eternal spirit. By this union, ancient Greek references lose the distance of historical, pagan origins. They are brought closer; they enter Hellenism's topography as signifiers of the people, who become veritable retainers of an indigenous tradition surviving from antiquity to the present. They achieve their modern incarnations in the form of condensed images of the everyday. These promise to reveal more about Hellenism than the ancient tradition could reveal about itself. By the miracle of incarnation, the modern literary palimpsest incorporates older layers of tradition; it then maps a transhistorical homeland, the nation's body and blood, the now and forever of Hellas.

Although the theology of Elytis's project may now be evident, we should spell out once again its aesthetic contradictions. Elytis persistently allied himself with the *protoporiakí* 'avant-garde', even though his work recenters poetic consciousness in the national body, the organic unity of which assumes a romantic proximity between voice and being. In his work, one discovers the difficult combination of artistic autonomy and a populist intention. One finds, too, as in Seferis's work, the systematic repression of the crisis of tradition that fueled the modernist revolution in Paris, Vienna, and other European cities. His effort to restructure the *topos* of literature as a *topos* of physical dwelling is romantic, though evidently not an anachronistic aberration if one considers his work in the light of Heidegger's philosophy of art. Finally, there is the conflation of poetry and people, language and landscape, orthography and geography, in blatant contradiction to the European modernist project that decentered poetic consciousness, depersonalized the text, disavowed external referents, and celebrated an abyss of linguistic signification that moves from signifier to signifier in endless play.

The contradictions of the project may become irrelevant, however, if one considers the phenomenon of modernist transpositions worldwide. What shape did modernism take outside the mainstream of European movements? Against what order did non-Western cultural revolutions rebel during the past two centuries? What did they achieve each time they updated, upgraded, or denounced traditional forms? One can answer these questions only through detailed studies of other literary histories, which may disclose complex patterns of appropriation, resistance, and change.

Regarding Greece, one may recall Virginia Woolf's identification of modern Greeks with "real" Greeks in her story "A Dialogue upon

Mount Pentelicus." When discussing that story, I speculated that Neo-hellenic modernism's own reworking of Western tradition might actually move to retake old territories. Works by Elytis and Seferis follow this pattern. I have described how the modernist revolution, with its revisions of Hellenism, traveled from some European centers to their outskirts, finding a place in the work of two preeminent poets residing in the world's archeological haven. Both poets offered a resting place for Hellenism in their work; they tried to give national roots to the very tradition that other modernists tried to destabilize or reinvent. They employed techniques of European and American modernism—ellipsis, the uncontextualized quotation from older texts, the spatial rather than narrative organization of literary material—to *ground* in the geopolitical territory of Hellas an internationalist movement that was largely a revolt against the tyranny of Hellas. And their grounding point was precisely the overly burdened *topos* of Hellenism: a physical site that promised to give new life to familiar textual citations.

Thus, during the years of what was for him an unmentionable civil war, Seferis attempted to stage a mystical leap from the darkness of agnosticism to "the light" of a cultural homing ground—that vague place of collective *nostos* where the origin of modern identity (the nation) arises out of the text's self-fulfilling nostalgia. Likewise in the period of reconstruction after World War II and the Greek civil war, Elytis depicted a landscape of the Aegean that implodes into a minute but ever so great *cosmos*. Indeed, both Seferis and Elytis invited compatriots and erstwhile invaders of Hellas to discover in their work the properly *Neo*-Hellenic beauty of the Hellenic landscape—to travel with them into what Elytis called "a far and sinless," "a far and unwrinkled country" (*The Axion Esti*, 56 and 57).

The *new* Grand Tour of Hellas passed through the modern vernacular as well as the ancient heritage. It promised recovery through contact with indigenous peoples. The new tourist could supersede all contingency precisely *because* she or he had descended from Mount Olympus to the erotic zone of the everyday. Elytis articulates the contemporary artist's responsibility very clearly when describing the contribution of his friend painter Yánnis Tsarúhis (1909–89):

The day he dared to search for Hermes not on Mount Olympus but in the coffeehouse [*kafenío*] "Olympus" was the day when a myth descended from books to life, while the eye of the artist became obligated to gaze at the *cosmos* differently. In other words, Neohellenic reality, distorted until then by a false philology, found its natural place in the artistic interests of our times. And the artist, located within [*entopis-ménos*] our limits, shouldered the responsibility of finding a singular expression that would harmonize with its particularity.[97]

Elytis's substitution of the *kafenío* 'coffeehouse' "Olympus" for the revered dwelling of the ancient pantheon suggests that the virtues of Hellenic culture, ancient and modern, might find not only their genuine residence but also their true *philology* in popular culture. On the site of the *kafenío* and in the figure of the *palikári* 'brave young man', one might locate the authentic descendants of a venerated lineage that began with the Homeric hero, moved through the archaic *kouros*, the Aeschylean Titan, the Byzantine hymnographer, and the hero of the Greek Revolution, and reached into the present. Obversely, one might make out the ancients as willful incarnations of the modern *laós* 'people'. Wayward Odysseus now wandered through modernity's "endless hotel" in search of home (Seferis); suffering Prometheus fought fire with the sun (Elytis); the archaic *kouros* frequented urban taverns (Tsarúhis);[98] the classical female nude acquired a Picasso-like solidity and eroticism (Nikoláu); the fragments of Sappho found their musical mode in upgraded popular melodies (Mános Hadzidákis). Any one of these famous personas, visual or acoustic reincarnations, *topoi* of the cultural past, would become a medium for spanning the entire historical spectrum of Hellenism.

Indeed, so expansive were Elytis's and some of his contemporaries' repossessions of Hellenism that they even claimed to divine the tastes of the ancient Greeks based on present-day popular preferences. In one

[97] Odysseus Elytis, Γιάννης Τσαρούχης (Yánnis Tsarúhis) (1988), 241. For Tsarúhis, too, Prometheus became the symbol of the artist as revolutionary. See Yánnis Tsarúhis, Λαϊκή και αριστοκρατική πρέπει να είναι η μεγάλη τέχνη (Great art must be popular and aristocratic) (1988).

[98] According to Aléxandros Xídis, Tsarúhis's paintings represent classical images of the urban male nude "as he had not appeared since ancient times" (Γιάννης Τσαρούχης, 1910–1989 [Yánnis Tsarúhis, 1910–1989], [1989], 47). Like Elytis's poetic persona, these images present popular, classical icons of native identity and authenticity: an interesting synthesis of the archaic *kouros* and the modern *palikári* 'brave young man'. Vakaló describes Tsarúhis's project in different terms; it involves continuous "evasions of the popular by way of the classical, and vice versa" (Ο μύθος της ελληνικότητας [The myth of Hellenicity], 75). Tsarúhis's interesting circumvention of Ellinismós by way of Romiosíni may indeed account for his success, if one judges from the universal praise that he has received throughout his career for the aesthetic purity, the "Hellenicity" of his work.

confident sweep they seemed to cross the enormous temporal chasm between modern and ancient sensibilities. Perhaps it is their confidence that gives continuing power and appeal to their outdated myth of Hellenicity. In an age that reflects with self-loathing on the precedence of archaic and classical Hellas, it is awkwardly refreshing to find Níkos Nikoláu speculating on what kind of art would appeal to ancient Hellenes based on what kind of art the modern Greek *laós* loves best:

> I think it loves music, especially the *rebétika* [urban blues]. This is what it likes to hear, Tsitsánis and the pure, untainted song of Bithikótsis. Beethoven is great, but we love something else deep inside us and this is what we need. While observing the Parthenon frieze, which represents the Panathenaic procession, one feels that this music—a *laikó* [popular] song of this sort—would also be suitable for the Hellenes of that epoch. Anyway, from the artists of our times, the one who would suit them best is Theófilos. Therein lies the myth of Hellenicity.[99]

[99] Nikoláu, Η περιπέτεια της γραμμής στην τέχνη (The adventure of line in art), 49–50.

Changing Topographies

Topographies are constantly undergoing change. They change not only as boundaries shift, countries unite or divide, or places take new names but also as we approach our world through different routes of knowledge. Old sites may lose their importance, even as new sites come to our attention or familiar sites become subject to new battles. As we redefine ourselves, our international communities, nations, states, cities, ethnic groups, neighborhoods, may erect new monuments while they dismantle the old, upgrade certain areas while they degrade others, make private property of formerly public lands while they nationalize formerly private holdings, carve new administrative districts while they dissolve the old, evacuate one place as they move into another. We are continuously redesigning, rebuilding, renovating, restoring, reinterpreting, the sites we administer. Even as we do this, we are periodically restructuring our knowledge about places and redefining the place of knowledge.

Topographies change because *topoi* change. New *topoi* may become *koinoi* in our *logos* about the world. We should remember that *topoi* are the commonplaces of topographies. They are *koinoi* 'common', and they are *epikoinoi* 'common ground', while they are also commonly contested territories in public debate. They are the territories we dispute precisely because they are the territories we hold in common. And they are the territories common to many precisely because they are the ones we dispute. Disputing parties, for example, Greece and the Former Yugoslav Republic of Macedonia (FYROM), have more in common when they are disputing the right to hold a name they share, "Macedonia," than they do when they compete for nothing at all. The communication becomes more intense as common ground is contested.

The *koinoi topoi* of topographies are the shared ground where communication takes shape. They are the territories where communication goes on even when it seems to stop—for communication never really stops until we no longer hold territories in common. Finally, they are the territories where communities take shape: where we imagine ourselves uniting, where we may find our tenuous alliances disintegrating. When *topoi* cease to be commonplace, then they no longer constitute common ground, they cease to be contested, and they stop playing a role in shaping communication and in forming or dividing communities.

During the past two centuries, Hellenism found its *koinos topos* in Hellas, the site of indisputably famous ruins, even though the qualities that made it famous remained subject to dispute. Hellenism found a place for itself in the space and knowledge of this site. Hellenism's project for the past two centuries has been to find answers to the questions, how does one reconstruct Hellas? what did Hellas once look like? how should it look today? what values did Hellas once stand for? what place do these values hold in the modern world? To answer these questions, people returned again and again to the commonplaces of Hellas. They revisited common citations: Ilissus, Marathon, the Acropolis, Eleusis, Crete, Mycene, the Sacred Way, philosophy, science, democracy, poetry, history, politics, ethnography, and ethics. Texts made way for travel; travel verified texts. Texts opened a site for the new nation-state; the nation-state verified its origins through texts. The fact that the Ilissus, Marathon, or the Acropolis revisited lay in a state of ruins at present only made it easier for people to imagine Hellas otherwise, not as it is today but as it appeared in texts.

The topography of Hellenism is changing, however. Old and new versions of a *logos* on the contours of Hellenism are heard today in the American academy and the European Union, as well as in everyday Greek conversation, whether this takes place in Athens, Florina, Porto Rafti, Paris, Frankfurt, Alexandria, Melbourne, Toronto, Astoria, Chicago, or even Columbus, Ohio. Clearly none of these contemporary *logoi* confine themselves to the *topoi* favored two centuries ago. Now there are *topoi* newly held in common, newly common, newly contested, newly under dispute, newly perpetuating conversation, newly shaping communities, newly marking communication's stopping point.

Some of the more interesting *topoi* of Hellenism's present-day topographies are found in Greek debates. During the past two centuries, the Greek *logos* never really centered solely on the meaning of classical Greece—although this was certainly a recurring theme, as I have argued. Greek discussions always had to do with the future of Hellenism, specifically the fate of the modern Panhellenic union, which, during the period I have examined most closely in this book, happened to have found its most fertile ground in the *topos* of Hellas. Today public discussions about Hellenism's future return to less commonly known *topoi* from Hellenism's past. Evidence appears on the streets, on the beaches, in public squares, on private balconies, in parliamentary debate, and in the daily press. To assess the present contours of Hellenism's topography, let us consider briefly some examples.

Architecture, urban planning, and the preservation of historical sites have involved political questions about Greece's modern beginnings. The poetics of space has been a preeminently political matter. Articles appear daily on the politics of restoration, the history and future of cities past and present. Decaying buildings from Greece's recent past constitute one *topos* in public debate. Neoclassical buildings dating from the 1800s are an important example. They continue to exist, frequently in a state of ruins, in most older neighborhoods of Athens, most areas of Attica, most regions of Greece. Ermúpolis, capital of the once prosperous island of Syros, boasts some four hundred remarkable examples dating from 1830 to 1870. "Unique in Hellas and in Europe, '. . . they combine the architectural, sculptural, and painting techniques of famous artists.' "[1] One might expect these neoclassical buildings to find their place comfortably next to the classical in Greece's culture of ruins. After all, archeologists are involved in preserving both these very distantly related layers of the Greek past. But Greek discussions about the future of the neoclassical are quite unlike the discourse that claimed Greece's classical ruins. Unlike ancient sites, which became places of appreciation when they were declared uninhabitable, decaying neoclassical buildings acquire a future only when they can be once again inhabited. Public debate has there-

[1] From the 1993 newspaper article Καταστρέφονται τα νεοκλασικά στην Ερμούπολη (Neoclassical buildings in Ermúpolis are being destroyed), quoting archeologist Méri Róta.

fore centered on problems encountered in their restoration, interpretations of the state's will to neglect them, and, more broadly, whether
the neoclassical finally has any inherent value for Greeks.

The *topos* of neoclassical buildings recurs not only in the *logos* of
historical preservation but, more poignantly, in a *logos* on the fate of
the nation, and, more in the spirit of Hellenicity, in the *logos* of
aesthetic nationalism. Why, some Neohellenes ask, is there such "an
absence of 'motives' for the protection of the buildings by private
owners? Whatever is the norm in Europe is considered a luxury here.
Neither tax breaks nor lower interest rates nor government subsi-
dies."[2] What future is there for Hellenism past or present, other Neohellenes wonder wistfully, if no one invests the money or energy to
restore even neoclassical buildings to an inhabitable state? Still others
wave the flag of skepticism. Why the intense interest in neoclassical
buildings when they represent nothing Hellenic but instead "the rationalism of Danish neoclassicism that imposed itself as the 'proper
dress' of the Neohellenic state"?[3]

Greek debates about the future of history and the history of the past
have found an even more potent *topos* in Makrónisos, an island located
northeast of Soúnion in Attica. From 1946 to 1949, Makrónisos was
the site of internal exile for some sixty thousand political prisoners.
Government officials nicknamed it the "National Baptismal Font"
because they imagined this to be the place where prisoners of the Greek
civil war would wash themselves clean of their political sins and so
refashion themselves into more conservative citizens. Philosopher and
politician Panayótis Kanelópulos called Makrónisos the place where
Greeks would build new Parthenons, because there, on an island suited
best for grazing, prisoners were forced to build out of local materials in
a span of three to four years not only administrative buildings, villas,
and a club for their persecutors but also a factory for nonalcoholic
beverages, a radio station, a convalescence area, kitchens, water reser-
voirs, roads, six churches, four theaters—where their ideological rehabilitation was to take place—arches, statues, bas-reliefs, monuments
with shells and mosaics, as well as miniature versions of the Parthenon
and of the Hagia Sophia.

During the decade of the 1980s, the Greek Ministry of Culture,

<hr>

[2] Dimítris Konstándios, Η προστασία των ιστορικών πόλεων, η ελληνική εμπειρία (The preservation of historical cities, the Greek experience) (1992), 44.

[3] Anastasia Pápari, Μακεδονία· Μορφή και τόπος (Macedonia: Form and *topos*)
(1992).

under the leadership of Melina Mercouri, declared Makrónisos a historical site, mandating its preservation and imagining its transformation into a *mnimío arhitektonikís tis vías* 'monument to the architecture of violence'. Many Greeks have disputed not only the message but also the history of Makrónisos. Yet the idea of preserving this unique site found favor with an important sector of the Greek population, including intellectuals, architects, and urban planners. Nonetheless Makrónisos remains today in a state of deterioration, something many Greeks bemoan, even as the builders of *paránoma* 'illegal' and *afthéreta* 'arbitrary' homes, a *koinos topos* of failed urban planning, dare to erect on this barren island their monuments to several decades of profiteering. Common to the discourse on Makrónisos are expressions of anxiety about its likely commodification in a country where tourism is the number one industry. How does one preserve historical memory without making an exhibition of its remains? intellectuals inquire of Makrónisos, as they failed to inquire of Greece's classical ruins. Under what conditions does the restoration of monuments assist in the preservation of history? Under what conditions does it become libelous or just plain kitsch? How, finally, does a state appropriately display ruins that bear witness to its own violence against its citizens?

In present-day topographies of Hellenism, Makrónisos has been a *koinos topos* of national soul-searching, as Greeks in their middle years, feeling the ominous threat of λήθη *líthi* 'oblivion', struggle to preserve the brutal memory of the Greek civil war, which so divided the country through the second half of the twentieth century. More acutely felt by Greeks of all generations is the threat that others to the north and west, including the FYROM, are conspiring to divest Neohellenes of their past by arbitrarily interpreting Hellenic history or rendering Hellenism insignificant—even as foreigners had previously overlooked Neohellenes when they treated Hellenism as something special: "Overlooking, undervaluing, ignoring all the particularities of Hellenic civilization, they pampered us, so that we came to believe our country to be the site of indisputably glorious ruins, unique and necessarily famous. In the meantime, times changed, a newer generation of practical studies and financial gain came into power, and with its first-rate realism and rationalism, its specialty, it judged matters differently. Hellas as encyclopedia entry is now just one among many."[4]

But there are other interesting changes in the contours of Helle-

[4] S. Vrahorítis, Γρέκικες τσόντες ([Skin] Flicks Grec) (1991).

nism's topography. Most remarkable in the present-day Greek world is the return to and of the diaspora. After having defensively secluded themselves in the territory of their state for over half a century, some Neohellenes, now feeling the need to escape the confines of state boundaries, or fearing the present lines of demarcation to be too tenuously drawn, are attending to Hellenism's forgotten *patrídes* 'homelands' outside Hellas. The outreach is conducted with an unsteady hand that withdraws at intervals, since the Greeks it finds "abroad" define their Hellenism otherwise. There is no consensus of opinion. At the same time, Greeks in Greece are again witnessing refugees' flooding their doorsteps—ethnic Greeks this time from Albania, Russia, and Georgia, who had never before in their lifetime stepped foot in Greece, are again "returning home" to Greece. Arms are not always extended wide. In a newly developing *logos*, diaspora becomes a *koinos topos*, commonly subject to agreement over its basic value but major disputes over its pragmatic consequences or real significance for the future of Hellenism. Around this *topos*, some organize a neo Byzantinist imperialist fantasy reminiscent of the Megáli Idéa; while others seek to "upturn . . . what is basically a nationalist insularity."[5] A minority are just working hard to find a place for diaspora.

The topography of Hellenism is changing. Beyond Greece, one finds the *logos* of Hellenism employing new commonplaces alongside the standard *topos* of Hellas's rich past. Contemporary Europe, seeking ways to verify its union while it also pays the necessary respects to difference, occasionally refers to Hellas as representative of the community's smaller nations. In the attenuated *logos* of a united Europe, Hellas becomes the *koinos topos* of a small country that has willingly opened its borders to currents from the north without allowing these to dilute its distinctive local color. Hellas represents the resurgence of diversity in the sea of sameness, or the power of unity over swelling waves of difference—have it as you will. Eminently quotable is the remarkable address delivered by president of the EU, Jacques Delors, in Athens in May 1992. In his speech Delors implored Neohellenes to "play a vanguard role in the Community. Introduce, suggest, and put into effect programs befitting small countries with flexible economies and a rich cultural past. Introduce to us Northern Europeans the personification of Europe of the future, united and without boundaries

[5] Stathis Gourgouris, "Nationalism and Oneirocriticism: Of Modern Hellenes in Europe" (1992), 65.

but with a multiple and diverse cultural identity. We are seeking the richness of a different destination of nations and peoples, and no one is in a better position to help us in this than you Hellenes."[6]

The academic *logos* in the United States has not been so flattering. Today we still find Hellenism envied for its contributions, though many question its originality. A few scholars, setting aside the complex issue of origins, describe interesting multicultural appropriations of Hellenism in the ancient world.[7] More and more frequently, however, scholars hold Hellenism accountable for the West's currently most despised vices: sexism, racism, colonialism, imperialism, metaphysics, the verb "to be." Yet little has been said of an obvious oversight in the more than two-hundred-year history of Hellenism's excavation: Hellas illustrates how the modern fetish for the ancient, the defunct, and the exotic operates at the expense of the contemporary Greek world, which has been struggling to control interpretations of its past. As we question the value of Hellenism for the present, perhaps we should consider ways to circumvent this obstacle in our own thinking.

The world that enabled Hellenism to emerge as a foundational civilization was a world that saw Hellas "only very partially cultivated and sparsely populated."[8] When it surveyed Hellas, it saw empty space—the kind of empty space burdened with history yet emptied of living descendants to fill it up. Two hundred years ago perhaps it was possible for travelers from the West to ignore the present as they brought into focus *topoi* from the Hellenic past. Today, however, Hellas is so densely populated and so richly cultivated that we can no longer afford to ignore its present. We find Neohellenes recycling even their most recent layers of history while they also turn an inquiring eye on Hellenism outside the confines of their borders. As the topography of Hellenism changes, it seems to me, it becomes increasingly useful for our academic *logos* to pass through layers of the *postclassical* as well as the preclassical and classical worlds. A good starting point is Neohellenism itself, including its diasporic dimension.

I am not arguing here that Neohellenism deserves "a modest place

---

[6] Quoted in Dimítris Petihákis, Φιλέλληνας ή κάτι παραπάνω; Ο Ζακ Ντελόρ στην Αθήνα και τι . . . άφησε πίσω του (Philhellene or something more? Jacques Delors in Athens and what . . . he left behind) (1992), E3.

[7] See Erich S. Gruen, "Cultural Fictions and Cultural Identity" (1993).

[8] Angelomatis-Tsougarakis, *Eve of the Greek Revival*, 207.

in the sun."[9] Neohellenism already holds that place, as the swarms of tourists annually prove. The physical necessity of traveling through modern Thessaloniki or Athens when revisiting Hellas merely underscores the fact that Neohellenism *is* a cardinal point of Hellenism. In searching the ruins of Hellas, in drafting new topographies of Hellenism, we may find Neohellenism unexpectedly crossing our path.

[9] David Ricks, "Greek *tout court?*" (1991), 31.

Works Cited

Alexander, Edward P. *Museum Masters: Their Museums and Their Influence*. Nashville: American Association for State and Local History, 1983.

Alexiou, Margaret. "Folklore: An Obituary?" *Byzantine and Modern Greek Studies* 9 (1984): 1–28.

——. *The Ritual Lament in Greek Tradition*. Cambridge: Cambridge University Press, 1974.

Alliès, Paul. *L'invention du territoire*. Critique du droit, vol. 6. Grenoble: Presses Universitaires de Grenoble, 1980.

Alonso, Carlos J. *The Spanish American Regional Novel: Modernity and Autochthony*. Cambridge Studies in Latin American and Iberian Literature. Cambridge and New York: Cambridge University Press, 1990.

Alsop, Joseph. *The Rare Art Traditions: The History of Art Collecting and Its Linked Phenomena Wherever These Have Appeared*. New York: Harper and Row, 1982.

Anderson, Benedict. *Imagined Communities: Reflections on the Origin and Spread of Nationalism*. London: Verso, 1983.

Anderson, James. "Nationalist Ideology and Territory." In *Nationalism, Self-Determination, and Political Geography*, ed. R. J. Johnston, David B. Knight, and Eleonore Kofman, 13–39. London: Croom Helm, 1988.

Angelomatis-Tsougarakis, Helen. *The Eve of the Greek Revival: British Travellers' Perceptions of Early Nineteenth-Century Greece*. London: Routledge, 1990.

Argyros, Alexander. "The Hollow King: A Heideggerian Approach to George Seferis's 'The King of Asine.'" *boundary 2* (fall and winter 1986–87): 305–21.

Arjomand, Said Amir. *The Turban for the Crown: The Islamic Revolution in Iran*. Studies in Middle Eastern History, ed. Bernard Lewis, Itamar Rabinovich, and Roger Savory. Oxford: Oxford University Press, 1988.

Arnold, Matthew. *Culture and Anarchy: An Essay in Political and Social Criticism*. 1868. New York: Bobbs-Merrill, 1971.

Augustinos, Olga. *French Odysseys: Greece in French Literature from the Renaissance to the Romantic Era.* Baltimore: Johns Hopkins University Press, 1993.

Barthes, Roland. *Writing Degree Zero.* Translated by A. Lavers and E. Ashton. 1953. New York: Hill and Wang, 1968.

Basch, Sophie. *Le voyage imaginaire: Les écrivains français en Grèce au XXe siècle.* Paris: Hatier, 1991.

Bate, Walter Jackson. *The Burden of the Past and the English Poet.* New York: Norton, 1972.

Baudrillard, Jean. *Simulations.* New York: Semiotext(e), 1983.

Bazin, Germain. *The Museum Age.* Translated by Jane Van Nuis Cahill. New York: Universe Books, 1967.

Becker, Howard S. *Art Worlds.* Berkeley: University of California Press, 1982.

Bloom, Harold. *The Anxiety of Influence.* Oxford: Oxford University Press, 1975.

Bourdieu, Pierre, and Alain Darbel, with Dominique Schnapper. *L'amour de l'articles musées europeéns et leur public.* Paris: Minuit, 1969.

Bové, Paul. "Discourse." In *Critical Terms for Literary Study,* ed. Frank Lentricchia and Thomas McLaughlin, 50–65. Chicago: University of Chicago Press, 1990.

Bradbury, Malcolm, and James MacFarlane. "The Name and Nature of Modernism." In *Modernism,* ed. Malcolm Bradbury and James McFarlane, 19–55. Harmondsworth: Penguin, 1976.

Brandes, Georg. *Hellas: Travels in Greece.* Translated by Jacob W. Hartmann. 1926. Reprint, Freeport, N.Y.: Adelphi, 1969.

Breuilly, John. *Nationalism and the State.* Chicago: University of Chicago Press, 1985.

Briggs, Asa. "The Image of Greece in Modern English Literature." In *Greek Connections: Essays on Culture and Diplomacy,* ed. J. T. A. Koumoulides, 58–74. Notre Dame: University of Notre Dame Press, 1987.

Browning, Robert. *Medieval and Modern Greek.* Cambridge: Cambridge University Press, 1969.

Buck-Morss, Susan. *The Dialectics of Seeing: Walter Benjamin and the Arcades Project.* Cambridge, Mass.: MIT Press, 1989.

——. "Semiotic Boundaries and the Politics of Meaning: Modernity on Tour—A Village in Transition." In *New Ways of Knowing: The Sciences, Society, and Reconstructive Knowledge,* ed. Marcus G. Raskin and Herbert J. Bernstein, 200–236. Totowa, N.J.: Rowman and Littlefield, 1987.

Bürger, Peter. *Theory of the Avant-Garde.* Translated by Michael Shaw. 1974. Minneapolis: University of Minnesota Press, 1984.

Burnet, John. *Early Greek Philosophy.* New York: Meridian, 1957.

Byron, George Gordon, Lord. *Byron's Works.* Vol. 1, *Letters and Journals,* edited by Rowland E. Prothero. London: John Murray, 1902.

——. *Byron's Works.* Vol. 2, *Poetry,* edited by Ernest Hartley Coleridge. London: John Murray, 1899. New York: Scribner, 1899.

——. *Lord Byron: Selected Letters and Journals.* Edited by Leslie A. Marchand. Cambridge, Mass.: Harvard University Press, Belknap Press, 1982.

——. *Poetical Works*. Edited by Frederick Page. Oxford: Oxford University Press, 1979.

Byron, Robert. *The Byzantine Achievement, an Historical Perspective, A.D. 330–1453*. 1929. New York: Russell and Russell, 1964.

Calinescu, Matei. *Five Faces of Modernity; Modernism, Avant-Garde, Decadence, Kitsch*. Durham: Duke University Press, 1987.

Calotychos, Vangelis. "The Art of Making Claques: Politics of Tradition in the Critical Essays of T. S. Eliot and George Seferis." In *Modernism in Greece? Essays on the Critical and Literary Margins of a Movement*, ed. Mary N. Layoun, 81–136. New York: Pella, 1990.

——. "Realizing and Resisting 'Self-Colonization': Ideology and Form in Modern Greek Poetics (1790–1960)." Ph.D. diss., Harvard University, 1993

Canovan, Margaret. *Populism*. New York: Harcourt Brace Jovanovich, 1981.

Castillo, Debra A. *The Translated World: A Postmodern Tour of Libraries in Literature*. Tallahassee: Florida State University Press, 1984.

Cavafy, C. P. Τα Ελγίνεια μάρμαρα (The Elgin Marbles). In Πεζά, ed. G. Α. Papoutsakis, 13–16. Athens: G. Féxi, 1963. (First published in the Athenian newspaper Εθνική, 30 March 1891.)

——. "'Give Back the Elgin Marbles'." In Πεζά, ed. G. A. Papoutsakis, 9–12. Athens: G. Féxi, 1963. (First published in *Rivista quindicinale* 10 [April 1891].)

——. Νεώτερα περί των Ελγινείων μαρμάρων (The latest on the Elgin Marbles). In Πεζά, ed. G. A. Papoutsakis, 17–22. Athens: G. Féxi, 1963. (First published in the Athenian newspaper Εθνική, 29 April 1891.)

Chantraine, Pierre. *Dictionnaire étymologique de la langue grecque*. Paris: Klincksieck, 1977.

Chateaubriand, François-René. *Itinéraire de Paris à Jérusalem et de Jérusalem à Paris, en allant par la Gréce, et en revenant par l'Egypte, la Barbarie et l'Espagne*. 3 vols. Paris: Le Normant, 1811.

Chinweizu, Onwuchekwa Jemi, and Ihechukwu Madubuike. *Decolonising the African Mind*. Lagos, Nigeria: Pero Press, 1987. London: Sundoor Press, 1987.

Clogg, Richard. *A Concise History of Greece*. Cambridge: Cambridge University Press, 1992.

——. *A Short History of Modern Greece*. Cambridge: Cambridge University Press, 1979.

Cobbah, Josiah A. M. "Toward a Geography of Peace in Africa: Redefining Sub-State Self-Determination Rights." In *Nationalism, Self-Determination, and Political Geography*, ed. R. J. Johnston, David B. Knight, and Eleonore Kofman, 70–86. London: Croom Helm, 1988.

Constantine, David. *Early Greek Travellers and the Hellenic Ideal*. Cambridge: Cambridge University Press, 1984.

——. "Poets and Travellers and the Ideal of Greece." *Journal of European Studies* 7 (1977): 253–65.

Cook, B. F. *The Elgin Marbles*. London: British Museum Publications, 1984.

Cowling, Elizabeth, and Jennifer Mundy. *On Classic Ground: Picasso, Leger, de Chirico, and the New Classicism, 1910–1930*. London: Tate Gallery, 1990.

Crimp, Douglas. "The End of Art and the Origin of the Museum." *Art Journal* 46, no. 4 (1987): 261–66.

——. "On the Museum's Ruins." *October* 14 (summer 1980): 41–58.

Cuddon, J. A. *A Dictionary of Literary Terms*. Harmondsworth: Penguin, 1979.

Curtius, Ernst Robert. *Essays on European Literature*. Translated by Michael Kowal. Princeton: Princeton University Press, 1973.

——. *European Literature and the Latin Middle Ages*. Translated by William Trask. 1948. Princeton: Princeton University Press, 1973.

Dállas, Yánnis. Μιά αίσθηση πέρα από τον Καβάφη· Με το κλειδή της Κίχλης (A feeling beyond Cavafy: With *Thrush* as key). In Για τον Σεφέρη· Τιμητικό αφιέρωμα στα τριάντα χρόνια της Στροφής, 292–303. Athens: Ermís, 1981.

Daniíl. Το φαινόμενο Θεόφιλος 40 χρόνια μετά την "ανακάλυψη του" (The phenomenon Theófilos 40 years after "his discovery"). Σήμα, 1975.

Davidson, J. "The Homeric Question." In *A Companion to Homer*, ed. Alan J. B. Wace and Frank H. Stubbings, 234–65. New York: Macmillan, 1969.

Davis, Mark. "Seferis' *Thrush*." *Neo-Hellenika* 2 (1975): 280–98.

Deleuze, Gilles, and Félix Guattari. *Kafka: Toward a Minor Literature*. Translated by Dana Polan. Minneapolis: University of Minnesota Press, 1986.

——. *A Thousand Plateaus: Capitalism and Schizophrenia*. Translated by Brian Massumi. 1980. Minneapolis: University of Minnesota Press, 1987.

de Man, Paul. "Literary History and Literary Modernity." In *Blindness and Insight*, ed. Lindsay Waters, 142–65. Theory and History of Literature, ed. Wlad Godzich and Jochen Schulte-Sasse. Minneapolis: University of Minnesota Press, 1983.

——. "Spacecritics: J. Hillis Miller and Joseph Frank." In *Critical Writings, 1953–1978*, 107–15. Theory and History of Literature, ed. Wlad Godzich and Jochen Schulte-Sasse. Minneapolis: University of Minnesota Press, 1989.

Dimarás, K. Th. Ελληνικός ρωμαντισμός (Greek romanticism). Athens: Deltíon Istorikís ke Ethnologikís Eterías Elládos, 1982.

——. Ιστορία της νεοελληνικής λογοτεχνίας (History of Neohellenic literature) 1948. Athens: Íkaros, 1972.

Dimirúlis, Dimítris. Το Άξιον της ιστορίας και το Εστί της ρητορικής· Κριτική φαντασία σε τοπίο ελληνικό (The "Worthy" of history and the "It is" of rhetoric: Critical imagination in a Greek landscape). Χάρτης 21–23 (November 1986): 314–34.

——. "The 'Humble Art' and the Exquisite Rhetoric: Tropes in the Manner of George Seferis." In *The Text and Its Margins,* ed. Margaret Alexiou and Vassilis Lambropoulos, 59–84. New York: Pella, 1985.

di Tella, Torcuato S. "Populism and Reform in Latin America." In *Obstacles to Change in Latin America*, ed. C. Veliz, 47–74. London: Oxford University Press, 1965.

Donato, Eugenio. "The Museum's Furnace: Notes toward a Contextual Reading of *Bouvard and Pécuchet*." In *Textual Strategies: Perspectives in Post-Structuralist Criticism*, ed. Josué V. Harari. Ithaca, N.Y.: Cornell University Press, 1979.

Dontos, George. *The Acropolis and Its Museum*. Athens: Clio Editions, 1979.

Douglas, F. S. North. *Essay on Certain Points of Resemblance between the Ancient and Modern Greeks*. London, 1813.

Doxiadis, Constantine A. *Building Entopia*. New York: Norton, 1975.

Dragúmis, Íon. Ελληνικός πολιτισμός (Hellenic civilization). In Έργα, σειρά B, κοινωνικά-πολιτικά, 161–235. 1914. Athens: Estia, 1927.

———. Ο Ελληνισμός μου και οι Έλληνες (My Hellenism and the Greeks). In Έργα, σειρά B, κοινωνικά-πολιτικά, 1–159. 1903–9. Athens: Estía, 1927.

———. Όσοι ζωντανοί (As many as survive). Athens: Néa Zoí, 1926.

Ducrot, Oswald, and Tzvetan Todorov. *Encyclopedic Dictionary of the Sciences of Languages*. Translated by Catherine Porter. Baltimore: Johns Hopkins University Press, 1972.

Duncan, Isadora. *The Art of the Dance*. Edited by Sheldon Cheney. New York: Theatre Arts Books, 1969.

Eagleton, Terry. *The Ideology of the Aesthetic*. Oxford: Basil Blackwell, 1990.

Eftaliótis, Aryíris. Ιστορία της Ρωμιοσύνης (History of Romiosíni). Athens: Estía, 1901.

Eikelman, Dale F. "Ideological Change and Regional Cults: Maraboutism and Ties of 'Closeness' in Western Morocco." In *Regional Cults*, ed. Richard P. Werbner, 3–27. African Studies Association Monograph, no. 16. New York and London: Academic Press, 1977.

Eisenstadt, S. N. "Continuity and Reconstruction of Tradition." *Daedalus* 102 (1973): 1–27.

Eisenzweig, Uri. "An Imaginary Territory: The Problematic of Space in Zionist Discourse." *Dialectical Anthropology* 5, no. 4 (May 1981): 261–85.

Eisner, Robert. *Travelers to an Antique Land: The History and Literature of Travel in Greece*. Princeton: Princeton University Press, 1991.

Eliot, T. S. "Tradition and the Individual Talent." In *The Sacred Wood: Essays on Poetry and Criticism*, 47–59. London: Faber, 1920.

———. "Ulysses, Order, and Myth." *The Dial* 75 (1923): 480–83.

———. *The Waste Land and Other Poems*. New York: Harcourt, Brace, and World, 1962.

Elytis, Odysseus. Η αισθητική και συναισθηματική καταγωγή του Θεοφίλου Χατζημιχαήλ (The aesthetic and emotional origin of Theófilos Hadzimihaíl). Αγγλοελληνική επιθεώρηση 3, no. 1 (May 1947). A revised and expanded version appeared in Ανοιχτά Χαρτιά (Athens: Íkaros, 1982), 191–231.

———. Το Άξιον Εστί (The Axion Esti). 1959. Athens: Íkaros, 1980.

———. *The Axion Esti*. Translated by Edmund Keeley and George Savidis. Pittsburgh: University of Pittsburgh Press, 1974.

——— Γιάννης Τσαρούχης (Yánnis Tsarúhis). In Εγώ ειμί πτωχός και πένης, by Yiánnis Tsarúhis, 241–42. Athens: Kastanióti, 1988.

———. Τα δημόσια και τα ιδιωτικά (The public and the private). Athens: Íkaros, 1990.

———. Ο ζωγράφος Θεόφιλος (The painter Theófilos). 1973. Athens: Gnósis, 1986.

———. Πρώτα-πρώτα (To begin). In Ανοιχτά χαρτιά, 13–41. Athens: Íkaros, 1982.

——. Η σύγχρονη ελληνική τέχνη και ο ζωγράφος Ν. Χατζηκυριάκος Γκίκας (Contemporary Greek art and the painter N. Hadzikiriákos Gíkas). In Ανοιχτά χαρτιά, 408–17. 1947. Athens: Íkaros, 1982.

——. Το χρονικό μιάς δεκαετίας (Chronicle of a decade). In Ανοιχτά χαρτιά, 234–329. 1973. Athens: Íkaros, 1982.

Errington, Shelly. "Fragile Traditions and Contested Meanings." *Public Culture: Bulletin of the Project for Transnational Cultural Studies* 1 (spring 1989): 49–59.

Euben, J. Peter. "Creatures of a Day: Thought and Action in Thucydides." In *Political Theory and Praxis: New Perspectives*, ed. Terence Ball, 28–56. Minneapolis: University of Minnesota Press, 1978.

Evans, Robert O. "Ellipse." In *Princeton Encyclopedia of Poetry and Poetics*, ed. Alex Preminger et al. Princeton: Princeton University Press, 1975.

Fallmerayer, Jacob Phillipp. *Geschichte der Halbinsel Morea während des Mittelalters* (History of the Morea peninsula during the Middle Ages). Stuttgart: Gotta, 1835.

——. Περί της καταγωγής των σημερινών Ελλήνων (Concerning the origin of contemporary Hellenes). Translated by Konstandínos Romanós. 1835. Athens: Neféli, 1984.

Fermor, Patrick Leigh. *Roumeli: Travels in Modern Greece*. 1966. London: Penguin, 1983.

Fessas-Emmanouil, Helen. *Public Architecture in Modern Greece, 1827–1992*. Athens: Papasotiríu, 1993.

Flaubert, Gustave. *The Letters of Gustave Flaubert, 1830–1857*. Translated by Francis Steigmuller. Cambridge, Mass.: Harvard University Press, 1980.

Foucault, Michel. "La bibliothèque fantastique." Introduction to *La Tentation de Saint Antoine*, by Gustave Flaubert. Paris: Gallimard, 1967.

——. *Discipline and Punish: The Birth of the Prison*. Translated by Alan Sheridan. 1975. New York: Vintage, 1979.

——. "Of Other Spaces." Translated by Jay Miskiewic. 1984. *Diacritics* 16 (spring 1986): 22–27.

——. "Questions on Geography." In *Power/Knowledge: Selected Interviews and Other Writings*, ed. Colin Gordon, 63–77. Brighton: Harvester, 1980.

——. "Space, Knowledge, and Power." In *The Foucault Reader*, ed. Paul Rabinow, 239–56. New York: Pantheon, 1984.

Fougères, Gustave. *Athènes*. Paris: H. Laurens, 1912.

Frame, D. *The Myth of Return in Early Greek Epic*. New Haven: Yale University Press, 1978.

——. "The Origins of Greek ΝΟΥΣ." Ph.D. diss., Harvard University, 1971.

Frank, Joseph. "Spatial Form in Modern Literature." In *The Widening Gyre: Crisis and Mastery in Modern Literature*, 3–62. 1945. New Brunswick: Rutgers University Press, 1963. Bloomington: Indiana University Press, 1968.

Freud, Sigmund. "A Disturbance of Memory on the Acropolis." In *The Standard Edition of the Complete Psychological Works of Sigmund Freud*. Vol. 22 (1932–36), edited and translated by James Strachey, 239–48. 1936. London: Hogarth Press and Institute of Psycho-Analysis, 1964.

Friar, Kimon. 'Αξιον Εστί το τίμημα (Worthy is the honor). Translated by Násos Vayenás. Athens: Kédros, 1979.

Frisk, Hjalmar. *Griechisches etymologisches Wörterbuch*. Heidelberg: Carl Winter, 1961.

Gauthier, Th. *L'Orient*. Vol. 1. In Τρεις Γάλλοι ρομαντικοί στην Ελλάδα (Three French romantics in Greece), trans. Váso Méntzu, 117–86. 1877. Athens: Olkos, 1990.

Gibbon, Edward. *The Decline and Fall of the Roman Empire*. Vol. 2. New York: Modern Library, 1932.

Gilbert, Sandra, and Susan Gubar. *No Man's Land: The Place of the Woman Writer in the Twentieth Century*. Vol. 1, *The War of the Words*. New Haven: Yale University Press, 1988.

Godzich, Wlad. "The Further Possibility of Knowledge." Foreword to *Heterologies: Discourse on the Other*, by Michel de Certeau. Minneapolis: University of Minnesota Press, 1986.

Gottman, Jean. *The Significance of Territory*. Charlottesville: University Press of Virginia, 1973.

———, ed. *Centre and Periphery: Spatial Variation in Politics*. London: Sage Publications, 1980.

Gourgouris, Stathis. Με τον Ed. Said (With Edward Said). Πλανόδιον 16 (June 1992): 392–401.

———. Η μυθοπλασία του Καραγκιόζη και το εθνικό ασυνείδητο (The mythification of Karagiózis and the national unconscious). Πλανόδιον 7 (summer 1988): 358–66.

———. "Nationalism and Oneirocriticism: Of Modern Hellenes in Europe." *Diaspora: A Journal of Transnational Studies* 2, no. 1 (spring 1992): 43–71.

———. "The Simulations of the *Center*: Lorentzatos's Neohellenism against the Modernist Phantom." In *Modernism in Greece? Essays on the Critical and Literary Margins of a Movement*, ed. Mary N. Layoun, 59–80. New York: Pella, 1990.

———. "Writing the National Imaginary: The Memory of Makriyánnis and the Miracles of Neohellenism." *Emergences*, fall 1989, 95–130.

Goux, Jean-Joseph. "Politics and Modern Art—Heidegger's Dilemma." *Diacritics* 19, nos. 3–4 (fall–winter 1989): 10–24.

Green, Tamara M. "*Black Athena* and Classical Historiography: Other Approaches, Other Views," *Arethusa* special issue, fall 1989, 55–65.

Gregory, Derek. "Chinatown, Part Three? Soja and the Missing Spaces of Social Theory." *Strategies: A Journal of Theory, Culture, and Politics* 3 (1990): 40–104.

Griffith, M., ed. *Aeschylus, Prometheus Bound*. Cambridge: Cambridge University Press, 1983.

Gruen, Erich S. "Cultural Fictions and Cultural Identity." *Transactions of the American Philological Association* 123 (1993): 1–14.

Guillory, John. *Poetic Authority: Spenser, Milton, and Literary History*. New Haven: Yale University Press, 1983.

Gusfield, Joseph R. "Tradition and Modernity: Misplaced Polarities in the Study of Social Change." *American Journal of Sociology* 72 (1967): 351–62.

Hadzidákis, Geórgios N. Νεωτάτη φάσις του γλωσσικού ζητήματος (The newest phase of the language question). Παναθήναια 3 (April–September 1902): 216–18, 249–52.

Hadzidákis, Manólis. Έκθεσις Νικολάου (The Nikoláu exhibit). In Η περιπέτεια της γραμμής στην τέχνη (The adventures of line in art), by Níkos Nikoláu, 69–70. 1948. Athens: Sakellaríu, 1986.

Hadzidákis, Mános. Ο μεγάλος ερωτικός (The great erotic [God]). Athens: Nótos, 1972. (Distributed by Aliki Publishing, New York.)

Harvey, David. The Condition of Postmodernity. Oxford: Basil Blackwell, 1989.

Heidegger, Martin. "The Origin of the Work of Art." In Poetry, Language, Thought, trans. Albert Hofstadter, 15–81. 1935–36. New York: Harper and Row, 1971.

———. "The Origin of the Work of Art: Addendum." In Poetry, Language, Thought, trans. Albert Hofstadter, 82–87. New York: Harper and Row, 1971.

Herington, C. J. "A Study in the Prometheus, Part I: The Elements in the Trilogy." Phoenix 17 (1963): 180–97.

Herzen, A. J. From the Other Shore and The Russian People and Socialism. Translated by Moura Budberg. London: Weidenfeld and Nicolson, 1956.

Herzfeld, Michael. Anthropology through the Looking Glass: Critical Ethnography in the Margins of Europe. Cambridge: Cambridge University Press, 1987.

———. Ours Once More: Folklore, Ideology, and the Making of Modern Greece. Austin: University of Texas Press, 1982.

High, Steven S. "The Significance of Place." In the exhibition catalogue Alfredo Jaar: Geography = War. Richmond: Anderson Gallery, Virginia Commonwealth University and the Virginia Museum of Fine Arts, 1991.

Highet, Gilbert. The Classical Tradition: Greek and Roman Influences on Western Literature. 1949. Oxford: Oxford University Press, 1976.

Hirschon, Renée. Heirs of the Greek Catastrophe: The Social Life of Asia Minor Refugees in Piraeus. Oxford: Clarendon Press, 1989.

Hobhouse, John Cam. A Journey through Albania, and Other Provinces of Turkey in Europe and Asia, to Constantinople, during the Years 1809 and 1810. Vols. 1 and 2. London: James Cawhorn, 1813.

Hobsbawm, Eric, and Terence Ranger, eds. The Invention of Tradition. Past and Present Publication Series. Cambridge: Cambridge University Press, 1983.

Hofmannsthal, Hugo von. "Moments in Greece." In Selected Prose, trans. Mary Hottinger, Tania Stern, and James Stern, 165–87. New York: Pantheon, 1952.

Hudson, Kenneth. A Social History of Museums: What the Visitors Thought. Atlantic Highlands, N.J.: Humanities Press, 1975.

Hutchinson, Peter. Games Authors Play. London and New York: Methuen, 1983.

Ibsch, Elrud. "Historical Changes of the Function of Spatial Description in Literary Texts." Poetics Today 3, no. 4 (autumn 1982): 97–113.

Iliú, Fílipos. Ιδεολογικές χρήσεις του κοραϊσμού (Ideological uses of Koraïsmós). Athens: Polítis, 1989.

Impey, Oliver, and Arthur MacGregor, eds. The Origins of Museums: The Cabinet of Curiosities in Sixteenth- and Seventeenth-Century Europe. Oxford: Clarendon Press, 1985.

Ionescu, Ghita, and Ernest Gellner, eds. *Populism: Its Meaning and National Characteristics*. New York: Macmillan, 1969.

Jackson, Richard. *The Dismantling of Time in Contemporary Poetry*. Tuscaloosa. University of Alabama Press, 1988.

Jameson, Fredric. "Beyond the Cave: Demystifying the Ideology of Modernism." In *The Ideologies of Theory: Essays, 1971–1986*. Theory and History of Literature, ed. Wlad Godzich and Jochen Schulte-Sasse, 2: 115–32. 1975. Minneapolis: University of Minnesota Press, 1988.

Jay, Gregory S. *T. S. Eliot and the Poetics of Literary History*. Baton Rouge: Louisiana State University Press, 1983.

Jenkyns, Richard. *The Victorians and Ancient Greece*. Cambridge, Mass.: Harvard University Press, 1980.

Jezierski, Louise. "The Politics of Space." Review of *Postmodern Geographies*, by Edward Soja, and *The Condition of Postmodernity*, by David Harvey. *Socialist Review* 21, no. 2 (April–June 1991): 177–84.

Johnston, R. J., David B. Knight, and Eleonore Kofman, eds. *Nationalism, Self-Determination, and Political Geography*. London: Croom Helm, 1988.

Jusdanis, Gregory. *Belated Modernity and Aesthetic Culture: The Making of a National Literature*. Theory and History of Literature, ed. Wlad Godzich and Jochen Schulte-Sasse. Minneapolis: University of Minnesota Press, 1991.

——. *The Poetics of Cavafy. Textuality, Eroticism, History*. Princeton: Princeton University Press, 1987.

Kafétsi, Ánna. Ελληνικότητα και εικαστική δημιουργία (Hellenicity and artistic creation). Δεκαπενθήμερος πολίτης 59 (January 1986): 35–37.

Kaklamánis, Gerásimos. Ανάλυση της νεοελληνικής αστικής ιδεολογίας (Analysis of the ideology of the Neohellenic middle class). Athens: Róis, 1989.

Kakridís, J. Th. Στρατηγός Μακρυγιάννης· Μια ελληνική καρδιά (General Makriyánnis: A Greek heart). 1964. Athens: Konstandinídis and Mihalás, 1972.

Kant, Immanuel. *The Critique of Judgment*. Translated by James Creed Meredith. 1790. Oxford: Clarendon Press, 1982.

Kapsális, Dionísis. Κριτική του ελληνικού μοντερνισμού, Μέρος Α'· Στο φως της απομυθοποίησης (Critique of Hellenic modernism, part A: In the light of demythologization). Καθημερινός πολίτης 25 (19 October 1984): 30–31.

——. Κριτική του ελληνικού μοντερνισμού, Μέρος Β'· Στη σκιά του μύθου (Critique of Hellenic modernism, part B: In the shadow of myth). Καθημερινός πολίτης 26 (2 November 1984): 44–46.

Karandónis, Andréas. Γύρω από το "'Αξιον Εστί" (Surrounding the "Axion Esti"). Ιn Για τον Οδυσσέα Ελύτη (For Odysseus Elytis). Athens: Papadímas, 1980.

——. Εισαγωγή στη νεώτερη ποίηση (Introduction to contemporary poetry). Athens: Galaxia, 1958.

——. Η ελληνική αίσθηση στην ποίηση του Σεφέρη και του Ελύτη (Hellenic feeling in the poetry of Seferis and Elytis). In Για τον Οδυσσέα Ελύτη (For Odysseus Elytis), 143–60. 1962. Athens: Papadímas, 1980.

——. Ο ποιητής Γιώργος Σεφέρης (The poet George Seferis). Athens: Galaxia, 1963.

Καταστρέφονται τα νεοκλασικά στην Ερμούπολη (Neoclassical buildings in Ermúpolis are being destroyed). In the Greek newspaper Τα Νέα, 12 April 1993.

Kazantzakis, Nikos. *Report to Greco*. Translated by P. A. Bien. New York: Simon and Schuster, 1965.

Kearns, George. *Guide to Ezra Pound's Selected Cantos*. New Brunswick: Rutgers University Press, 1980.

Kedourie, Elie, ed. *Nationalism in Asia and Africa*. New York: World Publishing, 1970.

Keeley, Edmund. "Seferis and 'Mythical Method.' " In *Modern Greek Poetry: Voice and Myth*. 1968. Princeton: Princeton University Press, 1983.

Kermode, Frank. *The Sense of an Ending: Studies in the Theory of Fiction*. New York: Oxford University Press, 1967.

Kern, Stephen. *The Culture of Time and Space, 1880–1918*. Cambridge, Mass.: Harvard University Press, 1983.

Kiriakídis, Stílpon. "The Language and Folk Culture of Modern Greece." In *Two Studies on Modern Greek Folklore*, trans. Robert A. Georges and Aristotle A. Katranidis, 45–127. 1946. Thessalonica: Institute for Balkan Studies, 1968.

Kiriakídu-Néstoros, Alki. Λαογραφικά μελετήματα (Folklore studies). Athens: Néa Sínora, 1975.

Kirk, G. S., and J. E. Raven. *The Presocratic Philosophers: A Critical History with a Selection of Texts*. Cambridge: Cambridge University Press, 1957.

Kitching, Gavin. *Development and Underdevelopment in Historical Perspective*. New York: Methuen, 1982.

Kitromilides, Paschalis M. "The Last Battle of the Ancients and Moderns: Ancient Greece and Modern Europe in the Neohellenic Revival." *Modern Greek Studies Yearbook* 1 (1985): 79–91.

Klironomos, Martha E. "Formation of the Nation/State: Hellenism in the Poetry of Ezra Pound, William Butler Yeats, and Odysseas Elytis." Ph.D. diss., Ohio State University, 1993.

——. "George Theotokas' *Free Spirit*: Reconfiguring Greece's Path toward Modernity?" *Journal of the Hellenic Diaspora* 18, no. 1 (1992): 79–97.

Knight, D. B. "Identity and Territory: Geographical Perspectives on Nationalism and Regionalism." *Annals of the Association of American Geographers* 72 (1982): 514–31.

Knight, D. B., and Maureen Davies, eds. *Self-Determination: An Interdisciplinary Annotated Bibliography*. New York and London: Garland, 1987.

Knox, Bernard. *The Oldest Dead White European Males and Other Reflections on the Classics*. New York and London: W. W. Norton, 1993.

Konstandás, Grigórios, and Daniíl Filippídis. Νεωτερική γεωγραφία (Neoteric geography). In Βασική βιβλιοθήκη. Vol. 9, Ο Κοραής και η εποχή του, 71–77. Athens: Vasikí Vivliothíki, n.d.

Konstándios, Dimítris. Η προστασία των ιστορικών πόλεων, η ελληνική εμπειρία (The preservation of historical cities, the Greek experience). Πολίτης 118 (April 1992); 43–45.

Kranáki, Mimíka. Φιλέλληνες· Είκοσι τέσσερα γράμματα μιάς Οδύσσειας (Philhellenes: Twenty-four letters of an odyssey) Athens: Íkaros, 1992.

Krumbacher, Karl. Το πρόβλημα της νεωτέρας γραφομένης Ελληνικής (The problem of modern written Greek). Athens: Sakellaríu, 1905.

Kubayanda, Josaphat B. "Minority Discourse and the African Collective: Some Examples from Latin American and Caribbean Literature." Cultural Critique 6 (spring 1987): 113–50.

Kuhn, Thomas S. "Postscript—1969." In The Structure of Scientific Revolutions. 2d ed. International Encyclopedia of Unified Science, vol. 2, no. 2, pp. 174–210. Chicago: University of Chicago Press, 1970.

Lachmann, Karl K. F. W. Betrachtungen über Homers Ilias. Berlin: G. Reimer, 1974.

Ladiá, Eléni. Ποιητές και αρχαία Ελλάδα· Σικελιανός, Σεφέρης, Παπαδίτσας (Poets and ancient Greece: Sikelianós, Seferis, Papadítsas). Athens: Ekdósis ton Fílon, 1983.

Lamartine, Alphonse de. Voyage en Orient. 1855–56. In Τρεις Γάλλοι ρομαντικοί στην Ελλάδα (Three French romantics in Greece), trans. Váso Méntzu, 31–81. Athens: Ólkos, 1990.

Lambropoulos, Vassilis. Literature as National Institution: Studies in the Politics of Modern Greek Criticism. Princeton: Princeton University Press, 1988.

——. The Rise of Eurocentrism: Anatomy of Interpretation. Princeton: Princeton University Press, 1992.

Layoun, Mary N. Travels of a Genre: The Modern Novel and Ideology. Princeton: Princeton University Press, 1990.

——, ed. Modernism in Greece? Essays on the Critical and Literary Margins of a Movement. New York: Pella, 1990.

Lazer, Harry. "British Populism: The Labour Party and the Common Market Parliamentary Debate." Political Science Quarterly 91 (1976): 259–77.

Le Corbusier (Charles-Edouard Jeanneret). Journey to the East. Edited by Ivan Zaknic and translated by Ivan Zaknic and Nicole Pertuiset. Cambridge, Mass., and London: MIT Press, 1989.

Leontis, Artemis. " 'The Lost Center' and the Promised Land of Greek Criticism." Journal of Modern Greek Studies 5, no. 2 (October 1987): 175–90.

——. "Modernist Criticism: Greek and American Defenses of the Autonomous Literary Text in the 1930s." In Modernism in Greece? Essays on the Critical and Literary Margins of a Movement, ed. Mary N. Layoun, 21–58. New York: Pella, 1990.

Lesky, Albin. A History of Greek Literature. Translated by James Willis and Cornelis De Heer. New York: Methuen, 1963.

——. Die Homerforschung in der Gegenwart. Vienna: Verlag, 1952.

Levenson, Michael H. A Genealogy of Modernism: A Study of English Literary Doctrine, 1908–1922. Cambridge: Cambridge University Press, 1984.

Lignádis, Tásos. Το Άξιον Εστί του Ελύτη (Elytis's "Axion Esti"). Athens: N. and S. I. Rosse, 1976.

Lihnará, Lína. Το μεσογειακό τοπίο στην ποίηση του Γιώργου Σεφέρη και του Οδυσσέα Ελύτη (The Mediterranean landscape in the poetry of George Seferis and Odysseus Elytis). Athens: Estía, 1986.

Likiardópulos, Gerásimos. Ρωμιοσύνη· Ιδεολογία και αθλιότητα του νέου εθνικισμού (Romiosíni: Ideology and paltriness in the new nationalism). In Η Ρωμιοσύνη στον παράδεισο, 11–17. Athens: Érasmos, 1983.

List, F. The National System of Political Economy. Translated by Sampson Lloyd. 1841. London: Longman, 1904.

Longenbach, James. Modernist Poetics of History: Pound, Eliot, and the Sense of the Past. Princeton: Princeton University Press, 1987.

Lorentzátos, Zísimos. Δοκίμιο 1 (Essay 1). Athens: Tipografío Stéfanou N. Tarusópulu, 1947.

———. "The Lost Center." In The Lost Center and Other Essays in Greek Poetry, trans. Kay Cicellis, 85–146. 1961. Princeton: Princeton University Press, 1980.

———. "Solomos." In The Lost Center and Other Essays in Greek Poetry, trans. Kay Cicellis, 3–69. 1945–46. Princeton: Princeton University Press, 1980.

Lucy, Sean. T. S. Eliot and the Idea of Tradition. London: Cohen and West, 1960.

Lukács, Georg. The Theory of the Novel. Translated by Anna Bostock. 1920. Cambridge, Mass.: MIT Press, 1971.

MacEwen, Gwendolyn. Mermaids and Ikons: A Greek Summer. Toronto: Anani, 1978.

MacNeal, R. A "Archaeology and the Destruction of the Later Athenian Acropolis." Antiquity 65 (March 1991): 49–63.

MacRae, Donald. "Populism as an Ideology." In Populism: Its Meaning and National Characteristics, ed. Ghita Ionescu and Ernest Gellner, 153–65. New York: Macmillan, 1969.

Maharaj, Sarat. "The Congo Is Flooding the Acropolis: Art in Britain of the Immigrations." Third Text: Third World Perspectives on Contemporary Art and Culture 15 (summer 1991): 77–90.

Makriyánnis, Yánnis. Απομνημονεύματα (Memoirs). 2 vols. Edited by Yánnis Vlahoyánnis. Athens: E. G. Vayonáki, 1947.

Malakis, Emile. "French Travellers in Greece (1770–1820): An Early Phase of French Philhellenism." Ph.D. diss., University of Pennsylvania, 1925.

Malkki, Liisa. "National Geographic: The Rooting of Peoples and the Territorialization of National Identity among Scholars and Refugees." Cultural Anthropology 7 (February 1992): 24–44.

Malraux, André. The Voices of Silence. Translated by Stuart Gilbert. 1953. Frogmore, St. Albans, Herts: Paladinh, 1974.

Mango, Cyril. "Antique Statuary and the Byzantine Beholder." Dumbarton Oaks Papers 17 (1963): 55–75.

Mani, Lata. "Contentious Traditions: The Debate on SATI in Colonial India." Cultural Critique 7 (fall 1987): 119–56.

Mantuvála, María. Ρωμαίος, Ρωμιός και Ρωμιοσύνη (Roman, Romiós, and Romiosíni). Μαντατοφόρος 22 (1983): 34–73.

Mantzúfas, G. Z. Ιδεολογία και κατευθύνσεις εις το νέον κράτος (Ideology and directions in the new state). Το νέον κράτος 16 (December 1938): 1327–29.

Maronítis, Dimítris N. Η νέκυια της "Κίχλης" (The nekuia of Thrush). In Η ποίηση του Γιώργου Σεφέρη· Μελέτες και μαθήματα, 15–28. Athens: Ermís, 1984.

Mellor, Roy E. H. Nation, State, and Territory: A Political Geography. London and New York: Routledge, 1989.

Méntzu, Váso. Σημείωμα της μεταφράστριας (Translator's note). In Τρεις Γάλλοι ρομαντικοί στην Ελλάδα (Three French romantics in Greece), 21–28. Athens: Ólkos, 1990.

Metaxás, Ioánnis. Το προσωπικό του ημερολόγιο (Private journal). Vol. 4. Athens. Govóstis, 1960.

Mileur, Jean-Pierre. Literary Revisionism and the Burden of Modernity. Berkeley: University of California Press, 1985.

Miller, Henry. The Colossus of Maroussi: A Celebration of the Uninhibited Pagan Spirit of Greece. 1941. Harmondsworth: Penguin, 1985.

Minogue, Kenneth. "Populism as a Political Movement." In Populism: Its Meaning and National Characteristics, ed. Ghita Ionescu and Ernest Gellner, 197–211. New York: Macmillan, 1969.

Mitchell, W. J T. "Diagrammatology." Critical Inquiry 7 (spring 1981): 622–33.

———. "Spatial Form in Literature: Toward a General Theory." Critical Inquiry 6 (spring 1980): 539–67.

Mosse, George L. Nationalism and Sexuality: Middle-Class Morality and Sexual Norms in Modern Europe. Madison: University of Wisconsin Press, 1985.

Myrsiades, Linda. "Aristophanic Comedy and the Modern Greek Karaghiozis Performance." Comparative Modern Literature 7, no. 2 (winter 1987): 45–59.

———. "The Karaghiozis Performance in Nineteenth-Century Greece." Byzantine and Modern Greek Studies 2 (1976): 83–97.

———. "The Karaghiozis Tradition and Greek Shadow Puppet Theatre: History and Analysis." Ph.D. diss., Indiana University, 1973.

Myrsiades, Linda, and Kostas Myrsiades. Karagiozis: Culture and Comedy in Greek Puppet Theater. Lexington: University Press of Kentucky, 1992.

Nagy, Gregory. The Best of the Achaeans: Concepts of the Hero in Archaic Greek Poetry. Baltimore: Johns Hopkins University Press, 1979.

———. Comparative Studies in Greek and Indic Meter. Cambridge, Mass.: Harvard Studies in Comparative Literature 33, 1974.

———. "Homeric Questions." Transactions of the American Philological Association 122 (1992): 17–60.

———. Pindar's Homer: The Lyric Possession of an Epic Past. Baltimore: Johns Hopkins University Press, 1990.

———. "Sēma and Nóēsis: The Hero's Tomb and the 'Reading' of Symbols in Homer and Hesiod." In Greek Mythology and Poetics. Ithaca, N.Y.: Cornell University Press, 1990.

Nerval, G. de. Oeuvres complètes. In Τρεις Γάλλοι ρομαντικοί στην Ελλάδα

(Three French romantics in Greece), trans. Váso Méntzu, 83–115. Athens: Ólkos, 1990.

Nikolareízis, Dimítris. Η παρουσία του Ομήρου στη νέα ελληνική ποίηση (The presence of Homer in modern Greek poetry). In Δοκίμια κριτικής, 209–36. 1947. Athens: G. Féxi, 1962.

Nikoláu, Níkos. Η περιπέτεια της γραμμής στην τέχνη (The adventure of line in art). Athens: Sakellaríu, 1986.

Notopoulos, James A. "Mnemosyne in Oral Literature." *Transactions of the American Philological Association* 69 (1938): 465–93.

Padel, Ruth. "Homer's Reader: A Reading of George Seferis." *Proceedings of the Cambridge Philological Association* n.s. 31 (1985): 74–132.

Palamás, Kostís. Ρωμιός και Ρωμιοσύνη (Romiós and Romiosíni). In Άπαντα, 6: 273–81. 1907. Athens: Bíris Govóstis, 1962.

Pállis, Aléxandros. Η Ιλιάδα μεταφρασμένη από τον Αλέξανδρο Πάλλη (The *Iliad* translated by Alexandros Pállis). 1904. Athens: Estía, 1932.

Panourgia, Nenny. *Fragments of Death, Fables of Identity: An Athenian Anthropography.* New Directions in Anthropological Writing, ed. George E. Marcus and James Clifford. Madison: University of Wisconsin Press, forthcoming.

Panúsis, Jimmy. Η ζάλη των τάξεων (Class muddle). Athens: Gnósis, 1989. (Book and cassette from forty radio broadcasts, May 1988–March 1989.)

Pápari, Anastasia. Μακεδονία· Μορφή και τόπος (Macedonia: Form and *topos*). In the Greek newspaper To Βήμα, 26 July 1992, 27.

Paparrigópulos, Konstandínos. Ιστορία του ελληνικού έθνους (History of the Hellenic nation). Edited by K. Th. Dimarás. Athens: Ermís, 1970.

Pemble, John. *The Mediterranean Passion: Victorians and Edwardians in the South.* Oxford: Clarendon Press, 1987.

Perl, Jeffrey M. *The Tradition of Return: The Implicit History of Modern Literature.* Princeton: Princeton University Press, 1984.

Petihákis, Dimítris. Φιλέλληνας ή κάτι παραπάνω; Ο Ζακ Ντελόρ στην Αθήνα και τι . . . άφησε πίσω του (Philhellene or something more? Jacques Delors in Athens and what . . . he left behind). In the Greek newspaper To Βήμα, 31 May 1992, E2–3.

Pikiónis, Dimítris. Το πρόβλημα της μορφής (The problem of form). In Κείμενα, ed. Zísimos Lorentzátos, 204–46. 1946. Athens: Morfotikó ídrima ethnikís trapézis, 1985.

Plamenatz, John. "Two Types of Nationalism." In *Nationalism, the Nature and Evolution of an Idea*, ed. Eugene Kamenka, 3–20. Sydney: Australian National University Press, 1973.

Polis, Adamantia. "Notes on Nationalism and Human Rights in Greece." *Journal of Modern Hellenism* 4 (1988): 147–60.

Polítis, Línos. Ιστορία της νεοελληνικής λογοτεχνίας (History of Neohellenic literature). Athens: Morfotikó ídrima ethnikís trápezis, 1979.

Polítis, Nikólaos G. Έλληνες ή Ρωμιοί (Hellenes or Romií). In Λαογραφικά σύμμεικτα. 1901. Athens: Akadimía Athinón, 1931.

Portugali, Juval. "Nationalism, Social Theory, and the Israeli/Palestinian Case."

In *Nationalism, Self-Determination, and Political Geography*, ed. R. J. Johnston, David B. Knight, and Eleonore Kofman, 151–65. London: Croom Helm, 1988.

Pratt, Mary Louise. *Imperial Eyes: Travel Writing and Transculturalism*. London and New York: Routledge, 1992.

Proudhon, P. J. *What Is Property? An Inquiry into the Principle of Right and Government*. Translated by Benjamin Tucker. 1840. London: Reeves, 1898.

Psiháris, Yánnis. Ρωμιός και Ρωμιοσύνη (Romiós and Romiosíni). Ρόδα και μήλα, 1: 39–51. Athens: Estía, 1903.

———. Το ταξίδι μου (My journey). 1888. Athens: Ermís, 1979.

Rámfos, Stélios. Τόπος υπερουράνιος (Transcendental topos). 1975. Athens: Kédros, 1983.

Reinhold, Meyer, and Emily Albu Hanawalt. *The Classical Tradition: Teaching and Research*. American Philological Association Educational Papers, no. 4. Bronx, N.Y.: American Philological Association Committee on Education, 1987.

Renan, Ernest. "Prière sur l'Acropole." *Souvenirs d'enfance et de jeunesse*. 1865. Paris: Calmann-Lévy, 1925.

———. Προσευχή επάνω στην Ακρόπολη (Prayer on the Acropolis). Translated by Xenofóntas Steph. Dántis. Athens: Cultura, 1960.

Rice, W. G. "Early English Travellers in Greece and the Levant." *Essays and Studies in English and Comparative Literature* 10 (1933): 205–60.

Ricks, David. "Greek *tout court?*" *Arion: A Journal of Humanities and the Classics* 1, no. 3 (fall 1991): 29–44.

———. *The Shade of Homer. A Study in Modern Greek Poetry*. Cambridge: Cambridge University Press, 1989.

Ross, Kristin. *The Emergence of Social Space: Rimbaud and the Paris Commune*. Minneapolis: University of Minnesota Press, 1988.

Rudolph, Lloyd I., and Susanne Hoeber Rudolph. *The Modernity of Tradition: Political Development in India*. Chicago: University of Chicago Press, 1967.

Sack, R. "Human Territoriality: A Theory." *Annals of the Association of American Geographers* 73 (1983): 55–74.

———. *Human Territoriality: Its Theory and History*. Cambridge: Cambridge University Press, 1986.

Said, Edward. "Traveling Theory." In *The World, the Text, and the Critic*, 226–47. Cambridge, Mass.: Harvard University Press, 1983.

St. Clair, William. *Lord Elgin and the Marbles*. London, New York, and Toronto: Oxford University Press, 1967.

Sakai, Naoki. "Modernity and Its Critique: The Problem of Universalism and Particularism." *South Atlantic Quarterly* 87 (summer 1988): 475–504.

Savídis, Yórgos P. Άξιον Εστί το ποίημα του Ελύτη (Worthy is the poem by Elytis). In Πάνω νερά. 1960. Athens: Ermís, 1974.

Savvópulos, Dionísis. Γεννήθηκα στη Σαλονίκη (I was born in Thessaloníki). On the album Η Ρεζέρβα. Athens: Líra, 1979.

———. Χρειάζονται συντηρητικές λύσεις (Conservative solutions are necessary). Interview with Vasílis Angelikópulos. In the Greek newspaper Η Καθημερινή, 12 February 1989.

Schiller, Friedrich. *On the Aesthetic Education of Man, in a Series of Letters.* Translated by Reginald Snell. New York: Frederick Ungar, 1965.

——. *On the Naive and Sentimental in Literature.* Translated and introduced by Helen Watanabe-O'Kelley. 1795–96. Manchester: Carcanet, 1981.

Seferis, George. Ἀντιγραφές (Copyings). Athens: Íkaros, 1965.

——. Για τον I. A. Σαρεγιάννη (For I. A. Sarayánnis). In Δοκιμές, 2: 153–58. 1963. Athens: Íkaros, 1981.

——. "Γλώσσες" στον Ἀρτεμιδώρο τον Δαλδιανό ("Commentary" on Artemidoros Daldianos). In Δοκιμές, 2:313–32. 1970. Athens: Íkaros, 1981.

——. Γράμμα σ' έναν ξένο φίλο (Letter to a foreign friend). In Δοκιμές, 2: 9–24. 1948. Athens: Íkaros, 1981.

——. Δελφοί (Delphi). In Δοκιμές, 2: 136–52. 1961. Athens: Íkaros, 1981.

——. Δεύτερος πρόλογος στο βιβλίο μου Θ. Σ. Ἔλιοτ· Η Ἔρημη Χώρα και άλλα ποιήματα (Second prologue to my book T. S. Eliot, *The Wasteland and Other Poems*). In Δοκιμές, 2:25–29. 1949. Athens: Íkaros, 1981.

——. Διάλογος πάνω στην ποίηση (Dialogue on poetry). In Δοκιμές, 1: 82–104. 1938. Athens: Íkaros, 1981.

——. "Dialogue on Poetry: What Is Meant by Hellenism?" In *On the Greek Style,* trans. Rex Warner and Th. Frangopoulos, 73–99. 1938–39. Boston and Toronto: Little, Brown, 1966.

——. Ἕνας Ἕλληνας—ο Μακρυγιάννης (A Hellene—Makriyánnis). In Δοκιμές, 2:228–63. 1943. Athens: Íkaros, 1981.

——. Ezra Pound, Τρία "Canto" (Ezra Pound, Three "Cantos"). Τα νέα γράμματα, April–June 1939, 187–200.

——. Θεόφιλος (Theófilos). In Δοκιμές, 1: 458–66. 1947. Athens: Íkaros, 1981.

——. Κ. Π. Καβάφης, Θ. Σ. Ἔλιοτ· Παράλληλοι (C. P. Cavafy, T. S. Eliot: Parallel Cases). In Δοκιμές 1: 324–63. 1947. Athens: Íkaros, 1981.

——. Μέρες (Days). Vol. 5, 1 January 1945–19 April 1951. Athens: Íkaros, 1986.

——. Μιά σκηνοθεσία για την Κίχλη (Stage directions for Thrush). In Δοκιμές, 2:30–56. 1949. Athens: Íkaros, 1981.

——. Πάντα πλήρη θεών (All is full of gods). In Δοκιμές, 2: 339–48. 1971. Athens: Íkaros, 1981.

——. *A Poet's Journal, Days of 1945–1951.* Translated by Athan Anagnostopoulos. Cambridge, Mass.: Harvard University Press, Belknap Press, 1974.

——. Ποιήματα (Poems). Athens: Íkaros, 1974.

——, trans. Η Ἀποκάλυψη του Ιωάννη (The apocalypse of John). Athens: Íkaros, 1975.

Segal, Charles. "Orpheus, Agamemnon, and the Anxiety of Influence: Mythic Intertexts in Seferis, *Mythistorema 3.*" *Classical and Modern Literature* 9 (summer 1989): 291–98.

Seling, H. "The Genesis of the Museum." *Architectural Review* 141 (1967): 103–14.

Seton-Watson, Hugh. *Nations and States.* Boulder: University of Colorado Press, 1977.

Shafer, Boyd C. *Faces of Nationalism: New Realities and Old Myths.* New York: Harcourt Brace Jovanovich, 1972.

Shils, Edward. *The Torment of Secrecy.* London: William Heinemann, 1969.

——. *Tradition.* Chicago: University of Chicago Press, 1981

Simópulos, Kiriákos. Ξένοι ταξιδιώτες στην Ελλάδα (Foreign travelers to Hellas). Athens: n.p., 1970.

Skopetéa, Éli. Το πρότυπο βασίλειο και η Μεγάλη Ιδέα (The model kingdom and the Megáli Idéa). Athens: Polítipo, 1988.

Skopetéa, Sofía. Μυστήρια και αποκαλύψεις (Mysteries and apocalypses). Σημειώσεις 29 (March 1987): 22–43.

Slatkin, Laura. "*Oedipus at Colonus*: Exile and Integration." In *Greek Tragedy and Political Theory*, ed. J. Peter Euben, 210–21. Berkeley: University of California Press, 1986.

Smith, Anthony D. *The Ethnic Origin of Nations.* Oxford: Basil Blackwell, 1988.

Snyder, Louis L., ed. *Encyclopedia of Nationalism.* New York: Paragon House, 1990.

Soja, Edward W. "Heterotopologies: A Remembrance of Other Spaces in the Citadel-LA." *Strategies* 3 (1990): 6–39.

——. *Postmodern Geographies: The Reassertion of Space in Critical Social Theory.* London: Verso, 1989.

Solomós, Dionísios. Διάλογος (Dialogue). In 'Απαντα, ed. Línos Polítis, 2: 9–30. 1824. Athens: Íkaros, 1979.

Sommer, Doris. *One Master for Another: Populism as Patriarchal Rhetoric in Dominican Novels.* New York: University Press of America, 1983.

Sotiriádis, G. Ιστορία της Ρωμιοσύνης (History of Romiosíni). In the Greek newspaper Ακρόπολις, 5 August 1901.

Spanos, William. "Modern Literary Criticism and the Spatialization of Time." *Journal of Aesthetics and Art Criticism* 29 (fall 1970): 87–104.

Spender, Harold. *Byron and Greece.* New York: Charles Scribner's Sons, 1924.

Stein, Rokkan, and Derek W. Urwin. *The Politics of Territorial Identity.* London, Beverly Hills, and New Delhi: Sage Publications, 1982.

Steiner, George. *Extraterritorial: Papers on Literature and the Language Revolution.* Harmondsworth: Penguin, 1975.

Stewart, Angus. "The Social Roots." In *Populism: Its Meaning and National Characteristics*, ed. Ghita Ionescu and Ernest Gellner, 180–96. New York: Macmillan, 1969.

Stivale, Charles J. "The Literary Element in *Mille Plateaus*: The New Cartography of Deleuze and Guattari." *Substance* 44/45 (1985): 20–34.

Stoessl, F. "Aeschylus as a Political Thinker." *American Journal of Philology* 73 (1957): 113–39.

Stone, James. "A Letter on Thrush." *Journal of the Hellenic Diaspora* 7 (1980): 5–26.

Stoneman, Richard, ed. *Land of Lost Gods: The Search for Classical Greece.* London: Hutchinson, 1987.

——. *A Literary Companion to Travel in Greece.* London: Penguin, 1984.

Σύναξη 34 (April–June 1990).

Tennenhouse, Leonard. "Simulating History: A Cockfight for Our Times." *The Drama Review* 34, no. 4 (winter 1990): 137–55.

Terdiman, Richard. *Discourse/Counter-Discourse: The Theory and Practice of Symbolic Resistance in Nineteenth-Century France*. Ithaca, N.Y.: Cornell University Press, 1985.

Thackeray, William Makepeace. *Notes of a Journey from Cornhill to Grand Cairo*. Introduction by Sarah Searight. 1844. Heathfield: Cockbird Press, 1991.

Thaniel, George. "George Seferis' *Thrush*: A Modern 'Descent.'" *Canadian Review of Comparative Literature* 4 (1977): 89–102.

———. "George Seferis' *Thrush* and the Poetry of Ezra Pound." *Comparative Literary Studies* 11 (1974): 326–36.

———. "George Seferis' *Thrush* and T. S. Eliot's *Four Quartets*." *Neohelicon* 4 (1976): 261–82.

———. "The Moon, the Heron, and *The Thrush*: George Seferis, Douglas Lepan, and Greek Myth." *Classical and Modern Literature* 9, no. 4 (summer 1989): 315–25.

Thasítis, Pános K. Επτά δοκίμια για την ποίηση (Seven essays on poetry). 1960. Athens: Kédros, 1979.

Theodorakópulos, Ioánnis. Το πνεύμα του Νεοελληνισμού (The spirit of Neohellenism). In Φιλοσοφία και ζωή· Μικρά φιλοσοφικά κείμενα, 119–91. 1945. Athens: n.p., 1967.

Theotokás, Yórgos. Η διαύγεια (Clarity). Ο Κύκλος, November 1931, 30.

———. Ελεύθερο πνεύμα (Free spirit). 1929. Athens: Ermís, 1988.

———. Ο Στρατηγός Μακρυγιάννης (General Makriyánnis). In Πνευματική πορεία, 141–66. 1945. Athens: Estía, 1961.

Thomson, George. "The Continuity of Hellenism." *Greece and Rome* 18 (1971): 18–29.

———. *The Greek Language*. Cambridge: Cambridge University Press, 1972.

Τί θα γίνει με το μουσείο της Ακρόπολης (What will become of the Acropolis Museum?). In the Greek newspaper Το Βήμα, 26 September 1993.

Tregaskis, Hugh. *Beyond the Grand Tour: The Levant Lunatics*. London: Ascent Books, 1979.

Tsarúhis, Yánnis. Λαϊκή και αριστοκρατική πρέπει να είναι η μεγάλη τέχνη (Great art must be popular and aristocratic). In Εγώ ειμί πτωχός και πένης, 18–32. Athens: Kastanióti. 1988.

Tsátsos, Konstandínos. Ένας διάλογος για την ποίηση (A dialogue on poetry). Προπύλαια 1, nos. 8–10 (October–December 1938): 246–61.

———. Πριν από το ξεκίνημα I (Before setting out I). Προπύλαια 1 (April 1938): 49–57.

———. Πριν από το ξεκίνημα II (Before setting out II). Προπύλαια 1, nos. 3–4 (May–June 1938): 89–104.

Tsifopoulos, Yánnis. "Pausanias as a Steloskopas: An Epigraphical Commentary on Pausanias' ELIAKON A and B." Ph.D. diss., Ohio State University, 1991.

Tsigakou, F. M. *The Rediscovery of Greece: Travellers and Painters of the Romantic Era*. Introduction by Steven Runciman. London: Thames and Hudson, 1981.

Tsiómis, Yánnis. Επιστρέφοντας από την έκθεση (Returning from the exhibition). In Αθήνα πρωτεύουσα πόλη (Athens capital city). Athens: Office of Foreign Affairs, 1985.

Turner, Frank M. *The Greek Heritage in Victorian Britain*. New Haven and London: Yale University Press, 1981.

Turnikiótis, Panayótis. Ο Ιλισσός του Πλάτωνα· Για την ιδεολογική παρουσία του παρελθόντος στη σύγχρονη Αθήνα (Plato's Ilissus: On the ideological presence of the past in modern Athens). Σύγχρονα θέματα 45 (June 1991): 81–89.

Twain, Mark. *Innocents Abroad*. 1869. New York: Library of America, 1984.

"Two Romans Have Been Chosen to Design the New Acropolis Museum." *New York Times*, 28 December 1990, B2.

Tynjanov, Jurij. "On Literary Evolution." In *Twentieth-Century Literary Theory: An Introductory Anthology*, ed. Vassilis Lambropoulos and David Neal Miller, 152–62. 1927. Albany: State University of New York Press, 1987.

Tzióvas, Dimítrios. "George Thomson and the Dialectics of Hellenism." *Byzantine and Modern Greek Studies* 13 (1989): 296–304.

——. Οι μεταμορφώσεις του εθνισμού και το ιδεολόγημα της Ελληνικότητας στο μεσοπόλεμο (The transformations of nationism and the ideologeme of Hellenicity during the interwar period). Athens: Odiséas, 1989.

——. *The Nationism of the Demoticists and Its Impact on Their Literary Theory (1885–1930)*. Amsterdam: Hakkert, 1986.

Vakaló, Eléni. Ο μύθος της ελληνικότητας· Η φυσιογνωμία της μεταπολεμικής τέχνης στην Ελλάδα (The myth of Hellenicity: The physiognomy of postwar art in Greece). Vol. 2. Athens: Kédros, 1983.

Vasiliev, A. A. *History of the Byzantine Empire*. Madison: University of Wisconsin Press, 1928.

Vayenás, Násos. Η γενεαλογία της "Κίχλης" (Genealogy of *Thrush*). Παρνασσός 16 (1974): 484–507.

Vergópulos, Kóstas. Η δυναμική του 1821 (The dynamic of 1821). Θεωρία και κοινωνία 2 (1990): 75–99.

Vermeule, Emily. "The World Turned Upside Down." Review of *The Archaeological and Documentary Evidence*, vol. 2 of *Black Athena: The Afroasiatic Roots of Classical Civilization*, by Martin Bernal. *New York Review of Books*, 27 March 1992, 40–43.

Vitti, Mario. Η γενιά του τριάντα· Ιδεολογία και μορφή (The generation of the thirties: Ideology and form). Athens: Ermís, 1979.

Vrahorítis. S. Γρέκικες τσόντες ([Skin] Flicks Grec). In the Greek newspaper To Βήμα, 1991.

Vryonís, Speros, Jr. "Recent Scholarship on Continuity and Discontinuity of Culture: Classical Greeks, Byzantines, Modern Greeks." In *The "Past" in Medieval and Modern Greek Culture*, ed. Speros Vryonis, Jr., 237–56. Malibu: Undena, 1978.

Wagner, Philip. "Rank and Territory." In *The Structure of Political Geography*, ed. Roger E. Kasperson and Julian V. Minghi, 89–93. Chicago: Aldine Publishing Company, 1969.

Waldman, Marilyn. "Tradition as a Modality of Change: Islamic Examples." *History of Religions* 25, no. 4 (May 1986): 318–40.

Watson, Stephen. "Criticism and the Closure of 'Modernism.'" *Substance* 42 (1983): 15–30.

Weimann, Robert. *Structure and Society in Literary History: Studies in the History and Theory of Historical Criticism.* Baltimore and London: Johns Hopkins University Press, 1984.

Wellek, René. "The Concept of Evolution in Literary History." In *Concepts of Criticism.* 1956. New Haven: Yale University Press, 1963.

Werblowsky, R. J. Zwi. *Beyond Tradition and Modernity: Changing Religions in a Changing World.* Jordon Lectures in Comparative Religions, no. 11. London: Athlone, 1976.

White, Hayden. "The Problem of Change in Literary History." *New Literary History* 7, no. 1 (autumn 1975): 97–111.

Whitman, Cedric H. *The Vitality of the Greek Language and Its Importance Today.* New York: The Greek Archdiocese Publication Department, 1954.

Wilber, J. B., and H. J. Allen. *The Worlds of the Early Greek Philosophers.* New York: Prometheus Books, 1979.

Wiles, Peter. "A Syndrome, Not a Doctrine: Some Elementary Theses on Populism." In *Populism: Its Meaning and National Characteristics,* ed. Ghita Ionescu and Ernest Gellner, 166–79. New York: Macmillan, 1969.

Wilson, David L. "Researchers Hope to Lead Students into 'Virtual Reality.'" *Chronicle of Higher Education,* 22 April 1992, A23–25.

Wolf, F. A. *Prolegomena to Homer.* Translated by Anthony Grafton, Glenn W. Most, and James E. G. Zetzel. 1795. Princeton: Princeton University Press, 1985.

Woof, Virginia. "A Dialogue upon Mount Pentelicus." Edited by S. P. Rosenbaum. *Times Literary Supplement,* 11–17 September 1987, 979.

——. Ένας διάλογος στην Πεντέλη (A dialogue upon Mount Pentelicus). Translated by Aris Berlis. Εντευκτήριο 14 (March 1991): 5–10.

——. *The Letters of Virginia Woolf.* Vol. 4, 1932–1935. Edited by Nigel Nicolson and Joanne Trautmann. New York and London: Harcourt Brace Jovanovich, 1978.

Worsley, Peter. "The Concept of Populism." In *Populism: Its Meaning and National Characteristics,* ed. Ghita Ionescu and Ernest Gellner, 215–50. New York: Macmillan, 1969.

——. *The Third World.* London: Weidenfeld and Nicolson, 1967.

Xenópoulos, Gregórias. Ιστορία της Ρωμιοσύνης υπό Αργύρη Εφταλιώτη τόμος πρώτος (History of Romiosíni by Aryíris Eftaliótis, volume 1). Παναθήναια 3 (April–September 1902): 26–29.

Xidís, Aléxandros. Γιάννης Τσαρούχης, 1910–1989 (Yánnis Tsarúhis, 1910–1989). Αντί, 7 July 1989, 47.

Yannópulos, Periklís. Η ελληνική γραμμή, το ελληνικό χρώμα (Hellenic line, Hellenic color). In Άπαντα, 93–158. 1904. Athens: Eléftheri Sképsis, 1988.

——. Νέον πνεύμα (New spirit). Athens: Sakellaríu, 1906.

———. Η σύγχρονος ζωγραφική (Contemporary painting). In Άπαντα, 7–65. 1902. Athens: Eléftheri Sképsis, 1988.

Zahareas, Anthony N. "George Seferis: Myth and History." *Books Abroad* 42, no. 2 (spring 1968): 190–98.

Zambélios, Spirídon. Πόθεν η κοινή λέξις τραγουδώ; Σκέψεις περί ελληνικής ποιήσεως (Whence the common word, to sing? Thoughts on Hellenic poetry). In Βασική βιβλιοθήκη, vol. 42, Νεοελληνική κριτική, 1–46. 1859. Athens: Vasikí Vivliothíki, n.d.

Ζυγός 1, no. 7 (May 1956).

Index

MYTH AND POETICS

A series edited by GREGORY NAGY